An Illustrated Handbook of

ART
HISTORY

THIRD EDITION

FRANK J. ROOS, JR.

College of Fine and Applied Arts, University of Illinois

THE MACMILLAN COMPANY
COLLIER-MACMILLAN LIMITED, LONDON

PREFACE TO THE THIRD EDITION

Much of the preface to the revised edition applies equally well to today's art scene, and the choice of the illustrations has been no less difficult. There is little need for amplification of the previous preface.

May I, however, express my appreciation to those of my late husband's colleagues who aided in the choice of examples, and to the staffs of the Krannert Art Museum and the Ricker Architectural Library at the University of Illinois for their help. I also wish to thank the museums, galleries, collectors, artists, and photographers who kindly gave me permissions for use of their material.

Especially my gratitude goes to the photographer, Mr. James H. Rutledge, and to Mr. Donald C. Neville and Mrs. Edwin R. Phillips, Jr., who have helped me in numerous ways.

Beatrice Adams Roos
(Mrs. Frank J. Roos, Jr.)

CHAMPAIGN-URBANA, ILLINOIS

PREFACE TO THE REVISED EDITION

In the preface to the first edition we said that "The choice of men and examples constituting the modern section was particularly difficult." When it was determined to enlarge and bring the latter section of the book more nearly up to date, the problem of selection was no less difficult than it was for the first edition. Schools of painting and sculpture have become increasingly numerous in the past fifteen years, to the point where it has sometimes seemed that each artist tended to become a school in his own right.

It has been our purpose in choosing the illustrations to identify the numerous directions in which modern painting and sculpture have gone. Fifteen years from now some of the illustrations in this section will doubtless seem less important or of historic interest only, just as some of the last illustrations in the Modern Painting Section of the first edition no longer seem as important as when they were selected. On the other hand, architecture has had a more consistent and logical development than have painting and sculpture in the decade and a half since the appearance of the first edition.

Since the relative importance of examples in the pre-modern sections of the book have changed little, and the contemporary scene is changing continuously, the earlier sections have been left as they were, except for a few minor details.

Within the last fifteen years more and more works of contemporary art have become known to the public through numerous art publications, such as those of the Museum of Modern Art, through dramatic and well-staged exhibitions in the larger museums, and through the many color reproductions appearing in non-art journals that have a wide circulation. It will be found that the modern section in this revision has a wider variety of examples than did the same section in the previous edition.

We have made little attempt to bring the locations of works of art in the pre-modern sections up to date, as it would be an almost impossible task. Also, it has not been possible in all cases to locate paintings and sculpture in the modern section; they move around even in peacetime, and, like architecture, their location and condition tend to be affected by war.

May I again express my thanks to the numerous colleagues who have helped me with their advice and criticism in the matter of the choice of examples, to the artists, owners of objects of art, photographers, publications, and museum personnel who have been so gracious with their time and permissions. In particular I wish to thank my wife, Beatrice Adams Roos, and Donald C. Neville.

Urbana, Illinois   *F. J. R., Jr.*

PREFACE TO THE FIRST EDITION

The aim of this handbook is to put into the hands of students useful illustrations of as many works of art, together with reference charts, as can be encompassed in the covers of a book selling for a comparatively low price. It is the result of a need felt by myself and other teachers of art history, not for another history of art, since several good ones exist, but for a profusely illustrated reference book, which might be used independently or in conjunction with another art book. The handbook is organized primarily for students of art history and appreciation courses, particularly for the instructor or student who is handicapped by a small budget for illustrative material and who might find in this book enough examples for a short course.

Before the actual work on the volume was begun, a survey was made of the type and content of art history and appreciation courses in a great number of colleges and art schools. From this survey it was found, unfortunately, that Oriental art and the more anthropological phases of art as a whole were seldom considered. In view of the aim of the book, which is the greatest usefulness to the greatest number of students, these phases of art, particularly the former, were reluctantly eliminated.

An attempt was made, also, to determine the examples that would be best known and therefore most useful, to both instructor and student. A master list was made from an examination of the most commonly used histories of art and of its various phases. Examples illustrated in two or more books were automatically placed on the list which formed the basis of the final list. The master list could not be rigidly followed in all instances, although most of it is here present.

Some readers will feel that too much emphasis has been placed on the Italian Renaissance, or the American or Modern sections, or too little on the Baroque. Here again, usefulness, in the light of the survey of existing courses, was the aim. The choice of men and examples constituting the Modern section was particularly difficult. Although there are as many men of great importance left out as are included, the choice of the names to be considered was here guided by the necessity of using men typical of certain trends and by the availability of material. The examples as a whole have been placed in an order easily suited to a comparative study of the history of art.

Enlargements of details have been used frequently to facilitate an understanding of the techniques involved. Attributions and dates, often problematical, may sometimes be considered in error. Every effort, however, has been made to eliminate such errors. Whenever a choice was possible, American-owned examples were used in preference to those in European museums, and often several works of a similar type, by the same artist, were used for emphasis, in preference to the addition of an isolated work by another man.

Such a handbook as this could not have been produced without the aid of a great number of persons. I wish to thank the various scholars who aided in compiling the parts of the master list and who checked over the finished book. I am grateful to the artists, owners of objects of art, authors, publishers and photographers whose works are here included. Whenever possible they are credited in parentheses where their examples appear.

I wish particularly to thank Mr. Jesse Zousmer for his assistance with all phases of the book, and the staff of the Metropolitan Museum of Art, especially the members of the Extension Division. Without the help of each of these persons and organizations, and the continued cooperation and consideration of the publishers, the production of the book could not have been accomplished.

F. J. R., Jr.

COLUMBUS, OHIO

v

CONTENTS

LIST OF MUSEUMS AND ABBREVIATIONS. viii

EXAMPLES ILLUSTRATING THE HISTORY OF ART
FROM THE PREHISTORIC PERIOD TO TODAY

Prehistoric Art 1
Egyptian Art 3
Mesopotamian Art 11
Early Aegean Art 14
Greek Art 17
Roman Art 42
Early Christian and Byzantine Art 53
Romanesque Art 62
Gothic Art 74
Italian Renaissance Art 98
Flemish Art, Fifteenth to Seventeenth Centuries 155
German Art, Fifteenth to Eighteenth Centuries 166
Spanish Art, Sixteenth to Nineteenth Centuries 171
Dutch Art, Seventeenth Century 176
English Art, Sixteenth to Twentieth Centuries 184
European and American Minor Arts, Sixteenth to Nineteenth Centuries 195
French and Other European Art, Thirteenth to Twentieth Centuries . 200
Mexican Art, Eighteenth to Twentieth Centuries 248
American Art, Seventeenth to Twentieth Centuries 251
Twentieth Century Sculpture 312

APPENDIX

Print Techniques 320
Charts
A. Chronological Development of Art Periods, 4000 B.C.–1 A.D. . . 321
B. Chronological Development of Art Periods, 1 A.D.–1937 A.D. . . 322
C. The Major Architectural Styles and Influences 323
D. Sculpture During the Renaissance in Italy 324
E. Painting During the Renaissance in Italy 325
F. Painting in Europe, 1350–1700 326
G. Painting in Europe, 1700–1930 327
H. Basic European Furniture Styles 328

INDEX 329

LIST OF MUSEUMS AND ABBREVIATIONS

The locations of the following art museums are not always given in the captions:

Acropolis Museum, Athens; Albertinum, Dresden; Art Institute, Chicago; The Bargello, Florence; Bibliothèque Nationale, Paris; Borghese Gallery, Rome; British Museum, London; Candia Museum, Crete; Capitoline Museum, Rome; Cleveland Museum, Cleveland, Ohio; Cluny Museum, Paris; Fogg Museum of Art, Harvard University, Cambridge, Mass.; Church of the Frari, Venice; The Glyptothek, Munich; The Hispanic Society of America, New York City; Kaiser Friedrich Museum, Berlin; Lateran Museum, Rome; The Louvre, Paris; Luxembourg Museum, Paris; Metropolitan Museum of Art, New York City; Museum of Fine Arts, Boston, Mass.; Pennsylvania Academy of Fine Arts, Philadelphia; Pennsylvania Museum of Fine Arts, Philadelphia; Pergamon Museum, Berlin; Phillips Memorial Art Gallery, Washington, D. C.; Pitti Gallery, Florence; Prado Museum, Madrid; Rijksmuseum, Amsterdam; Terme Museum, Rome; Toledo Art Museum, Toledo, Ohio; Uffizi Gallery, Florence; Victoria and Albert Museum, London.

The credit lines of the following photographic sources are sometimes abbreviated in the captions:

(Al) Alinari; (And) Anderson; (Arch. Photo.) Les Archives Photographiques d'Art et d'Histoire; (Berlin) Berlin Museum; (Bib. Nat.) Bibliothèque Nationale; (Bruck) Bruckmann; (Cario) Cario Museum; (Can) Candia Museum; (Clev. Mus.) Cleveland Museum of Art; (Fogg) Fogg Museum of Art; (Gir) Giraudon; (Hanf) Hanfstaengl; (Lux) Luxembourg Museum; (Man) Mansell; (Met) Metropolitan Museum of Art; (M.F.A.) Museum of Fine Arts; (N.D.) Neurdein; (Nat. Gall.) National Gallery, London; (Nat. Mus.) National Museum, Athens, Naples; (Taft) Taft Museum, Cincinnati; (Vict. Alb.) Victoria and Albert Museum.

A. Stonehenge Today. Salisbury Plain, England. From a model in the Stonehenge Museum.

B. Stonehenge Restored. From a model in the Stonehenge Museum.

C. Wooly Rhinoceros. Polychrome drawing from Font-de-Gaume cave. Aurignacian. (American Museum of Natural History)

D. Horse. Drawing from Font-de-Gaume cave. Aurignacian. (American Museum of Natural History)

E. Galloping Horse. From a cave at Altamira. (Stoedtner)

F. Reindeer and Salmon. Engraving in Reindeer Horn, from Lorthet, in the Pyrenees. Magdalenian. (American Museum of Natural History)

G. Stag Hunt. From cave at Alpera. (American Museum of Natural History)

A. Bison with Turned Head. Paleolithic. Reindeer Horn. La Madeleine, Dordogne. Louvre. (Louvre)

B. Egyptian Early Dynastic Jar decorated with Gazelles and Ostriches. Metropolitan Museum. (Met)

C. Prehistoric. Reindeer. Paleolithic. (Stoedtner)

D. The Sphinx. Gizeh. IV Dynasty. (Sebah)

E. Stepped Pyramid at Sakkâra. III Dynasty. (Sebah)

F. Pyramids of Gizeh: Kheops, Khephren, Mykerinos. IV Dynasty. 2900–2750 B.C. (Sebah)

EGYPTIAN ARCHITECTURE AND SCULPTURE
OLD KINGDOM · 3400–2475 B.C.

3

A. Valley Temple of the Pyramid of Khephren. c. 2850 B.C.

B. Palette of Narmer. Museum, Cairo. I Dynasty. (Cairo)

C. Palette of Narmer. King and Prisoner. Museum, Cairo.

D. Ranofer as a Priest of Phtah. V Dynasty, 2750–2625 B.C. Museum, Cairo.

E. "Sheik el-Beled." IV Dynasty, 2900–2750 B. C. Museum, Cairo. (Met)

F. "Sheik el-Beled." Detail of E.

G. Khephren. Museum, Cairo.

H. Khephren. Detail of figure similar to G.

I. Statue of a Lady, probably a princess. IV Dynasty, 2900–2750 B.C. Metropolitan Museum. (Met)

J. Bust of a Woman. Museum, Cairo.

A. Rahotep and Nofret. III Dynasty. From Meidum. (Met)

B. Rahotep. Detail of A.

C. Seated Scribe. V Dynasty, 2750–2625 B.C. Louvre. (Gir)

D. Seated Scribe. Side view of C.

E. Woman Grinding Grain. Archaeological Museum, Florence. (Al)

F. Man Making Beer. Metropolitan Museum. (Met)

G. Cattle Scene. Tomb of Ptahhotep, Sakkâra. V Dynasty, 2750–2625 B.C.

H. Sailing Through Marshes. From Tomb of Mereruka, Sakkâra. V Dynasty.

I. Panel of Hesire. Detail. c. 2800 B.C.

EGYPTIAN ARCHITECTURE

5

MIDDLE KINGDOM · 2160–1788 B.C. AND NEW EMPIRE · 1580–1090 B.C.

A. Façade of Tomb of Khnûmhotep II at Benihasan. XII Dynasty.

B. Restoration of Temple of Queen Hatshepsut at Deir el-Bahri. XVIII Dynasty, 1580–1350 B.C. (Charles Chipiez)

C. Typical Plan of an Egyptian Temple.

D. Plan of Temple of Amon, Karnak. 1633–323 B.C. (Charles Chipiez)

E. Temple of Amon, Karnak. The Avenue of Sphinxes leading to the Temple. XIX Dynasty, 1350–1205 B.C.

F. Temple of Amon, Karnak. Granite piers bearing the Lily of Upper Egypt and the Papyrus of Lower Egypt.

G. Temple of Amon, Karnak. Side aisle, Hypostyle hall. XIX Dynasty, 1350–1205 B.C.

H. Temple of Amon, Karnak. Hypostyle hall. Restored. Metropolitan Museum. (Met)

A. Hathor Capital from the Temple at Denderah. Saïte Period.
(Rosengarten)

B. Palm Leaf Capital from the Temple at Edfu. Saïte Period.
(Rosengarten)

C. Lotus Bell Capital from the Temple at Edfu. Saïte Period.
(Rosengarten)

D. Lotus Bud Column of Thotmes III from Ambulatory of
Thotmes at Karnak. (Chipiez)

E. Temple of Amon, Luxor. Restored by Charles Chipiez.
XVII and XIX Dynasties, 1580–1205 B.C.

F. Plan of Temple of Amon, Luxor. (Perrot and Chipiez)

G. Temple of Amon, Luxor. Pylon with Colossi of Ramses II
and Obelisk. XIX Dynasty, 1350–1205 B.C.

H. Temple of Amon, Luxor. Court of Amenophis III. XVIII
Dynasty, 1580–1350 B.C.

I. Temple of Amon, Luxor. Principal façade restored by
Charles Chipiez. XIX Dynasty, 1580–1350 B.C.

J. Hypostyle hall. Temple of Seti I, Abydos. 1350 B.C.

EGYPTIAN ARCHITECTURE AND SCULPTURE
NEW EMPIRE · 1580–1090 B.C.

7

A. Temple of Khons, Karnak. XIX Dynasty, 1350–1205 B.C.

B. Colossi of "Memnon," Thebes. (Langani)

C. Temple of Ramses II, Abu Simbel. 1300 B.C.

D. Temple of Ramses II, Abu Simbel. Entrance hall. 1300 B.C.

E. Guardian Figure. XIX Dynasty, 1350–1205 B.C. Louvre. (Gir)

F. Ikhnaton. c. 1375 B.C. New Museum, Berlin. (Grantz)

G. Queen Nofretete. 1375–1358 B.C. New Museum, Berlin. (Grantz)

H. Ikhnaton. c. 1375 B.C. New Museum, Berlin. (Grantz)

8

EGYPTIAN SCULPTURE AND PAINTING
NEW EMPIRE · 1580–1090 B.C.

A. Relief from Wall of Temple of Seti I, Abydos. XIX Dynasty, 1350–1205 B.C.

B. Man and Horse. XVII–XVIII Dynasty. Metropolitan Museum. (Met)

C. Gold Portrait Mask of King Tutankhamon. 1350 B.C. Museum, Cairo. (Cairo)

D. Painted Relief in Tomb of Seti I. XIX Dynasty, 1305–1205 B.C. Archaeological Museum, Florence. (Al)

E. Banquet Scene. Slave Arranging an Ear-ring. Tomb of Nakht, Thebes. XVII Dynasty, 1580–1350 B.C.

F. Wall Painting. Tomb of Nakht, Thebes. XVII Dynasty. (Met).

G. Ramses II in Battle. XIX Dynasty, 1350–1205 B.C. (Champollion)

H. Relief from Second Hypostyle Hall, Temple of Seti I, Abydos. XIX Dynasty, 1350–1205 B.C.

EGYPTIAN SCULPTURE AND MINOR ARTS
NEW EMPIRE · 1580 1090 B.C.; SAÏTE PERIOD · 663–525 B.C.

9

A. Seti I. Necropolis, Thebes. XIX Dynasty, 1350–1205 B.C.

B. Comb and Handle. Louvre. (Gir)

C. Chair. Wood. Louvre. (Gir)

D. Spoons. Louvre. (Gir)

E. Pectoral of Ramses II. XIX Dynasty, 1350–1205 B.C. Louvre. (Gautier)

F. Basalt Head of a Priest. Saïte Period, XXVI Dynasty, 663–525 B.C. New Museum, Berlin. (Grantz)

G. Side View of F.

H. Sculptor's Model of a Goddess. Saïte Period, XXVI Dynasty, 663–525 B.C. Metropolitan Museum. (Met)

A. Sculptor's Model of Queen or Goddess. Ptolemaic Period.
Metropolitan Museum. (Met)

B. Walking Figure. Saïte Period. Vatican Museum. (Al)

C. Sculptor's Model. Ram's Head. Early Ptolemaic Period.
Metropolitan Museum. (Met)

D. Temple of Horus, Edfu. 237–212 B.C., in part.

E. Temple of Horus, Edfu. Pylon from the forecourt. 237–212
B.C., in part

F. Temple of Isis, Philae. Ptolemaic Period. (Rosengarten)

G. Bell Shaped Capitals, Temple at Esneh. c. 280 B.C.

EARLY BABYLONIAN SCULPTURE C. 3000–1275 B.C.
ASSYRIAN SCULPTURE · C. 1650–606 B.C.

11

A. Gudea Head. Early Babylonian, c. 2450 B.C. Louvre.

B. Winged Man-Headed Bull. From Palace of Ashurnasirpal II. IX century B.C. Metropolitan Museum. (Met)

C. Head of a Figure similar to B. British Museum. (Man)

D. Ashurbanipal Hunting. 668–626 B.C. British Museum. (Man)

E. Winged Being Offering Branch with Pomegranates. From

Palace of Ashurnasirpal II. IX century B.C. Metropolitan Museum. (Met)

F. Ashurbanipal Hunting. 668–626 B.C. British Museum. (Man)

G. Eagle-Headed Winged Being Pollenating the Sacred Tree. From Palace of Ashurnasirpal II. IX century B.C. Metropolitan Museum. (Met)

A. Palace of Sargon II, Khorsabad. Restored. 722–705 B.C.
(Thomas)

B. Plan of Palace of Sargon II. (Place)

C. Palace of Sargon II. Main Gateway. Restored. (Thomas)

D. Head of Royal Attendant from Palace of Sargon II. VIII
century B.C. Metropolitan Museum. (Met)

E. Palace of Sargon II. Harem Court. Restored. (Thomas)

F. Archers of King Darius. Glazed Tile from Palace of Darius
at Susa. 521–484 B.C. Louvre. (Gir)

ASSYRIAN SCULPTURE · 1650–606 B.C.
PERSIAN ARCHITECTURE AND SCULPTURE · 530–225 B.C.

13

A. A Mede Bringing a Tribute of Horses. From Palace of Sargon II, Khorsabad. 722–705 B.C. Metropolitan Museum. (Met)

B. Tomb of Darius, above the Great Temple at Persepolis. (Texier)

C. Palace of Darius, Persepolis. Reconstruction. c. 521 B.C.

D. Sculptured Capital from interior of Palace of Artaxerxes, Susa. 521–485 B.C. Louvre. (Gir)

E. Wounded Lioness. From Palace at Nineveh. 668–626 B.C. British Museum. (Man)

F. Lion Frieze. From Palace at Susa. Glazed Tile. Louvre. (Louvre)

A. Palace of Minos, Knossus. Plan. c. 1500 B.C.

B. Palace of Minos, Knossus. Colonnaded Hall. Restored. c. 1500 B.C. (Maroghiannis)

C. Corbeled Gallery of Citadel, Tiryns. c. 1500 B.C. (Perrot and Chipiez)

D. "Treasury of Atreus," Mycenae. 1185 B.C.

E. "Treasury of Atreus." Mycenae. Reconstruction by Charles Chipiez.

F. Priestess Bearing a Casket. Fresco from Tiryns. c. 1450 B.C. National Museum, Athens. (Met)

G. Lion Gate, Mycenae. Detail. c. 1300 B.C.

A. Dolphins. Fresco from Palace of Minos, Knossus. c. 1500 B.C. (Met)

B. Cupbearer. Fresco from Palace of Minos, Knossus. c. 1500 B.C. Candia Museum. (Met)

C. Chariot Scene. Fresco from Knossus. c. 1500 B.C. Candia Museum. (Met)

D. Throne Room. Palace of Minos, Knossus. c. 1500 B.C. (Met)

E. Painted Sarcophagus from Hagia Triada. 1400–1200 B.C. Candia Museum. (Met)

F. Gold Cups from Vaphio. 1600–1500 B.C. National Museum, Athens.

G. Detail of F. (Schuchardt)

A. Vase from Hagia Triada. Candia Museum. (Can)

B. Amphora of the Palace Style from Knossus. 1500–1350 B.C. (Buschor)

C. Snake Goddess. Detail of E. (M.F.A.)

D. Kamares Style Vase from Knossus. 2000–1800 B.C. (Buschor)

E. Snake Goddess. Gold and Ivory. c. 1500 B.C. Museum of Fine Arts. (M.F.A.)

F. Snake Goddess. Side view of E.

G. Greek Architecture. The Three Orders: Doric, Ionic, Corinthian. (D'Espouy)

H. The Doric Order. R. to L.: Temple of Apollo, Corinth, c. 540 B.C.; Parthenon, 447–432 B.C.; Temple of Delos, c. 373 B.C. (Borrmann)

A. Doric Order. Detail. From the Propylaea, Athens. 437–432 B.C.

B. Cypriote Stele. VI century B.C. (Met)

C. The Heraeum, Olympia. c. 700 B.C.

D. Temple of Apollo, Corinth. VII century B.C. (See 16 H.)

E. Treasury of the Siphnians, Delphi. Reconstruction. Delphi Museum. c. 525 B.C. (See 27 B., C.)

F. Temple of Demeter, Paestum. c. 520 B.C.

G. Treasury of the Athenians, Delphi. c. 515 B.C.

A. Order of the Olympieum, Acragas. Conjectural restoration by Koldewey. 480 B.C.

B. Conjectural restoration of the type of the Temple of Zeus, Olympia. c. 465 B.C.

C. Temple of Poseidon, Paestum. Plan. c. 460 B.C. (Koldewey)

D. Temple of Poseidon, Paestum. c. 460 B.C. Left: The Basilica, 550 B.C. (Al)

E. Temple of Apollo Epicurius, Bassae. c. 450 B.C. Ictinus, architect.

F. Temple of Apollo Epicurius, Bassae. Plan. c. 450 B.C.

G. The Parthenon, Athens. Plan. 447–432 B.C. Ictinus and Callicrates, architects. (Dörpfeld)

A. The Acropolis, Athens. Restoration. (Bell)

B. The Acropolis, Athens. Detail of plan. (A) The Old Temple of Athena, c. 527 B.C.; (B) The Parthenon, 447–432 B.C.; (C) The Erechtheum, 420 B.C.

C. The Parthenon, Athens, 447–432 B.C. Ictinus and Callicrates, architects. (Fred L. Ball)

D. The Parthenon, Athens. E. façade. Model. Metropolitan Museum. (See pp. 31, 32.) (Met)

E. The Erechtheum, Athens. E. side. Restoration. 420–409 B.C., and later. Mnesicles, architect. (Tetaz)

F. The Erechtheum, Athens. N. porch. (Al)

A. The Erechtheum, Athens. S. side. 420–409 B.C., and later. (See 34 C.) (Clarence Kennedy)

B. Temple of Athena Nike, Athens. E. façade. c. 426 B.C.

C. Temple of Athena Nike, Athens. Corner capital.

D. Frieze from the Erechtheum with Honeysuckle, Egg and Dart, Bead and Reel, Leaf and Dart motifs. Acropolis Museum. (Al)

E. The Propylaea, Athens. W. side. Mnesicles, architect. Begun c. 437 B.C. (Al)

F. The Propylaea, Athens. E. side. (Al)

GREEK ARCHITECTURE · GOLDEN AGE · 470–338 B.C.
HELLENISTIC PERIOD · 323–146 B.C.

21

A. The Theseum, Athens. E. façade. Restored. 421 B.C. (André)

B. The Mausoleum, Halicarnassus. Conjectural restoration. 353–340 B.C. (See 37 B.) (Bühlmann)

C. Theatre, Epidaurus. Plan. c. 350 B.C. (Dörpfeld)

D. Precinct of Demeter, Eleusis. Restored. Graeco-Roman. (Gaudy-Deering)

E. Theatre, Epidaurus. From S.W.

F. Corinthian Capital from the Tholos. Epidaurus. c. 350 B.C.

A. Choragic Monument of Lysicrates, Athens. 335–334 B.C.

B. Choragic Monument of Lysicrates, Athens. Restoration by Stuart and Revett.

C. Corinthian Order of the Choragic Monument of Lysicrates. (Stuart and Revett)

D. The Acropolis, Pergamon. Restoration by F. Thiersch, 1882.

A painting in the Pergamon Museum, Berlin. (See 39 A.)

E. Tower of the Winds, Athens. I century B.C.

F. Temple of Jupiter Olympus, Athens. Roman, 174 B.C.–117 A.D. (Al)

G. Oinochoë. Rhodian. VII century B.C. Museum of Fine Arts. (M.F.A.)

A. Geometric Amphora from the Dipylon Cemetery, Athens. VII century B.C. National Museum, Athens. (Nat. Mus.)

B. Chief Design on an Amphora from Melos. VII century B.C. National Museum, Athens. (Conze)

C. Slaying of Kyknos by Herakles. From a Chalkidian black-figured Amphora. VII century B.C. Munich. (Münch Vasens)

D. Francois Vase. Krater from Chiusi. By Klitias and Ergotimos. VI century B.C. National Museum, Florence. (Furtwängler)

E. Details of a Kylix by Epictetus. VI century B.C. British Museum. (Furtwängler)

F. Amphorae. VI century B.C. Vatican Museum. (Al)

A. Athena and Herakles. From an Amphora in the style of the Andokides painter. VI century B.C. Munich. (Furtwängler)

B. Women Celebrating a Festival of Dionysus. An early Stamnos attributed to the Menelaos painter. Metropolitan Museum. (Met)

C. The Argonauts (?). Detail of a Krater of the Polygnotan Period. V century B.C. Louvre. (Furtwängler)

D. Combat of the Greeks and the Amazons. Volute-Krater. V century B.C. National Museum, Naples. (Al)

E. Pelops and Hippodameia. Detail from a red-figured Amphora. V century B.C. Museum, Arezzo. (Furtwängler)

F. Polyneikes Offers Eriphyle the Necklace. Detail from red-figured Pelike. V century B.C. Lucca. (Furtwängler)

GREEK VASES · V–IV CENT. B.C.
GREEK SCULPTURE · ARCHAIC PERIOD · 750–510 B.C.

25

A. Herakles and Antaeus. Detail of a Kylix-Krater by Euphronius. V century B.C. Louvre. (Furtwängler)

B. Apulian Volute-Krater. Achilles and Thersites. IV century B.C. Museum of Fine Arts. (M.F.A.)

C. Theseus, Athena and Amphitrite. Kylix by Euphronius. V century B.C. Louvre. (Furtwängler)

D. Volute-Krater. Shrine of Athena. IV century B.C. National Museum, Naples. (Nat. Mus.)

E. Artemis from Delos. c. 650 B.C. National Museum, Athens. (Al)

F. Hera of Samos. c. 550 B.C. Louvre. (Gir)

G. Kitylos and Dermys. VII century B.C. National Museum, Athens. (Al)

H. Sepulchral Stele from Sparta. Berlin.

I. Winged Figure from Delos. Early VI century B.C. National Museum, Athens. (Al)

J. Seated Figure of Chares from Branchidae. VI century B.C. British Museum. (Br. Mus.)

A. Spartan Stele. Mid-VI century B.C. Old Museum, Berlin. (Bruck)

B. Perseus Decapitating the Gorgon. Metope from Selinus. Early Series. Early VI century B.C. Museum, Palermo. (See 28 H.)

C. Apollo from Melos. Early VI century B.C. National Museum, Athens. (Al)

D. Apollo. VI century B.C. National Museum, Athens. (Al)

E. Apollo. Late VI century B.C. National Museum, Athens. (Al)

F. Figure found on the Acropolis. Late VI century B.C. Acropolis Museum. (Al)

G. Figure found on the Acropolis. Late VI century B.C. Acropolis Museum. (Al)

H. Figure found on the Acropolis. Late VI century B.C. Acropolis Museum. (Al)

I. Figure found on the Acropolis. Late VI century B.C. Acropolis Museum. (Al)

J. Detail of I.

K. Figure found on the Acropolis. Early V century B.C. Acropolis Museum. (Al)

L. Stele of Aristion. By Aristocles. Early VI century B.C. National Museum, Athens. (See 27 A) (Al)

A. Stele of Aristion. (Detail of 26 L.) (Al)

B. Treasury of the Siphnians. Frieze. c. 525 B.C. Delphi Museum. (See 17 E.) (Al)

C. Treasury of the Siphnians. Frieze. Delphi Museum. (Al)

D. Archaic Head. VI century (?) B.C. Terme Museum. (Al)

E. Frieze of Six Youths Playing Ball. c. 510 B.C. National Museum, Athens. (Clarence Kennedy)

F. Palaestra Scene with Jumper, Wrestlers, Spear Thrower. Frieze. c. 510 B.C. National Museum, Athens. (Clarence Kennedy)

G. Naxian Sphinx. c. 550–540 B.C. Delphi Museum. (Al)

A. Fragment of a Pediment, Athens. The Typhon. Late VI century B.C. Acropolis Museum. (Bruck)

B. Wounded Warrior from W. Pediment of the Temple of Aegina. Late VI century B.C. Glyptothek, Munich. (Bruck)

C. Warrior from E. Pediment of the Temple of Aegina. Late VI century B.C. Glyptothek, Munich. (Bruck)

D. Wounded Warrior from E. Pediment of the Temple of Aegina. Late VI century B.C. Glyptothek, Munich. (Bruck)

E. Archaic Head. School of Aegina (?). VI century B.C. Archaeological Museum, Florence. (Al)

F. The Calf Bearer (Hermes Moscophorus). c. 536 B.C. Acropolis Museum.

G. Head of a Youth. Late VI century B.C. Acropolis Museum. (Al)

H. Hercules and an Amazon. Metope from Selinus. Later Series. (See 26 B.)

A. Harmodius and Aristogeiton. Probably by Critius and Nesiotes. 477 B.C. Copy. National Museum, Naples. (Al)

B. Harmodius. Detail of A.

C. Augeian Stable Metope. E. side. From Temple of Zeus, Olympia. Olympia Museum. c. 460 B.C. (Al)

D. Detail of W. Pediment, Temple of Zeus, Olympia. Battle of Centaurs and Lapiths. c. 460 B.C. Olympia Museum. (Al)

E. Detail of E. Pediment, Temple of Zeus, Olympia. "Alpheios." c. 460 B.C. Olympia Museum. (Al)

F. Detail of W. Pediment, Temple of Zeus, Olympia. Centaur Biting a Boy. c. 460 B.C. Olympia Museum. (Al)

G. Detail of W. Pediment, Temple of Zeus, Olympia. Centaur and Lapith Woman. c. 460 B.C. Olympia Museum. (Al)

H. Detail of E. Pediment, Temple of Zeus, Olympia. Oinomaos and Sterope. c. 460 B.C. Olympia Museum. (Al)

A. "Ludovisi Throne." Relief from R. side. c. 480 B.C. Terme Museum. (Al)

B. "Ludovisi Throne." The back. c. 480 B.C. Terme Museum. (Al)

C. "Ludovisi Throne." Relief from L. side. Terme Museum. (And)

D. "Aphrodite" (?). Detail of B. (Al)

E. Charioteer of Delphi. Detail of F. (Al)

F. Charioteer of Delphi. c. 470 B.C. Delphi Museum. (Al)

G. Mourning Athena. Acropolis Museum. (Al)

H. Myron. Athena, from a Roman Athena and Marsyas group. c. 450 B.C. Gallery, Frankfurt. (Frankfurt Gallery)

I. Myron. Marsyas, from a Roman Athena and Marsyas group. c. 450 B.C. Lateran Museum. (See 31 A.) (Al)

A. Myron. Marsyas. British Museum (See 30 I.) (Br. Mus.)

B. Phidias (?). W. Pediment. The Parthenon. 447–432 B.C. After a drawing by Jacques Carrey in 1674 in the Bibliothèque Nationale, Paris. (Michaelis)

C. Phidias (?). "The Three Fates." E. Pediment. The Parthenon. 447–432 B.C. British Museum. (See p. 19.) (Br. Mus.)

D. Myron. Discobolus. Reconstruction. Terme Museum.

E. Phidias (?). Nike and a Fate. E. Pediment. The Parthenon.

F. Myron. Discobolus. Vatican Museum. (Al)

G. Myron. Discobolus. Another view of D. Terme Museum.

H. Lapith Conquering a Centaur. S. Metope, The Parthenon. 447–432 B.C. British Museum. (See pp. 19, 32.) (Br. Mus.)

A. Lapith and Centaur. S. Metope, The Parthenon. 447–432
B.C. British Museum. (See 19 D.) (Br. Mus.)

B. Youths Bearing Wine Jars. Parthenon frieze. N. side.
Acropolis Museum. (Al)

C. Bulls Being Led to Sacrifice. Parthenon frieze. N. side.
Acropolis Museum. (Al)

D. Group of Men. Parthenon frieze. N. side. Acropolis Museum. (Al)

E. Horsemen. Parthenon frieze. W. side. Acropolis Museum.
(Al)

F. Poseidon, Dionysus, Demeter (?). Parthenon frieze. E. side.
Acropolis Museum. (Al)

A. Parthenon Frieze. N. side. Acropolis Museum. (Al)

B. Parthenon Naos. Restored. (Met)

C. Phidias' Influence. The Varvakeion Athena. A Roman copy. National Museum, Athens. (Al)

D. Phidias' Influence. Side view of C.

E. Phidias' Influence. Detail of D.

F. Phidias' Influence. Roman copy of Athena Parthenos. Prado.

G. Phidias' Influence. Athena Farnese. National Museum, Naples. (Brogi)

H. Phidias' Influence. The Velletri Athena. Roman copy. Louvre. (Louvre)

I. Phidias (?) Athena Lemnia. Albertinum.

J. Phidias (?) Athena Lemnia Head. Civic Museum, Bologna. (Clarence Kennedy)

A. Demeter. Vatican Museum. (Bruck)

B. Athena. Capitoline Museum, Rome. Late V century B.C.

C. Caryatid Porch. Erechtheum, Athens. 420–409 B.C. (See 20 A.)

D. Venus Genetrix. Probably after Arkesilaos. Terme Museum. (Al)

E. Nike Fastening Her Sandal. From the balustrade of the Temple of Athena Nike. 421–415 B.C. Acropolis Museum.

F. Figure from the balustrade of the Temple of Athena Nike. 421–415 B.C. Acropolis Museum. (Al)

G. Paionius. Nike. Olympia Museum. (Bruck)

H. Paionius. Nike. Restored. Olympia Museum. (Olympia Mus.)

I. Polyclitus. Diadoumenos. Roman copy. National Museum (Al)

J. Polyclitus. Diadoumenos. Copy. Metropolitan Museum. (Met)

K. Polyclitus. Copy of Spearbearer (Borghese Mars). Louvre. (Louvre)

A. Polyclitus, School of. Youth. National Museum, Athens. (Al)

B. Polyclitus, School of. Doryphorus Bust. National Museum, Naples.

C. Polyclitus, School of. Amazon, Mattei type. Vatican Museum. (Al)

D. Polyclitus, School of. Amazon, Capitoline type. Capitoline Museum. (Bruck)

E. Polyclitus, School of. Amazon. Berlin Museum.

F. Praxiteles. Hermes with the Infant Dionysus. c. 350 B.C. Olympia Museum.

G. Praxiteles. Hermes. Detail of F. (Olympia Museum)

H. Praxiteles. Copy. "Apollo" Sauroctonos. 370–340 B.C. Vatican Museum. (Traldi)

I. Praxiteles. Copy. Satyr (Marble Faun). Capitoline Museum. (Traldi)

J. Praxiteles. Copy. Satyr. Detail of I.

A. Praxiteles' Influence. Hermes of Andros. Vatican Museum.
(Al)

B. Hermes of Andros. Detail of A.

C. Praxiteles. Copy. Venus of Cnidos. Vatican Museum.

D. Venus of Cnidos. Detail of C. (Al)

E. Praxiteles' Influence. Aphrodite Anadyomene. National
Museum, Naples. (Al)

F. Praxiteles' Influence. Aphrodite of Cyrene. I century B.C.
Copy. Terme Museum. (Al)

G. Praxiteles' Influence. Capitoline Venus. Capitoline Museum.

H. Aphrodite of Syracuse. Syracuse Museum. (Al)

I. Praxiteles' Influence. Artemis of Gabii. Louvre. (Louvre)

J. Lysippus. Copy. Apoxyomenos. Vatican. (Al)

K. Lysippus. Copy. Apoxyomenos. Other side of J.

L. Lysippus' Influence. Silenus and Bacchus. Louvre. (Louvre)

M. Glycon, after Lysippus. Farnese Hercules. I century B.C.
National Museum, Naples (Al)

A. Head of a Youth. Scopas' Influence. Museum of Fine Arts. (M.F.A.)

B. Battle of the Greeks and the Amazons. Frieze of the Mausoleum, Halicarnassus. c. 350 B.C. British Museum. (See 21 B.) (Br. Mus.)

C. Ares Ludovisi. Scopas' Influence. Terme Museum. (Grafia)

D. Meleager. Scopas' Influence. Fogg Museum. (Fogg)

E. Meleager. Vatican Museum. (Traldi)

F. Niobid. Terme Museum. (Grafia)

G. Niobe and Her Youngest Daughter. Uffizi.

H. Drum from Ephesus. British Museum. (Br. Mus.)

I. Kephisodotus. Eirene and Ploutos. Copy. Glyptothek. (Bruck)

A. Sophocles. IV century B.C. Lateran Museum. (Traldi)

B. "Alexander Sarcophagus." IV century B.C. Museum, Constantinople. (Constant. Mus.)

C. Grave Relief of Dexileos. Ceramicus, Athens. (Bruck)

D. Grave Relief of Hegeso. Detail. Ceramicus, Athens. (Bruck)

E. Grave Relief of Protonoe. Ceramicus, Athens. (Al)

F. Praying Boy. Influence of Lysippus (?). Old Museum,
Berlin. (Berlin)

G. Head of Aphrodite. IV century B.C. Francis Bartlett Collection, Museum of Fine Arts. (M.F.A.)

H. Head of Aphrodite. Side view of G.

I. Boy With a Goose. Bœthos. Capitoline Museum.

A. Frieze from the Altar of Zeus, Pergamon. c. 175 B.C. Pergamon Museum, Berlin. (See 22 D.)

B. Slave Sharpening Knife. Pergamon School. Uffizi. (Al)

C. Dying Gaul. Pergamon School. Capitoline Museum.

D. Dying Gaul. Detail of C.

E. Gaul and His Wife. Pergamon School. Terme Museum. (Al)

F. Boxer. By Apollonius. I century B.C. Terme Museum.

G. Muse Leaning Against a Rock. Berlin. (Bruck)

A. Pugilist. National Museum, Athens. (Bruck)

B. Laocoön. School of Rhodes. Vatican Museum.

C. Laocoön. Detail of B. (And)

D. "The Hellenistic Ruler." National Museum, Rome. (Al)

E. "The Hellenistic Ruler." Detail of D.

F. Zeus Otricoli. II century B.C. Vatican Museum. (Grafia)

G. Aphrodite of Melos. II century B.C. Louvre. (Louvre)

H. Tyche of Antiocheia. Vatican Museum.

I. Nike of Samothrace. After 306 B.C. Louvre. (Louvre)

J. Aphrodite of Capua. National Museum, Naples. (Al)

K. Artemis of Versailles. Louvre. (Louvre)

A. Apollo Belvedere. Vatican Museum. (Grafia)

B. Old Fisherman. Capitoline Museum.

C. Tanagra Figurine. IV century B.C. Museum of Fine Arts. (M.F.A.)

D. Old Market Woman. II century B.C. Metropolitan Museum. (Met)

E. Orestes and Electra. Pasiteles' Influence. I century B.C. National Museum, Naples.

F. Demosthenes. Vatican Museum. (And)

G. Hermes (Mercury) in Repose. National Museum, Naples. (Al)

H. Farnese Bull. School of Tralles. I century B.C. National Museum, Naples. (Al)

I. Sleeping Satyr (Barberini Faun). Glyptothek. (Bruck)

J. Archaistic Athena. National Museum, Naples. (Al)

A. Forum Romanum during the Imperial Period. Restored. From S.E. (L. to R.) Basilica Julia, 51 B.C. (behind columns); Temple of Jupiter Capitolinus, begun 509 B.C. (above); Temple of Saturn, 284 A.D. (facing R.); Temple of Vespasian, 94 A.D.; Temple of Concord, 27 B.C.–14 A.D.; Tabularium, 78 B.C. (with arch order); Arch of Septimius Severus, 204 A.D.; Temple of Juno Moneta, 146 B.C. (above R.); Basilica Aemilia, 54 B.C. (Tognetti)

B. Temple of Jupiter Capitolinus during the Imperial Period. Restored. (Tognetti)

C. Forum Romanum. From S.E. (L. to R.) Temple of Vespasian; Temple of Concord; Tabularium (above); Arch of Septimius Severus. (Al)

D. Forum Romanum during the Imperial Period. Restored. Detail of A. (Tognetti)

E. Forum Romanum during the Imperial Period. Restored. From E. (L. to R.) Temple of Divus Julius, 42–29 B.C.; Temple of Castor and Pollux, 6 A.D.; Basilica Julia; Temple of Jupiter Capitolinus (above R.). (Tognetti)

F. Temple of Vespasian. Forum Romanum. Fragment of cornice. 94 A.D.

A. Forum Romanum. From W. (L. to R.) Temple of Vespasian; Arch of Septimius Severus; Temple of Saturn.

B. Temple of the Sibyl, Tivoli. 27 B.C.-14 A.D. (And)

C. Temple of Fortuna Augusta, Pompeii. Restored. I century A.D. (Tognetti)

D. Temple of Mars Ultor, Rome. Restoration of Corinthian capital. (D'Espouy)

E. Baalbek. Reconstruction. R., Temple of the Sun, 131–161 A.D.; Temple of Jupiter, 273 A.D.

F. Baths (Temple) of Diana, Nîmes. 25 B.C.

A. Maison Carrée, Nîmes. I or II century A.D. (N.D.)

B. Temple of Fortuna Virilis, Rome. I century B.C. (Al)

C. The Pantheon, Rome. 120–124 A.D. Portico, 27 B.C.–14 A.D. (Al)

D. The Pantheon, Rome. Interior. (Brogi)

E. Round Temple Near the Tiber, Rome. I century A.D.

F. Baths of Diocletian, Rome. Restored. 302 A.D. (Paulin)

BASILICAS · CIRCUSES · HOUSES · AMPHITHEATRES

A. Basilica of Maxentius (Constantine), Rome. 306–12 A.D.

B. Circus Maximus during the Imperial Period, Rome. I century B.C.

C. House of Menandro, Pompeii. The Atrium. I century A.D.

D. House of Pansa, Pompeii. Plan. I century B.C.

E. The Colosseum (Flavian Amphitheatre), Rome. 70–82 A.D.

F. The Colosseum. Isometric section.

A. Amphitheatre, Nîmes. I–II century A.D. (L.N.)

B. Porta Nigra, Trèves. 275 A.D.

C. The Little Theatre, Herculaneum. Restored. I century A.D.

D. The Theatre, Orange. (N.D.)

E. Arch of Titus, Rome. 81 A.D. (See 48 G, 49 B.) (Grafia)

F. Arch of Constantine, Rome. Re-erected, 312 A.D. (See 49 F.) (And)

A. Arch of Septimius Severus. 204 A.D. (And)

B. Arch at Orange. 27 B.C.–14 A.D. (N.D.)

C. Columbaria. The Appian Way, Rome. (Al)

D. Tomb of Hadrian (Castel S. Angelo), Rome. 135 A.D. (Grafia)

E. Aqueduct, Segovia. I–II century A.D.

F. Pont du Gard, Nîmes. 27 B.C.–14 A.D.

A. Apollo. Found at Pompeii. National Museum, Naples. (Al)

B. Dancing Faun from the House of the Faun, Pompeii. I century B.C. (?). National Museum, Naples.

C. Boy With a Dolphin. Found at Pompeii. National Museum, Naples. (Al)

D. Caesar Augustus. From the Prima Porta. 27 B.C.–14 A.D. Vatican Museum. (Al)

E. Horse of St. Mark's, Venice. Detail of head. (c. 480 B.C. (?).) Once on Arch of Nero, Rome. (See 56 E.)

F. Augustus from the Via Labicana. 27 B.C.–14 A.D. Terme Museum. (Al)

G. Spoils of Jerusalem. Arch of Titus, Rome. 81 A.D. (See 46 E, 49 B.)

H. Triumphal Procession. Arch of Titus, Rome. 81 A.D.

A. Ara Pacis. Procession. 13 B.C. Uffizi. (See 50 D.) (Al)

B. Arch of Titus, Rome. Spandrels. 81 A.D. (See 46 E, 48 G.)

C. Column of Trajan, Rome. Detail of lower drums. 113 A.D.

D. Equestrian Statue of Marcus Aurelius (161–180 A.D.). Campidoglio, Rome. (See 103 A.)

E. Marcus Aurelius. British Museum. (Br. Mus.)

F. Medallions. N. side, Arch of Constantine, Rome. Rededicated 312 A.D. (See 46 F.) (Al)

G. Sarcophagus of St. Helena. IV century A.D. Vatican Museum. (Grafia)

A. Sacrifice of Marcus Aurelius (161–180 A.D.). Capitoline Museum. (Al)

B. Caracalla. 211–17 A.D. Berlin. (Berlin Museum)

C. The Portland Vase. Probably I century A.D. British Museum. (Br. Mus.)

D. Ara Pacis. Detail of decoration. 13 B.C. Uffizi. (See 49 A.) (Al)

E. Battle Between Romans and Barbarians. Sarcophagus. IV century A.D. Terme Museum.

F. The Battle of Issus, Between Darius and Alexander. c. 100 B.C. From a IV century B.C. original. Mosaic from House of the Faun, Pompeii. National Museum, Naples. (See 51 A.)

A. Battle of Issus. Detail of Alexander. Mosaic. (See 50 F.)

B. Hercules Discovers His Son Telephos. Painting. From Pompeii. National Museum, Naples.

C. Wall Paintings from Boscoreale. (Met)

D. Putto (Cupid) Riding a Crab. Painting from the House of the Vetii, Pompeii. National Museum, Naples.

E. Pirithous Rescuing Ippotamia from the Centaur. Painting on marble from Herculaneum. V century B.C. type. National Museum, Naples.

F. Portrait of Paquius Proculus and Wife. National Museum, Naples. (See 52 A.) (Al)

A. Wife of Paquius Proculus. Detail of 51 F.

B. The Aldobrandini Marriage. Painting. I century A.D. Detail. Vatican Museum. (Al)

C. The Aldobrandini Marriage. Detail of B.

D. Doves. Mosaic. From the Villa of Hadrian. II century A.D. Capitoline Museum.

E. Hercules with the Serpents. Painting. House of the Vetii, Pompeii. I century A.D.

F. Three Graces. Painting from Pompeii. National Museum, Naples. (Al)

G. Portrait of a Young Woman. Egyptian painting. III century A.D. Archaeological Museum, Florence. (Al)

A. Section of the Old Basilica of St. Peter, Rome. Consecrated 326 A.D. Destroyed XV century. (See 139 C for façade.) (Fontana)

B. St. Paul's Outside the Walls, Rome. Founded 386 A.D. Rebuilt 1823. (See 64 C.) (And)

C. Old St. Peter's, Rome. Plan. 326 A.D. (See A.)

D. Basilica of San Clemente, Rome. Plan. 385 A.D. Rebuilt 1108.

E. S. Stefano Rotondo, Rome. Interior. 470 A.D. (See G.) (Al)

F. Basilica of San Lorenzo Outside the Walls, Rome. Façade. Rebuilt 578 A.D. Remodeled 1216–1227. (Al)

G. S. Stefano Rotondo, Rome. Restoration. 468–483 A.D.

A. Santa Costanza, Rome. Interior. 323–37. Rebuilt 1256. (See 60 B.) (Al)

B. Tomb of Galla Placidia, Ravenna. Interior. c. 450 A.D. (Al)

C. Tomb of Galla Placidia, Ravenna. Exterior. c. 450 A.D.

D. Tomb of Galla Placidia, Ravenna. Plan. c. 450 A.D.

E. Tomb of Theodoric, Ravenna. Restored. 526 A.D. (Haupt-Hannover)

F. Basilica of Tourmanin, Syria. Restored. VI century A.D. (De Vogüe)

A.　San Vitale, Ravenna. Interior. 526 A.D. (See 57 B, 60 E.)
(Al)

B.　San Vitale, Ravenna. Interior. 526 A.D. (Al)

C.　San Vitale, Ravenna. Plan. (Dehio)

D.　Santa Sophia, Istanbul. 532–537 A.D. Section without dome.
(Choisy)

E.　Santa Sophia, Istanbul. Plan.

F.　Santa Sophia, Istanbul. Exterior.

G.　Santa Sophia, Istanbul. Interior.

A. Sant' Apollinare Nuovo, Ravenna. The Nave. 549 A.D. (See 61 A.) (Al)

B. Chapel, Aix-la-Chapelle (Aachen). Plan. 796–804 A.D.

C. Chapel, Aix-la-Chapelle. Elevation. (See 89 A.)

D. St. Mark's, Venice. Plan. 1042–1071.

E. St. Mark's, Venice. Façade. (And)

F. St. Mark's, Venice. Capitals. (And)

BYZANTINE ARCHITECTURE · XI CENT.
EARLY CHRISTIAN AND BYZANTINE SCULPTURE · IV–VI CENT.

57

A. St. Mark's, Venice. Section. 1042–1071. (See p. 56.)

B. San Vitale. Byzantine capital. 526 A.D. (Al)

C. The Miracles of Christ. Early Christian Sarcophagus. IV century A.D. Lateran Museum.

D. The Good Shepherd. III century A.D. Lateran Museum.

E. Junius Bassus Sarcophagus. 350 A.D. St. Peter's, Rome.

F. "The Throne of Maximian." c. 550 A.D. Ravenna, Archiepiscopal Palace. (See 58 A.)

A "Throne of Maximian." Detail. c. 550 A.D. Ravenna, Archiepiscopal Palace. (See 57 F.)

B. Diptych of Consul Anastasius. 517 A.D. Bibliotheque Nationale. (Gir)

C. Mshatta Façade from Syria. IV–VI century A.D. Pergamon Museum.

D. Diptych Leaf. The Consul Magnus Seated with Symbolic Figures of Rome and Constantinople. 518 A.D. Bibliothèque Nationale. (Gir)

E. Sarcophagus Relief. Sant' Apollinare Nuovo, Ravenna. VII century A.D. (Al)

F. Empress Eudosia. VI century A.D. Bargello. (See 60 C.)

A. The Harbaville Triptych. X century A.D. Louvre.

B. Byzantine Ivory Book Cover. X century A.D. Cluny Museum. (Cluny Museum)

C. Ivory Triptych. X century A.D. Bargello.

D. French Ivory Book Cover. IX or X century A.D. Cluny Museum. (Cluny Museum)

E. Ivory. Late XI or early XII century A.D. The Visitation and the Magi Before Herod. Salerno Cathedral. (Gir)

F. Byzantine Ivory Coffer. X century A.D. The Nativity and the Presentation in the Temple. Louvre. (Louvre)

G. Virgin and Child. Byzantine Ivory. Late X century or early XI century A.D. Metropolitan Museum. (Met)

A. The Stroganoff Ivory. XI century. Cleveland Museum.
(Cleveland Mus.)

B. Making Wine. Early Christian Mosaic. IV century A.D.
Santa Costanza, Rome. (See 54 A.)

C. Christ Blessing Romanus IV, Emperor of Constantinople
and His Wife Eudosia. 1068–71 A.D. Bibliothèque Nationale.
(See 58 F.) (Gir)

D. The Good Shepherd. 440 A.D. Mausoleum of Galla Placidia,
Ravenna. (See 54 B.) (Al)

E. The Empress Theodora and Her Attendants. Mosaic, San
Vitale, Ravenna. (See 55 A, B.) (Al)

F. The Empress Theodora. Detail of E. (Al)

A. Sant' Apollinare Nuovo, Ravenna. Mosaic. Virgins Bearing Their Crowns as Offerings to the Virgin. VI century A.D. (See 56 A.) (Al)

B. St. Castrensis Freeing the Possessed from a Devil and Saving a Ship in Distress. Mosaic. XII century A.D. Monreale Cathedral. (Al)

C. Christ Entering Jerusalem. Mosaic. XII century A.D. Royal Chapel, Palermo. (Al)

D. Angels Appearing to Joshua Before the Walls of Jericho. Manuscript. V–VI century A.D. Vatican. (Muñoz)

E. Apse Mosaic. Monreale Cathedral. XII century A.D. (See 64 D.) (Al)

F. Crossing the Red Sea. Manuscript. X century A.D. Bibliothèque Nationale. (Gir)

A. Sant' Ambrogio, Milan. XII century. (Al)

B. Sant' Ambrogio, Milan. The Atrium and Façade. XII century. (Al)

C. Sant' Ambrogio, Milan. Interior. XII century. (Al)

D. Sant' Ambrogio, Milan. Plan. XII century. (Ferrario)

E. Modena Cathedral. 1099–1184. (Al)

F. Modena Cathedral. 1099–1184. (Al)

G. S. Zeno Maggiore, Verona. Façade. Begun 1138.

A. San Michele, Pavia. XII–XIII centuries. (And)

B. Cathedral and Baptistry, Parma. XII–XIII centuries. Baptistry, 1196. (Al)

C. Cathedral Group, Pisa. Cathedral, begun 1063; Baptistry, 1153–1278; Campanile, begun 1174.

D. Cathedral, Pisa. Plan. Begun 1063.

E. Campanile, Pisa. Begun 1174.

F. Cathedral, Pisa. Nave. Looking E. (Brogi)

G. San Miniato, Florence. Begun 1013. (See 64 A.) (Al)

A. San Miniato, Florence. Begun 1013. (See 63 G.) (Al)

B. Baptistry, Florence. Remodeled c. 1200.

C. St. Paul's Outside the Walls, Rome. Cloister. 1220–1241.
(See 53 B.) (And)

D. Monreale Cathedral. 1174–89. (See 61 E.) (Al)

E. Monreale Cathedral. Exterior of apse. 1174–89.

F. San Niccolo, Bari. 1197. (Al)

G. Monreale. Cloister of the Benedictine Monastery. (Al)

A. Bonannus of Pisa. Bronze Doors, Monreale. Detail. 1186.

B. Bonannus of Pisa. Bronze Doors, Pisa. Detail. 1180.

C. Bonannus of Pisa. Bronze Doors, Pisa. Detail of B. The Magi.

D. Christ on the Cross. Museum, Arezzo.

E. Marble Pavement. Baptistry, Florence. c. 1200. (Al)

F. Pulpit. San Miniato, Florence. XI century. (Al)

G. Pontifical Throne. San Lorenzo Fuori le Mura, Rome. XII century. (Al)

H. Pulpit. Cathedral, Ravello. XIII century. (Al)

A. Germiny-les-Prés. 801–806.

B. St. Front. Périgueux. c. 1120. (Aquitaine)

C. St. Front, Périgueux. Plan.

D. St. Sernin, Toulouse. Plan. Begun 1080, continued XII–XIII centuries. (Languedoc)

E. St. Sernin, Toulouse. Restoration.

F. Notre Dame la Grande, Poitiers. XI century. (Aquitaine)

G. Notre Dame la Grande, Poitiers. Facade. XI century. (Gir)

A. Angoulême Cathedral. Plan. 1105–1128. (Aquitaine)

B. Angoulême Cathedral. Façade. 1105–1128. (N.D.)

C. St. Gilles. Portico detail. Late XII century. (Provence)

D. St. Trophîme, Arles. Façade. Second half XII century. (Provence) (N.D.)

E. Abbey Church, Vézelay. Tympanum of Narthex Portal. 1132–40. (Burgundy) (See 68 B.) (Gir)

F. St. Trophîme, Arles. Detail of D. Second half XII century. (Provence) (N.D.)

G. St. Trophîme, Arles. Detail of D. Second half XII century. (N.D.)

H. French Romanesque Madonna. Metropolitan Museum. (Met)

A. Moissac. Tympanum from S. Portal. c. 1100. (Languedoc)

B. Abbey Church, Vézelay. Interior. Rebuilt 1132. (Burgundy) (See 67 E.) (Gir)

C. Autun Cathedral. Detail of Tympanum. XII century. (Burgundy)

D. Romanesque System of Vaulting.

E. St. Etienne, Caen. Façade. Begun 1064. (Normandy) (Clarence Ward)

F. St. Etienne, Caen. Interior. Vaulting. c. 1135. (See 69 A.)

G. St. Etienne, Caen. Exterior. Begun 1064. (Clarence Ward)

A. St. Etienne, Caen. The Gallery. c. 1135. (See 68 F.)

B. La Trinité, Caen. Begun 1062. Remodeled c. 1140. (N.D.)

C. La Trinité, Caen. Interior. Remodeled c. 1140. (N.D.)

D. Morienval. North aisle. c. 1080. (Ile de France)

E. Bury. XII century. (Clarence Ward)

F. Earl's Barton. Anglo-Saxon. Early XI century (?).

G. Earl's Barton. XI century. (Britton)

H. The Bayeux "Tapestry." Embroidery of Queen Matilda. XI century. Bayeux Library.

A. Iffley. Late XII century.

B. Canterbury. Exterior Stairway. XII century. (Man.)

C. Prior's Door, Ely. XII century. (Clayton)

D. Durham Cathedral, Nave. 1096–1133. (See 85 F.)

E. The Galilee, Durham Cathedral. 1096–1133.

F. Monogram Page from the Book of Kells. c. 700. Celtic. Trinity College Library, Dublin.

G. Quoniam Page from the Book of Lindisfarne. c. 700. British Museum. (Br. Mus.)

H. Muirdach's Cross. Celtic. X century. Monsterboice, Co. Louth, Irish Free State. (Ralph Fanning)

ENGLISH MEDIEVAL MANUSCRIPTS · XI–XII CENT.
SPANISH ROMANESQUE PAINTING · SCULPTURE · XII CENT.

71

A. Pages from the Liber Vitae. XI century. British Museum. (Br. Mus.)

B. Page from the Huntingfield Psalter. Tower of Babel and Abraham Avenging Lot. XII century. Pierpont Morgan Library, N. Y. (Morgan Library)

C. Huntingfield Psalter. Detail of B. (Morgan Library)

D. Portico de la Gloria, Santiago Cathedral. XII century.

E. Portico de la Gloria, Santiago Cathedral. Detail of D.

F. Catalonian Fresco from S. Maria de Mura. XII century. Museum of Fine Arts. (M.F.A.)

G. Apse Fresco from S. Clement de Tahull. XII century. Barcelona Museum.

A. Worms Cathedral. XII century.

B. Speyer Cathedral. Founded 1030. Remodeled XII century.

C. Worms Cathedral. Plan. XII century. (Geier and Görz)

D. Mainz Cathedral. Largely XIII century

E. Echternach Codex. The Ivory Cover. XI century. Library, Gotha.

F. Gertrudis Portable Altar. Brunswick. Middle XI century. Cleveland Museum. (Clev. Mus.)

G. Gertrudis Portable Altar. Detail of F. (Clev. Mus.)

A. Cloisonné Medallion of Christ. Frankish, VII century. Cleveland Museum. (Clev. Mus.)

B. The Second Gertrudis Cross. Brunswick, c. 1040. Cleveland Museum. (Clev. Mus.)

C. The Bronze Doors, Hildesheim Cathedral. XI century (?).

D. The Magi. Detail of C.

E. Page from Codex Egberti. Adoration of the Magi. 977–993. Trier Library. (Trier Library)

F. Throne of Dagobert. Merovingian. VII century. Louvre.

G. Copy of a Norwegian Chair of IX or X century. University of Christiana.

H. German Chair. XIII century or later. (Schmitz)

A. **Gothic Vaulting Scheme.** (Colas)

B. **Gothic System.** Section. St. Germer. 1130–60. (Dehio)

C. **Cathedral of Notre Dame, Paris.** Section.

D. **St. Leu d Esserant.** XII century. (Clarence Ward)

E. **Chartres Cathedral.** Plan. XII–XIII centuries. (Chapu)

F. **Chartres Cathedral.** Façade. Chiefly 1194–1260. Earlier spire c. 1250. Later spire 1507–14. Royal portal 1145. (Clarence Ward)

G. **Chartres Cathedral.** Buttress. XIII century. (Clarence Ward)

H. **Chartres Cathedral.** Transept. XIII century. (N.D.)

I. **Chartres Cathedral.** Choir. c. 1220. (See 75 A.)

A. Chartres Cathedral. Vaulting of the Choir. c. 1220. (Clarence Ward)

B. Chartres Cathedral. Royal (West) Portal. c. 1145. (N.D.)

C. Chartres Cathedral. Royal Portal detail. Kings, Queens and Saints. (N.D.)

D. Chartres Cathedral. Royal Portal detail. Christ of the Apocalypse. (Laillet)

E. Chartres Cathedral. Royal Portal detail. Saints. Detail of C.

F. Chartres Cathedral. Royal Portal detail. Head of a figure. (N.D.)

G. Chartres Cathedral. Royal Portal detail. Life of the Virgin. (Houvet)

A. Chartres Cathedral. Royal Portal detail. Pythagoras. 1145. (Houvet)

B. Chartres Cathedral. S. Porch. Late XII, early XIII century. (Clarence Ward)

C. Chartres Cathedral. S. Porch. (N.D.)

D. Chartres Cathedral. S. Porch. (N.D.)

E. Chartres Cathedral. S. Porch. Detail of saints. (N.D.)

F. Chartres Cathedral. S. Porch. Detail of saints. (N.D.)

G. Chartres Cathedral. N. Porch. c. 1205–70. (Clarence Ward)

H. Chartres Cathedral. N. Porch detail. c. 1205–70.

I. Chartres Cathedral. N. Porch detail. (Houvet)

J. Paris Cathedral. Plan. 1163–1235. (Chapu)

A. Paris Cathedral. Façade. 1163–1235.

B. Paris Cathedral. Façade detail. (Al)

C. Paris Cathedral. The Nave System. (Viollet-le-Duc)

D. Paris Cathedral. Nave. (Al)

E. Paris Cathedral. Façade detail. c. 1235. (Colas)

F. Paris Cathedral. Façade detail. c. 1235. (Al)

G. Paris Cathedral. Grotesque. (Al)

H. Reims Cathedral. W. front 1380. W. towers 1420. (Colas)

A. Reims Cathedral. XIII–XIV centuries.

B. Reims Cathedral. S. side. (Arch. Photo.)

C. Reims Cathedral. Flying buttresses. (Clarence Ward)

D. Reims Cathedral. Apsidal chapel. 1211–90. (Viollet-le-Duc)

E. Reims Cathedral. Side aisle. 1211–90. (Arch. Photo.)

F. Reims Cathedral. W. façade. Saints. XIV century. (Arch. Photo.)

G. Reims Cathedral. Capital of a clustered pier. XIII century. (Colas)

A. Plans. Left, Reims; right, Amiens. (Chapu)

B. Amiens Cathedral. 1220–1288. (Clarence Ward)

C. Amiens Cathedral. Portal of Vierge Dorée. Second half XIII century. (Colas)

D. Amiens Cathedral. W. front. 1220–1248. (Clarence Ward)

E. Amiens Cathedral. Christ (Le Beau Dieu). Detail of D.

F. Amiens Cathedral. Head of Christ. Detail of E.

G. Amiens Cathedral. Detail of W. portal. Detail of D.

H. Amiens Cathedral. The Months. Detail of G.

A. Amiens Cathedral. Nave. 1220–1248. (Clarence Ward)

B. Amiens Cathedral. Vaulting at the crossing. (Clarence Ward)

C. Beauvais Cathedral. 1225–1548.

D. La Sainte Chapelle, Paris. 1242–47. (Arch. Photo.)

E. La Sainte Chapelle, Paris. Interior. (Arch. Photo.)

F. La Sainte Chapelle, Paris. The Crypt.

G. Mont St. Michel. Hall of the Chevaliers. XIII century (N.D.)

A. Mont St. Michel. The Cloister. 1225–28. (N.D.)

B. Rouen Cathedral. N. Porch detail. Begun 1280. (Arch. Photo.)

C. Rouen Cathedral. N. Porch detail with St. Michael. Begun 1280.

D. Rouen Cathedral. Façade. XIV–XVI centuries. Central section, 1507. (Arch. Photo.)

E. Rouen Cathedral. Detail of D. XVI century.

F. Rouen Cathedral. S. aisle.

G. Rouen Cathedral. Butter Tower. 1497–1509. (N.D.)

H. Palais de Justice, Rouen. 1499–1508. (Arch. Photo.)

A. St. Vulfrand, Abbeville. 1488–1539. (Arch. Photo.)

B. St. Eustache, Paris. Vaulting. XVI century. (Clarence Ward)

C. Papal Palace, Avignon. XIV century. (N.D.)

D. Albi Cathedral. 1282–1512. (N.D.)

E. Hôtel de Ville, Brussels. 1377.

F. Hôtel de Cluny, Paris. 1490. (See 83 A.) (Al)

G. House of Jacques Coeur, Bourges. Late XV century.

A. Hôtel de Cluny, Paris. 1490 (See 82 F.) (Gir)

B. Medieval Town House. Romanesque. (Viollet-le-Duc)

C. House at Compiègne. (Pagolnet)

D. The Château, Carcassonne. Late XII century. (N.D.)

E. Ivory Madonna. XIV century. Metropolitan Museum. (Met)

F. Ivory Madonna and Child. End of XIII century. Metropolitan Museum. (Met)

G. Claus Sluter and Claus de Werve. Moses Well. Burgundian School. Carthusian Monastery near Dijon. c. 1389.

H. Claus Sluter and Claus de Werve. Mourners from Tomb of Philip the Bold. 1384–1411. Museum, Dijon. (Gir)

A. Reliquary. Limoges Enamel. XIII century. Metropolitan Museum. (Met)

B. Ivory Diptych. XIV century. Louvre. (Louvre)

C. Ivory Casket. XIV century. Metropolitan Museum. (Met)

D. Stained Glass, Chartres Cathedral. Tree of Jesse. XII century.

E. Festival of Roses. Tapestry. 1435–40. Metropolitan Museum. (Met)

F. Story of Alexander. Flemish Tapestry, School of Tournai. XV century. Palazzo Doria, Rome.

G. St. Matthew. Middle XIII century. Louvre. (Louvre)

FRENCH GOTHIC MINOR ARTS · XII–XV CENT.
ENGLISH GOTHIC ARCHITECTURE · XII–XIII CENT.

85

A. Pol de Limbourg and Brothers. February Page from the "Très Riches Heures" of the Duc de Berri. 1412–16. Musée Condé, Chantilly. (Gir)

B. Church Bench. XV century. (Schmitz)

C. Credence. XV century. (Met)

D. Chair. XV century. (Met)

E. Crozier. Limoges Enamel. Second half of XIII century. Metropolitan Museum. (Met)

F. Durham Cathedral. XI–XIV centuries. (See 70 D.)

G. Canterbury Cathedral. Plan. 1175–1503.

H. Canterbury Cathedral. Begun 1175. Central tower 1495–1503. (See 86 B.)

I. Wells Cathedral. From E. 1190–1239. (See 86 A.)

A. Wells Cathedral. Façade. 1220–39. (See 85 I.) (Man)

B. Canterbury Cathedral. S. side. 1175–84. (See 85 G, H.) (Man)

C. Ely Cathedral. Choir looking E. 1229–54. (Bolas)

D. Lincoln Cathedral. Façade. Rebuilt 1192–1200. (Bolas)

E. Lincoln Cathedral. Rose Window. S. Transept. Early XIII century.

F. Lincoln Cathedral. Nave looking E. c. 1250. (Bolas)

G. Salisbury Cathedral. 1220–60. Tower, XVI century. (See 87 A.) (Man)

A. Salisbury Cathedral. Plan. XIII–XVI centuries. (See 86 G.)

B. York Minster. Nave looking E. 1291–1394.

C. York Minster. Façade. 1241–1423.

D. Exeter Cathedral. Nave looking W. 1331–50.

E. Exeter Cathedral. Façade. 1328–94.

F. Exeter Cathedral. Flying buttresses and transept tower. XIII–XIV centuries. (Bolas)

G. Gloucester Cathedral. Choir looking E. Rebuilt 1331–37. (See 88 A.) (Bolas)

A. Gloucester Cathedral. S. side. XII–XIV centuries. (See 87 G.) (Bolas)

B. Chapel of Henry VII, Westminster Abbey. Fan vaulting. 1503–20. (Bolas)

C. Compton Wynyates, Warwickshire. S. wing. Detail of E. 1520. (Call)

D. Chapel of Henry VII, Westminster Abbey. Exterior. 1503–20. (Bolas)

E. Compton Wynyates. S. wing. 1520. (Call)

F. Standing Cupboard. Middle XVI century. Victoria and Albert Museum. (Vict. Alb.)

G. Oak Cupboard. 1475–1500. Metropolitan Museum. (Met)

H. Madonna Enthroned. The Arundel Psalter. Early XIV century. British Museum. (Br. Mus.)

A. Aix-la-Chapelle (Aachen) Cathedral. Chapel, IX century. (See 56 B, C.) Cathedral, XIV–XV centuries. (von Stengel)

B. Church of St. Elizabeth, Marburg. 1233–83.

C. Cologne Cathedral. Plan. Mostly 1248–1322.

D. Cologne Cathedral. 1248–1322. Completed XIX century. (Hertel)

E. Frauenkirche, Nuremberg. 1354–61.

F. The Golden Door, Freiberg Cathedral. XIII century.

G. Freiberg Cathedral. Interior. Nave, 1260. Choir, 1354. (Rölicke)

H. Knochenhaueramthaus, Hildesheim. XVI century.

I. House, Hildesheim. XVI century.

A. Toledo Cathedral. 1227–1493.

B. Toledo Cathedral. Interior. 1227–1493.

C. Toledo Cathedral. Plan.

D. Burgos Cathedral. Spires begun 1442.

E. Burgos Cathedral. Vaulting. 1497–1512. (L.L.F.)

F. Giralda, Seville. Lower stages, 1194–96. Top, 1568. (Al)

G. Seville Cathedral. 1401–1506. (And)

H. The University, Salamanca. XV century. (See 170 E.) (Laurent)

A. Mosque, Córdova. Approach to the Mihrab. Begun VIII century. (Gonzalez)

B. Mosque, Córdova. Interior. Begun VIII century. (And)

C. Alhambra, Granada. Court of the Lions. 1354. (And)

D. Alhambra, Granada. Court of the Lions at L. 1354. (Mas)

E. Alhambra, Granada. Stucco detail. (Al)

F. Alhambra, Granada. Hall of the Two Sisters. Begun 1230. (And)

A. San Francesco, Assisi. 1228–53.

B. San Francesco, Assisi. Lower Church. (And)

C. San Francesco, Assisi. Upper Church. (See 120 B, C.) (And)

D. Siena Cathedral. c. 1245–1380. (Al)

E. Siena Cathedral. Façade. Detail of D. c. 1245–1380.

F. Siena Cathedral. Interior. (Al)

G. Orvieto Cathedral. Façade. Arnolfo di Cambio and Lorenzo Maitani. 1290–1310. (See 93 A, 97 H.) (Al)

A. Orvieto Cathedral. Interior. 1290–1310. (See 92 G.) (Al)

B. Florence Cathedral and Campanile. Arnolfo di Cambio, Brunelleschi, architects. 1296–1462. Campanile: 1334–87, Giotto and Andrea Pisano. Façade, 1875–87. (See 97 D, E.)

C. Florence Cathedral. Plan. (Isabelle)

D. Florence Cathedral. Interior. Arnolfo di Cambio, architect.

E. Santa Maria Novella, Florence. 1278–1350. Renaissance detail of façade by Alberti, 1470. (See 100 F.) (Brogi)

F. Santa Maria Novella, Florence. Interior. (Brogi)

A. Palazzo Vecchio, Florence. Arnolfo di Cambio, architect. 1298. R. and L., the Uffizi, Vasari, architect. 1560–74. (Al)

B. Palazzo Pubblico, Siena. 1289–1305. (See 118 A–D.) (Al)

C. Palazzo Loredan, Venice. XV century. (And)

D. Palazzo Cà d'Oro, Venice. XIV century. (And)

E. Palazzo Cà d'Oro Venice. Detail of D. (And)

F. Palazzo Foscari, Venice. XV century. (And)

G. Palazzo Foscari, Venice. Detail of F. (And)

H. Palazzo Contarini Fasan, Venice. XIV century. (And)

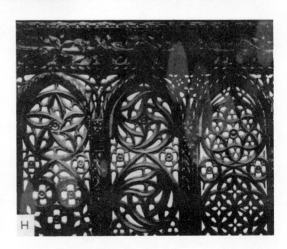

A. Palazzo Pisani, Venice. XIV century. (And)

B. Ducal Palace, Venice. XIV–XVI century. (And)

C. Ducal Palace, Venice. Detail of B. (Al)

D. Porta della Carta, Ducal Palace, Venice. 1438–43. (And)

E. Milan Cathedral. The Apse. XV century and later.

F. Milan Cathedral. Plan. Mainly 1385–1485.

G. Milan Cathedral. 1385–1485. Completed XIX century.

H. Gothic Wood Carving. Church of the Frari, Venice.

A. Niccolo Pisano (d'Apulia) Pulpit, Pisa Baptistry. 1260. (Al)

B. Niccolo Pisano. Crucifixion. Detail of A. (Al)

C. Niccolo Pisano Pulpit, Siena Cathedral. 1265–68. (Al)

D. Niccolo Pisano. Inferno. Detail of C. (Al)

E. Niccolo Pisano. Massacre of the Innocents. Detail of C. (Al)

F. Giovanni Pisano. Pulpit. Sant' Andrea, Pistoia. 1298–1302.

A. Giovanni Pisano. Madonna and Child. Pisa Cathedral. (Brogi)

B. Andrea Pisano. S. Doors, Baptistry, Florence. 1336. (Al)

C. Andrea Pisano. Visitation, Birth of John the Baptist. Detail of B. (Al)

D. Andrea Pisano. Painting. 1334–87. Campanile, Florence. (See 93 B.) (And)

E. Andrea Pisano. Architecture. Campanile, Florence. (Al)

F. Andrea Orcagna. Marriage of the Virgin. Tabernacle, Or San Michele, Florence. 1348–59. (Al)

G. Andrea Orcagna. Annunciation of the Death of the Virgin. Tabernacle, Or San Michele, Florence. (Al)

H. Lorenzo Maitani and others. The Last Judgment. Facade of the Orvieto Cathedral. 1320–30. (See 92 G.) (And)

I. Lorenzo Maitani and others. Inferno. Detail of H. (And)

A. **Loggia** of the Foundlings' Hospital, Florence. 1419–51. Brunelleschi, architect. (See 111 B.) (Al)

B. **Pazzi Chapel**, Florence. Façade begun 1429 by Brunelleschi. (From Moore, "The Character of Renaissance Architecture." Macmillan Co.)

C. **Pazzi Chapel**, Florence. Portico. (Al)

D. Pazzi Chapel, Florence. Interior. (Al)

E. Santo Spirito, Florence, 1436–87. Brunelleschi, architect.

F. San Lorenzo, Florence. 1425. Brunelleschi, architect.

G. Medici-Riccardi Palace, Florence. 1444. Michelozzo, architect.

A. Strozzi Palace, Florence. Begun 1489 by Benedetto da Maiano and Simone del Pollaiuolo, called Il Cronaca. Finished 1536. (Al)

B. Strozzi Palace, Florence. Detail of A. (Al)

C. Strozzi Palace, Florence. Detail of A. (Al)

D. Strozzi Palace, Florence. Iron Ring and Torch Holder. XV century. (Al)

E. Strozzi Palace, Florence. Court. Cronaca, architect. (Al)

F. Strozzi Palace, Florence. Detail of A. (Al)

G. Gondi Palace, Florence. Court. 1490. Giuliano da Sangallo, architect. (Al)

H. Gondi Palace, Florence. Capital of court column. Detail of G. (Al)

A. Quaratesi Palace, Florence. 1445. Brunelleschi, architect. (Al)

B. Rucellai Palace, Florence. 1451–55. Alberti, architect.

C. Sant' Andrea, Mantua. 1472–1512. Alberti, architect. Campanile, 1414. (Al)

D. Sant' Andrea, Mantua. Interior. XV–XVII century. (Al)

E. San Francesco, Rimini. 1447–1455. Alberti, architect.

F. Santa Maria Novella, Florence. Detail of façade by Alberti 1470. (See 93 E.) (Al)

G. Pitti Palace, Florence. Window. XV century.

H. Palazzo Vecchio, Florence. Interior door. Benedetto da Maiano, architect. (Al)

A. Church of San Satiro, Milan. Baptistry. 1472. Bramante, architect. (Al)

B. Church of San Satiro, Milan. Rotunda. 1472. Bramante, architect. (Al)

C. Sant'a Maria delle Grazie, Milan. Apse. 1492–97. Bramante, architect. (Al)

D. Church of San Satiro, Milan. Detail of Sacristy. 1472. Bramante, architect. (Al)

E. Massimi Palace, Rome. 1536. Baldassare Peruzzi, architect. (Al)

F. The Tempietto, San Pietro in Montorio, Rome. 1502. Bramante, architect. (Al)

G. Farnese Palace, Rome. 1530–80. Designed by Antonio da Sangallo the Younger. Top story by Michelangelo, 1546. (Grafia)

A. XVIII century view of Piazza of St. Peter's, Rome. Work of 14 architects. 1450–1667. Engraving by Piranesi.

B. St. Peter's, Rome. Façade by Carlo Maderna, 1606–12. (Al)

C. St. Peter's, Rome. Interior. 1606–12. Chief architects: Bramante, Michelangelo, Maderna. From an engraving.

D. Detail of C. The Crossing. Baldachino at L. by Bernini, 1633.

E. Model of St. Peter's, Rome, by Antonio da Sangallo, 1546. Vatican Museum. (Al)

F. Dome of St. Peter's, Rome. Rear view. Designed by Michelangelo. Finished 1590. (Al)

G. Cupola. Detail of F. Finished by Giacomo della Porta. 1590. (Grafia)

A. Senators' Palace, Rome. After 1546. Facade. 1592 after designs by Michelangelo. (See 49 D.)

B. Villa Madama, Rome. 1516. Raphael and Giulio Romano, architects. Paintings by Romano. (Al)

C. Villa Rotonda (Capra), near Vicenza. 1552. Engraving from Palladio's "Four Books of Architecture." Andrea Palladio, architect.

D. Plan of C.

E. Villa Rotonda today.

F. The Basilica, Vicenza. 1549. Engraving from Palladio's "Four Books of Architecture." Andrea Palladio, architect. (See 104 A.)

A. The Basilica, Vicenza. 1549. Arcades by Andrea Palladio.
(See 103 F.) (Al)

B. San Giorgio Maggiore, Venice. Andrea Palladio, architect.
1560. Facade by Scamozzi, 1575. (From Moore, "The Character of Renaissance Architecture." Macmillan Co.)

C. Logetta of the Campanile, Piazza of St. Mark's, Venice.
1540. Sansovino, architect. (Al)

D. Civil Hospital of St. Mark, Venice. 1485–90. Façade by
the Lombardi. (And)

E. Santa Maria dei Miracoli, Venice. 1480. Pietro Lombardo,
architect. (From Moore, "The Character of Renaissance Architecture." Macmillan Co.)

F. Library of St. Mark's, Venice. 1536. Andrea Sansovino,
architect. (And)

G. Grand Staircase, Court of the Ducal Palace, Venice. Finished c. 1550 by Scarpagnino and Rizzo. Flanking figures of
Mars and Neptune by Sansovino. (See 105 A.)

A. Court of the Ducal Palace, Venice. Begun 1486 by Rizzo, continued 1499–1511 by Pietro Lombardo. (See 104 G.) (And)

B. "Corner" Palace, on the Grand Canal, Venice. 1532. Sansovino, architect. (And)

C. Grimani Palace, Venice. 1549. Sanmichele, architect. (And)

D. Pesaro Palace, Venice. 1679. Longhena, architect. (And)

E. Scuola di San Rocco, Venice. 1517. Buon, architect.

F. Vendramin Palace, Venice. Detail of facade. 1481. Pietro Lombardo, architect. (Al)

A. Santa Maria della Salute, Venice. Façade detail. 1631–82. Longhena, architect. (See 153 E.) (AI)

B. Church of the Gesù, Rome. 1568–75. Vignola and della Porta, architects.

C. Santa Maria della Pace, Rome. Restored 1655 by Pietro da Cortona. (AI)

D. San Giovanni in Laterano, Rome. 1734. Designed by Alessandro Galilei. (AI)

E. Paolo Fountain, Rome. 1611. Designed by Giovanni Fontana and Carlo Maderna. (AI)

F. Trevi Fountain, Rome. 1735–62. Designed by Ferdinando Fuga (?). (AI)

G. Villa Medici, Rome XVI century. A. Lippi and Michelangelo, architects. (AI)

A. Brunelleschi. Competition panel for N. doors of Baptistry, Florence. Sacrifice of Isaac. 1402. National Museum, Florence.

B. Ghiberti. N. doors of Baptistry, Florence. 1403–24. (Al)

C. Ghiberti. Competition panel for N. doors of Baptistry, Florence. Sacrifice of Isaac. 1402. Bargello.

D. Ghiberti. Detail of C.

E. Ghiberti. Detail of B. L., Christ Bound to the Pillar; R., Christ Before Pilate.

F. Ghiberti. Detail of B. L., Christ Driving Money Changers from the Temple; R., Christ and Peter on the Water.

G. Ghiberti. E. doors of Baptistry, Florence. 1425–52. (See 108 A–C.) (Al)

A. Ghiberti. E. doors of Baptistry, Florence. 1425–52. (Detail of 107 G.) Abraham Entertains the Three Angels; Sarah at the Tent; Hagar in the Desert; Sacrifice of Isaac. (AI)

B. Ghiberti. (Detail of 107 G.) Finding of the Cup in Benjamin's Sack. (AI)

C. Ghiberti. (Detail of 107 G.) Solomon Receiving the Queen of Sheba in the Great Temple. (AI)

D. Jacopo della Quercia, attributed to. Tomb of Ilaria del Carretto. 1406. Lucca Cathedral. Detail of E. (AI)

E. Jacopo della Quercia, attributed to. Tomb of Ilaria del Carretto. 1406. Lucca Cathedral. (AI)

F. Jacopo della Quercia. Fall of Man. 1425. San Petronio, Bologna. (See 109 A.)

A. Jacopo della Quercia. Creation of Eve. 1425. San Petronio, Bologna.

B. Donatello. St. George. 1416. Bargello. (Al)

C. Donatello. Detail of B. (Al)

D. Donatello. David. 1416 (?). Bargello. (Al)

E. Donatello. King David (Zuccone). c. 1425. Campanile, Florence. (Al)

F. Donatello. John the Baptist. c. 1425. Bargello. (Al)

G. Donatello. John the Baptist. c. 1425. Bargello. (Al)

H. Donatello. David. After 1430. Bargello. (Al)

I. Donatello. Amorino in Breeches. Bargello.

J. Donatello. Detail of H.

K. Donatello (?). Niccolo da Uzzano. c. 1432. Bargello.

L. Donatello. Annunciation. 1430. Santa Croce. (Al)

A. Donatello and Michelozzo. Pulpit. 1434. Prato.

B. Donatello. Singing Gallery (Cantoria). 1433–38. Cathedral Museum, Florence.

C. Donatello. Gattamelata (Erasmo da Narni). 1447. Padua. (Al)

D. Donatello. Judith and Holfernes. c. 1440. Loggia dei Lanzi, Florence. (Al)

E. Luca della Robbia. Singing Gallery panel. 1431–38. Cathedral Museum, Florence. (Al)

F. Luca della Robbia. Singing Gallery. 1431–38. Cathedral Museum, Florence. (Al)

G. Andrea della Robbia. Madonna and Child. Bargello. (Al)

A. Luca della Robbia. Madonna and Child. Bargello.

B. Andrea della Robbia. Foundling. 1463–66. Hospital of the Innocents, Florence. (See 98 A.) (Al)

C. Andrea della Robbia. Altarpiece. S. Maria degli Angioli, Florence.

D. Bernardo Rossellino. Tomb of Leonardo Bruni. 1444. Santa Croce, Florence. (Al)

E. Bernardo Rossellino. Detail of D.

F. Desiderio da Settignano. Tomb of Carlo Marsuppini. c. 1455. Santa Croce, Florence. (Al)

G. Desiderio da Settignano. Detail of F.

BERNARDO ROSSELLINO · DESIDERIO DA SETTIGNANO · BENEDETTO DA MAIANO

A. Antonio Rossellino (?). Madonna and Child. Morgan Library.

B. Bernardo Rossellino. St. John the Baptist. Bargello. (Al)

C. Desiderio da Settignano. Bust of a Boy. Este Coll., Vienna. (Al)

D. Desiderio da Settignano. Tabernacle. San Lorenzo, Florence. (Al)

E. Desiderio da Settignano. Detail of D. (Al)

F. School of Donatello. John the Baptist. Bargello. (Al)

G. Desiderio da Settignano or Donatello. Madonna and Child. Bargello. (Al)

H. Benedetto da Maiano. Altarpiece. Annunciation. Mte. Oliveto, Naples. (Al)

A. Benedetto da Maiano. Pietro Mellini. 1474. Bargello. (Al)

B. Antonio Pollaiuolo. Hercules and Antaeus. Bargello. (Al)

C. Antonio Pollaiuolo. Giuliano de' Medici (?). 1470–78. Bargello. (Al)

D. Verrocchio. Incredulity of Thomas. 1463–83. Or San Michele, Florence. (Al)

E. Verrocchio. Bust of Unknown Woman. Bargello. (Al)

F. Verrocchio. David. Bronze. 1476. Bargello. (Al)

G. Verrocchio. Detail of F.

H. Verrocchio. Colleoni. Bronze. c.1481–88. Venice. (Al)

I. Verrocchio. Detail of H. (And)

A. Verrocchio. Madonna. Bargello. (Al)

B. Amadeo and Pupils of the Mantegazzi. Certosa of Pavia. Detail of S. side of façade. Visitation. Begun 1473.

C. Sansovino. Bacchus. 1513. Bargello. (Al)

D. Michelangelo. Madonna of Bruges. Notre Dame, Bruges.

E. Pisanello. Obverse and reverse of Medal to Isotta da Rimini. 1446. Bargello. (Al)

F. Pisanello. Obverse and reverse of Medal to John Paleologus. Bargello. (Al)

G. Michelangelo. Pietà. 1499–1500. St. Peter's, Rome. (Al)

H. Michelangelo. David. 1501–03. Academy, Florence.

I. Michelangelo. Detail of G.

J. Michelangelo. Detail of H.

K. Michelangelo. Medici Madonna. New Sacristy, San Lorenzo, Florence. (Al)

A. Michelangelo. Bacchus. 1496–1501. Bargello. (Al)

B. Michelangelo. Moses, for Tomb of Julius II. 1505–45.
S Pietro in Vincoli, Rome. (Al)

C. Michelangelo. Detail of B.

D. Michelangelo. Bound Slave, for Tomb of Julius II. 1513.
Louvre. (Al)

E. Michelangelo. Tomb of Giuliano de' Medici. L., Night;
R., Day. 1520–34. New Sacristy, San Lorenzo, Florence. (Al)

F. Michelangelo. Tomb of Lorenzo de' Medici. L., Twilight;
R., Dawn. 1520–34. New Sacristy, San Lorenzo, Florence. (Al)

G. Michelangelo. Madonna with the Book. Unfinished. Bargello. (Al)

H. Michelangelo. Giuliano de' Medici. Detail of E.

I. Michelangelo. Lorenzo de' Medici. Detail of F. (Al)

J. Michelangelo. Dawn. Detail of F.

A. Michelangelo. Madonna of the Stairs. Casa Buonarroti, Florence. (Al)

B. Bernini. Apollo and Daphne. 1616. Borghese Gallery. (Al)

C. Bernini. Detail of B.

D. Giovanni da Bologna. Mercury. 1574. Bargello. (Al)

E. Bernini. St. Therese in Ecstasy. 1646. S.M. della Vittoria, Rome. (Al)

F. Cellini. Nymph of Fontainebleau. 1543. Louvre. (Arch. Photo.)

G. Cellini. Rospigliosi Cup. Metropolitan Museum. (Met)

H. Cellini. Saltcellar of Francis I. Kunstgeschichte, Vienna. (Plon)

A. Italian School, XIII century. Madonna and Child. Fogg Museum. (Fogg)

B. Italian School, XIII century. Crucifixion. Uffizi.

C. Duccio. Detail of D.

D. Duccio. Majestà. 1308–11. Cathedral Museum, Siena. (Al)

E. Duccio. St. Agnes. Detail of D. (And)

F. Duccio. Deposition. Panel from back of D. (Al)

G. Duccio. Flagellation of Christ. Panel from back of D. (Al)

A. Simone Martini. Majestà. 1315. Palazzo Pubblico, Siena. (And)

B. Ambrogio Lorenzetti. Peace. Detail of Allegory of Good Government. 1337–43. Palazzo Pubblico, Siena. (Venturini)

C. Simone Martini. Guidoriccio da Fogliano. 1323. Palazzo Pubblico, Siena. (And)

D. Simone Martini. Detail of E.

E. Simone Martini and Lippo Memmi. Annunciation with SS. Ansano and Juliet. 1333. Uffizi. (Al)

F. Pietro Lorenzetti (?). Madonna and Child with Saints. San Francesco, Assisi. (Al)

A. Ambrogio Lorenzetti, attributed to the followers of. Triumph of Death. Between 1350 and 1375. Campo Santo, Pisa. (Al)

B. Sassetta. Betrothal of St. Francis to Poverty. 1444. Musée Condé, Chantilly. (Al)

C. Master of the Rucellai Madonna. Sometimes attributed to Duccio. Detail of the Rucellai Madonna. 1285? Santa Maria Novella, Florence. (And)

D. Cimabue. Detail of F. (Brogi)

E. Cimabue. Detail of F. (Brogi)

F. Cimabue. Virgin Enthroned. Uffizi. (Brogi)

G. Giotto. Virgin Enthroned. Uffizi. (And)

H. Giotto. Detail of G.

A. Giotto. Portrait of Dante. c. 1330. Bargello. (Al)

B. Giotto. St. Francis Preaching to the Birds. c. 1300. San Francesco, Upper Church, Assisi. (See 92 C.) (And)

C. School of Giotto. Body of St. Francis received by St. Clara before the Church of St. Damian. San Francesco, Upper Church, Assisi. (Al)

D. Giotto. Meeting of Joachim and Anna. c. 1305. Arena Chapel, Padua. (Al)

E. Giotto. Presentation of the Virgin in the Temple. c. 1305. Arena Chapel, Padua. (Al)

F. Giotto. Flight into Egypt. c. 1305. Arena Chapel, Padua. (Al)

G. Giotto. Last Supper. c. 1305. Arena Chapel, Padua. (See 121 A.) (Al)

A. Giotto. Detail of Last Supper. c. 1305. Arena Chapel, Padua. (See 120 G.) (Al)

B. Giotto. Pietà. Detail. c. 1305. Arena Chapel, Padua. (Al)

C. Giotto. Detail of the Vision of St. Francis. c. 1325. Santa Croce, Florence. (Al)

D. Giotto. Death of St. Francis. c. 1325. Bardi Chapel, Santa Croce, Florence. (And)

E. Taddeo Gaddi. Presentation of the Virgin in the Temple. c. 1335. Baroncelli Chapel, Santa Croce, Florence. (Al)

F. Taddeo Gaddi. Adoration of the Kings. c. 1335. Baroncelli Chapel, Santa Croce, Florence. (Al)

A. Agnolo Gaddi. Story of the True Cross. 1380. Santa Croce, Florence. (Al)

B. Orcagna. Detail of Christ Enthroned. 1357. Santa Maria Novella, Florence. (Brogi)

C. Agnolo Gaddi. Detail of Story of the True Cross. 1380. Santa Croce, Florence. (Al)

D. Andrea Bonaiuti (Andrea da Firenze). Dominican Allegory of Church Militant and Triumphant. c. 1370. Spanish Chapel, Santa Maria Novella, Florence. (And)

E. Fra Angelico. Annunciation. 1439–45. San Marco, Florence. (Al)

F. Fra Angelico. Coronation of the Virgin. 1439–45. San Marco, Florence. (Al)

A. Fra Angelico. Last Supper. 1439–45. San Marco, Florence.

B. Fra Angelico. Flight into Egypt. San Marco, Florence.

C. Fra Angelico. Coronation of the Virgin. 1435. Louvre. (Louvre)

D. Fra Angelico. Madonna of the Linaiuoli. 1433. San Marco, Florence. (And)

E. Fra Angelico. Angel Musician. Detail of Border of D.

F. School of Fra Angelico. Detail of Coronation of the Virgin. San Marco, Florence.

G. Fra Angelico. Detail of Madonna. Pinacotheca, Perugia.

H. Masaccio. Expulsion of Adam and Eve. c. 1425–28. Brancacci Chapel, Santa Maria del Carmine, Florence. (Al)

A. Masaccio. Detail of the Tribute Money. c. 1425–28. Brancacci Chapel, Santa Maria del Carmine, Florence. (And)

B. Masaccio. Detail of the Tribute Money. c. 1425–28. Brancacci Chapel, Santa Maria del Carmine, Florence. (Al)

C. Masaccio. SS. Peter and John Distributing Alms. c. 1425–28. Brancacci Chapel, Santa Maria del Carmine, Florence. (And)

D. Masaccio. St. Peter. Detail of C.

E. Masaccio or Filippino Lippi. Portrait of an Unknown Man. Uffizi.

F. Masolino. Feast of Herod. c. 1435. Castiglione d' Olona, Baptistry.

G. Uccello. Rout of San Romano. c. 1435. National Gallery, London.

A. Uccello. Tomb Portrait of Sir John Hawkwood. 1437. Cathedral, Florence. (AI)

B. Andrea del Castagno. Pippo Spano. c. 1434. Sant' Apollonia, Florence. (AI)

C. Domenico Veneziano. Madonna Enthroned. Uffizi.

D. Andrea del Castagno. Last Supper. 1450 Sant' Apollonia, Florence. (AI)

E. Baldovinetti. Also attributed to Pesellino. Annunciation. Uffizi.

F. Baldovinetti. Madonna and Child. c. 1460. Louvre. (AI)

G. Fra Filippo Lippi. Coronation of the Virgin. 1441. Uffizi. (See 126 A.) (AI)

FRA FILIPPO LIPPI · BENOZZO GOZZOLI

A. Fra Filippo Lippi. Self Portrait. (Detail of 125 G.)

B. Fra Filippo Lippi. Madonna and Child. Early work. Uffizi. (Al)

C. Benozzo Gozzoli. Detail of Journey of the Magi. Lorenzo de' Medici. 1459–63. Chapel of Medici Palace, Florence. (Al)

D. Fra Filippo Lippi. Funeral of St. Stephen. 1464. Cathedral, Prato. (Al)

E. Benozzo Gozzoli. Detail of Journey of the Magi. 1459–63. Chapel of Medici Palace, Florence. (Al)

F. Benozzo Gozzoli. Detail of E. Cosimo de' Medici, Salviati and Piero de' Medici. (Al)

G. Benozzo Gozzoli. Detail of E. Self Portrait. (Al)

A. Benozzo Gozzoli. Detail of Journey of the Magi. 1459–63. John Palæologus. Chapel of Medici Palace, Florence. (Ai)

B. Benozzo Gozzoli. St. Augustine as a Teacher of Rhetoric. 1463–67. San Gimignano. (Al)

C. Antonio Pollaiuolo. Tobias and the Angel. Turin.

D. Antonio Pollaiuolo. Battle of the Nudes. Engraving. 1465–80. Collection Paul J. Sachs. (Fogg)

E. Antonio Pollaiuolo. Apollo and Daphne. National Gallery, London.

F. Antonio Pollaiuolo. Hercules and the Hydra. 1460. Uffizi.

G. Antonio Pollaiuolo. Hercules and Antaeus. 1460. Uffizi.

A. Fiorenzo di Lorenzo. St. Sebastian. Early work. Perugia.

B. Piero della Francesca. Federigo da Montefeltro, Duke of Urbino. 1465. Uffizi. (And)

C. Piero della Francesca. Detail of Visit of Queen of Sheba. 1452–66. San Francesco, Arezzo. (Al)

D. Piero della Francesca. Sigismund Malatesta Kneeling Before his Patron St. Sigismund. 1451. San Francesco, Rimini. (Brogi)

E. Domenico Ghirlandaio. Old Man and Boy. Louvre. (Louvre)

F. Domenico Ghirlandaio. Adoration of the Shepherds. 1485. Academy, Florence.

G. Domenico Ghirlandaio. St. Jerome. c. 1480. Church of the Ognissanti, Florence. (Al)

A. Domenico Ghirlandaio and Pupils. Last Supper. c. 1480. San Marco, Florence.

B. Domenico Ghirlandaio and Pupils. Detail of C.

C. Domenico Ghirlandaio and Pupils. Birth of the Virgin. 1486–90. Santa Maria Novella, Florence.

D. Domenico Ghirlandaio and Pupils. Adoration of the Magi. 1488. Hospital of the Innocents, Florence. (And)

E. Domenico Ghirlandaio and Pupils. Detail of C.

F. Botticelli. Giovanni di Cosimo de' Medici (?). Early Work. Uffizi.

A. Botticelli. Spring (Primavera). c. 1475. Uffizi. (Al)

B. Botticelli. Detail of the Madonna of the Magnificat. c. 1466. Uffizi. (And)

C. Botticelli and Followers. Adoration of the Kings. 1478. Uffizi. (Al)

D. Botticelli. Detail of the Madonna of the Magnificat. Head of the Madonna. c. 1466. Uffizi. (Al)

E. Botticelli. Birth of Venus. c. 1485. Uffizi. (Al)

F. Botticelli. Judith with the Head of Holfernes. c. 1475. Uffizi.

A. Botticelli. Calumny of Apelles. c. 1490. Uffizi. (And)

B. Botticelli. Annunciation. 1490. Uffizi.

C. Botticelli. Madonna with Six Angels. 1478. Uffizi.

D. Masaccio and Filippino Lippi. Raising of King Theophilus' Son by St. Peter. 1484–85. Brancacci Chapel, Santa Maria del Carmine, Florence. (See p. 124.) (Al)

E. Filippino Lippi. Madonna Adoring Child. Uffizi. (Al)

F. Filippino Lippi. Detail of D.

G. Filippino Lippi. Madonna and Child with Angels. Early work. Corsini Palace, Florence. (And)

H. Filippino Lippi. Vision of St. Bernard. 1480. Badia, Florence.

PIERO DI COSIMO · LORENZO DI CREDI · VERROCCHIO · LEONARDO

A. Piero di Cosimo. Simonetta Vespucci (La Bella Simonetta). Musée Condé, Chantilly.

B. Lorenzo di Credi. Annunciation. Early work. Uffizi.

C. Verrocchio and Leonardo. Baptism of Christ. Before 1470. Uffizi.

D. Leonardo. Detail of C.

E. Leonardo. Mona Lisa. 1500–04. Louvre. (Al)

F. Leonardo. St. Anne, Madonna and Child. c. 1510. Louvre. (Louvre)

G. Leonardo. La Belle Ferronière. Louvre.

H. Leonardo. Madonna of the Rocks. Before 1499. National Gallery, London.

I. Leonardo. Study for Head of Leda. Windsor Castle, London.

A. Leonardo. Last Supper. c. 1495–98. Refectory of Monastery of Santa Maria delle Grazie, Milan. (And)

B. Attributed to Leonardo. Head of Christ. Brera, Milan. (Al)

C. Leonardo (?). Portrait of a Man. Attributed also to Ambrogio di Predis. Detail. Ambrosiana, Milan. (Al)

D Fra Bartolommeo. Madonna and Saints. 1509. San Martino, Lucca. (Al)

E. Fra Bartolommeo. Savonarola. Detail. San Marco, Florence.

F. Fra Bartolommeo. Virgin Enthroned. Uffizi

G. Andrea del Sarto. Madonna of the Harpies. 1517. Uffizi. (Al)

H. Andrea del Sarto. Detail of G.

A. Andrea del Sarto. Last Supper. 1527. San Salvi, Florence.

B. Andrea del Sarto. Annunciation. 1528. Pitti.

C. Andrea del Sarto. St. John the Baptist. Detail. Pitti. (Al)

D. Andrea del Sarto. Holy Family. Barberini Gallery, Rome.

E. Andrea del Sarto. Charity. c. 1520. Scalzo Cloister, Florence. (Al)

F. Pontormo. Cosimo de' Medici. Uffizi. (Traldi)

G. Bronzino. Don Garzia de' Medici. Uffizi.

H. Gentile da Fabriano. Detail of Adoration of the Magi. Uffizi. (See 135 A.) (Al)

A. Gentile da Fabriano. Adoration of the Magi. 1423. Uffizi. (See 134 H.) (Al)

B. Melozzo da Forli. Pope Sixtus IV Giving Audience to Platina. 1473–81. Vatican. (And)

C. Signorelli. Paradise. c. 1500. Cathedral, Orvieto. (And)

D. Melozzo da Forli. Angel with Tambourine. 1475–80. Vatican Museum. (And)

E. Signorelli. Detail of C. (And)

F. Signorelli. Church Fathers. c. 1500. Cathedral, Orvieto. (And)

A. Signorelli. The Damned. c. 1500. Cathedral, Orvieto. (Al)

B. Signorelli and Pupils. Madonna and Child with SS. Jerome and Bernard. Corsini Palace, Florence. (And)

C. Signorelli. Detail of the Overthrow of the Anti-Christ. Portraits of Signorelli and Fra Angelico. c. 1500. Cathedral, Orvieto. (And)

D. Signorelli. Detail of the Resurrection. c. 1500. Cathedral, Orvieto. (And)

E. Perugino. Madonna and Saints. Pinacotheca, Bologna. (And)

F. Perugino. Christ Delivering the Keys to St. Peter. c. 1481. Sistine Chapel, Vatican. (Traldi)

G. Perugino. (Detail of 137 A, B.)

A. Perugino. Detail of B.

B. Perugino. Mystical Crucifixion. 1495. Santa Maria Maddalena dei Pazzi, Florence. (Al)

C. Perugino. Vision of St. Bernard. 1496–1500. Munich.

D. Pinturicchio. Aeneas Silvius Piccolomini (Pius II) at Ancona. 1464. Cathedral Library, Siena.

E. Raphael. Madonna del Granduca. 1505. Pitti. (Al)

F. Pinturicchio. Madonna and Child. Ambrosiana, Milan. (Brogi)

G. Raphael. Maddalena Doni. 1505. Pitti. (Traldi)

H. Raphael. St. Cecilia. 1513. Bologna. (And)

A. Raphael. Detail of Sistine Madonna. 1515. Gallery, Dresden. (Al)

B. Raphael. Madonna del Cardellino. 1506. Uffizi. (Brogi)

C. Raphael. Detail of D.

D. Raphael. Madonna of the Chair. c. 1516. Pitti. (And)

E. Raphael. Marriage of the Virgin (Sposalizio). 1504. Brera, Milan. (Al)

F. Raphael. Detail of G. Plato and Aristotle.

G. Raphael. School of Athens. 1509–11. Camera della Segnatura, Vatican. (And)

H. Raphael, attributed to. Pope Julius II. 1511–13. Uffizi. (And)

A. Raphael. Dispute of the Sacrament. 1509–11. Camera della Segnatura, Vatican. (Al)

B. Raphael. Leo X with Cardinals Rossi and Giulio de' Medici. 1519. Pitti. (And)

C. Design by Raphael, executed by Giulio Romano. The Fire in the Borgo. Finished 1517. Stanze of Raphael, Vatican. (Al)

D. Raphael. Giuliano de' Medici, duc de Nemours. 1514–15. Collection of Jules S. Bache, New York. (Jules S. Bache)

E. Michelangelo. Detail of the Sistine Chapel. Creation of Adam. 1508–12. Vatican.

F. Michelangelo. Detail of E. Head of Adam.

A. Michelangelo. Detail of the Ceiling of the Sistine Chapel. Temptation and Expulsion of Adam and Eve. 1508–12. Vatican.

B. Michelangelo. Detail of the Ceiling of the Sistine Chapel. Head of Ezekiel. (And)

C. Michelangelo. Detail of the Ceiling of the Sistine Chapel. God Hovering over the Waters.

D. Michelangelo. Detail of the Ceiling of the Sistine Chapel. The Erythraean Sibyl. (Al)

E. Michelangelo. Detail of the Ceiling of the Sistine Chapel. The Cumaean Sibyl. (Al)

F. Michelangelo. Detail of the Ceiling of the Sistine Chapel. The Prophet Jeremiah.

G. Michelangelo. Detail of the Ceiling of the Sistine Chapel. The Prophet Joel.

A. Michelangelo. Detail of the Ceiling of the Sistine Chapel. Libyan Sibyl. 1508–12.

B. Michelangelo. Detail of the Ceiling of the Sistine Chapel. Delphic Sibyl.

C. Michelangelo. Detail of B.

D. Michelangelo. Last Judgment. 1534–41. Sistine Chapel, Vatican. (And)

E. Michelangelo. Detail of D. Christ and the Virgin.

F. Michelangelo. Holy Family of the Doni. 1505. Uffizi. (Traldi)

G. Michelangelo. Detail of F.

H. Michelangelo. Entombment of Christ. National Gallery, London.

I. Copy of a Michelangelo cartoon for the Battle of Pisa. An engraving by Marcantonio Raimondi. 1505 (?), (Al)

A. Vasari. Lorenzo de' Medici. Uffizi.

B. Carlo Crivelli. Annunciation. 1486. National Gallery, London.

C. Mantegna. Madonna and Child. Late work. Poldi-Pezzoli, Milan. (And)

D. Carlo Crivelli. Pietà. Metropolitan Museum. (Met)

E. Mantegna. Parnassus. c. 1500. Louvre.

F. Mantegna. Presentation of Christ in the Temple. Late work. Berlin.

G. Mantegna. Pietà. Late work. Brera, Milan. (And)

A. Mantegna. Agony in the Garden. Early work. National Gallery, London.

B. Mantegna. Holy Family. Late work. Gallery, Dresden.

C. School of Mantegna. Triumph of Caesar. Engraving.

D. Mantegna. St. Sebastian. Imperial Museum, Vienna. (Brogi)

E. Cosimo Tura. Annunciation. 1469. Duomo, Ferrara.

F. Francesco Cossa. Autumn. Berlin.

G. Antonello da Messina. Portrait of a Man (Il Condottière). 1475. Formerly Collection Somzée, Brussels.

H. Antonello da Messina. St. Jerome in his Study. National Gallery, London.

A. Jacopo da Barbari. Apollo and Diana. Engraving. Museum of Fine Arts. (M.F.A.)

B. Gentile Bellini. Sultan Mahomet II. 1480. National Gallery, London. (And)

C. Giovanni Bellini. Doge Loredano. 1505. National Gallery, London. (Hanf)

D. Giovanni Bellini. Madonna and Child. Collection of Carrara-Morelli, Bergamo.

E. Gentile Bellini. Detail of Corpus Christi Procession i Piazza San Marco, Venice. 1496. Academy, Venice. (And)

F. Giovanni Bellini. Madonna with SS. Paul and George Between 1490 and 1510. Academy, Venice.

G. Giovanni Bellini. Detail of the Madonna and Saints. 1488 Frari. (Al)

A. Giovanni Bellini. Agony in the Garden. c. 1470. National Gallery, London.

B. Giovanni Bellini. Madonna of the Trees. 1487. Academy, Venice. (Al)

C. Giovanni Bellini. Formerly attributed to Mantegna. Detail of Pietà. Heads of Christ and the Virgin. c. 1460. Brera, Milan.

D. Bartolommeo Vivarini. Madonna and Child with Saints. 1465. National Museum, Naples. (Al)

E. Carpaccio. Visitation. Late work. Academy, Venice. (Al)

F. Carpaccio. Legend of St. Ursula. The English Ambassadors Return to Their King. c. 1495. Academy, Venice. (And)

A. Carpaccio. Dream of St. Ursula. 1495. Academy, Venice. (And)

B. Carpaccio. Detail of C.

C. Carpaccio. Presentation of Christ in the Temple. 1510. Academy, Venice. (And)

D. Giorgione. Pastoral Symphony. Louvre.

E. Giorgione. Castelfranco Madonna. SS. Liberale and Francis. 1504. Castelfranco. (Al)

F. Giorgione. The Fire Ordeal of the Infant Moses. Early work. Uffizi.

G. Giorgione. Knight of Malta. Uffizi.

A. Giorgione. Also attributed to Titian. The Concert. c. 1510. Pitti. (Brogi)

B. Giorgione. Sleeping Venus. Landscape by Titian. Designed c. 1505. Gallery, Dresden. (Al)

C. Giorgione (?). Detail of A.

D. Giorgione (?). The Three Philosophers. Imperial Museum, Vienna. (Bruck)

E. Titian. Assumption of the Virgin. 1518. Frari, Venice. (And)

F. Titian. Detail of E.

G. Titian. Madonna of the Pesaro Family. 1526. Church of the Frari, Venice. (And)

H. Titian. Self Portrait. c. 1550. Berlin. (And)

A. Titian. Venus. Late work. Uffizi. (And)

B. Titian. The Forbidden Fruit. c. 1565–70. Prado, Madrid. (And)

C. Titian. Lavinia. c. 1550. Berlin.

D. Titian. Eleanora Gonzaga, Duchess of Urbino (La Bella). Pitti. (Traldi)

E. Titian. Pope Paul III. 1543. National Museum, Naples. (Al)

F. Titian. Detail of Portrait of an Unknown Man. Sometimes called the Duke of Norfolk. 1540–45. Pitti. (Al)

G. Lotto. Annunciation. Santa Maria sopra Mercanti, Recanati. (Al)

H. Correggio. Madonna and Child with Saints. 1515. Dresden. (Al)

A. Correggio. Detail of Vault of Convent of San Paolo, Parma. 1518. (Al)

B. Correggio. Detail of A.

C. Correggio. Detail of Cupola of the Cathedral, Parma. The Assumption of the Virgin. 1518. (Al)

D. Correggio. The Virgin Adoring Her Son. Uffizi. (And)

E. Correggio. Madonna of St. Jerome. Parma. (Al)

F. Moroni. Madonna with SS. Catherine and Jerome. Cathedral, Bergamo.

G. Primaticcio. Ulysses and Penelope. Castle Howard.

A. Tintoretto. The Crucifixion. c. 1575. San Cassiano, Venice. (And)

B. Tintoretto. Origin of the Milky Way. National Gallery, London.

C. Tintoretto. Mercury and the Three Graces. 1578. Anti-Collegio, Palace of the Doges, Venice. (Al)

D. Tintoretto. Presentation of the Virgin in the Temple. Early work. Santa Maria dell' Orto, Venice. (And)

E. Tintoretto. Last Supper. San Giorgio Maggiore, Venice.

F. Veronese. Rape of Europa. Detail. Anti-Collegio, Palace of the Doges, Venice. (And)

A. Veronese. Marriage at Cana. 1563. Louvre. (Al)

B. Veronese. Detail of Marriage at Cana. Head of Christ.
Gallery, Dresden.

C. Veronese. Detail of A.

D. Veronese. Feast in the House of Levi. 1573. Academy,
Venice. (Al)

E. Veronese. Detail of D.

F. Caravaggio. Conversion of St. Paul. Santa Maria del Popolo,
Rome. (Al)

A. Caravaggio. Death of the Virgin. Louvre.

B. Caravaggio. Entombment. Vatican.

C. Ludovico Caracci. Ecstasy of St. Catherine. Borghese.

D. Salvator Rosa. Port Scene. Pitti.

E. Guido Reni. Aurora. c. 1615. Rospigliosi Palace, Rome. (A

F. Guido Reni. Beatrice Cenci. Barberini Gallery, Rome.

G. Guido Reni. St. Sebastian. Palazzo Rosso, Genoa. (And)

H. Guido Reni. Archangel Michael Overcoming Satan. San
Maria della Concezione, Rome. (And)

A. Tiepolo. Ceiling Decoration. The Rosary of St. Dominic. Santa Maria del Rosario, Venice.

B. Canaletto. The Arno in Florence. Budapest.

C. Tiepolo. Wash Drawing. Holy Family. Detail. Fogg Museum. (Fogg)

D. Pietro Longhi. The Coffee Shop. Venice.

E. Guardi. Procession in Front of Santa Maria della Salute. Louvre.

F. Liberale da Verona. XVI Cent. St. Martin Dividing His Cloak. Initial from a Choir Book. Piccolomini Library, Cathedral, Siena. (Al)

A. Armor. Royal Palace, Turin. (Al)

B. Velvet. XVI cent. Museum of Fine Arts. (M.F.A.)

C. Chair. XVI cent. Metropolitan Museum. (Met)

D. Cassone of Carved and Gilded Wood. Demeter and Hecate

Searching for Persephone. 1450–1500. Metropolitan Museum. (Met)

E. Stool of Carved Wood. Late XVI or early XVII cent. Metropolitan Museum. (Met)

F. Chest from Venice. XVI cent. Metropolitan Museum. (Met)

G. Choir Stalls. 1487–98. The Certosa, Pavia. (Brogi)

A. Jean Malouel (French) and Henri Bellechose. The Martyrdom of St. Denis. c. 1415. Louvre. (Gir)

B. Hubert and Jan van Eyck. The Ghent Altarpiece, outer panel. Angel of the Annunciation. Above, Zacharias. 1415–32. Church of St. Bavon, Ghent.

C. Hubert and Jan van Eyck. The Ghent Altarpiece, outer panel. Madonna of the Annunciation. Above, Matthew. 1415–32. Church of St. Bavon, Ghent.

D. Hubert and Jan van Eyck. The Ghent Altarpiece, open. (Adoration of the Lamb.) 1415–32. Church of St. Bavon. Ghent.

E. Detail of D.

F. Detail of D.

G. Hubert van Eyck. The Three Marys at the Tomb. Collection of Sir Herbert Cook, Richmond.

H. Jan van Eyck. Portrait of His Wife Margaret. 1439. Bruges Museum.

THE VAN EYCKS · ROBERT CAMPIN · VAN DER WEYDEN

A. Jan van Eyck. Also attributed to Hubert. Madonna of Chancellor Rolin. c. 1432. Louvre. (X)

B. Jan van Eyck. Jan Arnolfini and His Wife. 1434. National Gallery, London.

C. Robert Campin. Portrait of a Man, perhaps Niccolo Strozzi. Kaiser Friedrich Museum.

D. Jan van Eyck. Detail of the Madonna with the Canon van der Paele. Portrait of the Canon. 1436. Bruges Museum. (Bruck)

E. Rogier van der Weyden. Portrait of a Lady. Collection of A. W. Mellon Educational and Charitable Trust. (Courtesy of the Trustees)

F. Robert Campin. The von Werl Altarpiece. Detail of one wing. St. Barbara. Prado. (And)

G. Rogier van der Weyden. Descent from the Cross. 1435–50. Escorial, Madrid.

H. Rogier van der Weyden. Madonna and Child. Kaiser Friedrich Museum.

A. Rogier van der Weyden. Adoration of the Magi. Gallery, Munich.

B. Petrus Christus. Legend of SS. Eligius and Godeberta. 1449. Collection of Philip Lehman, New York. (Philip Lehman)

C. Petrus Christus. Portrait of Dionysius the Carthusian (?). Collection of Jules S. Bache. (Duveen Brothers)

D. Petrus Christus. Portrait of a Lady of the Talbot Family. Kaiser Friedrich Museum.

E. Memlinc. R. panel from Diptych of Martin van Nieuwenhoven. 1487. Hospital of St. John, Bruges. (Bruck)

F. Justus of Ghent. The Last Supper. Ducal Gallery, Urbino.

G. Memlinc. Shrine of St. Ursula. 1489. Hospital of St. John, Bruges. (See 158 A, B)

A. Memlinc. Shrine of St. Ursula. 1489. Hospital of St. John, Bruges. (Bruck)

B. Memlinc. Shrine of St. Ursula. 1489. (Detail of 157 G.) Martyrdom of St. Ursula. (Bruck)

C. Memlinc. Central Panel of Altarpiece. Vienna, Imperial Museum.

D. Hugo van der Goes. Portinari Altarpiece. Central panel. Adoration of the Shepherds. 1476. Uffizi. (Brogi)

E. Hugo van der Goes. Detail of D.

F. Hugo van der Goes. Descent from the Cross. Copy. National Museum, Naples.

G. Hugo van der Goes. Portinari Altarpiece. Right panel. Wife and Daughter of the Donor with SS. Margaret and Mary Magdalene. 1476. Uffizi. (Brogi)

A. David. Canon and Saints. 1501. National Gallery, London.

B. David. Head of Christ. John G. Johnson Art Collection, Philadelphia. (John G. Johnson Art Coll.)

C. Massys (Matsys). Madonna and Child. Kaiser Friedrich Museum. (Berlin)

D. Massys. Banker and Wife. 1518. Louvre. (Gir)

E. Massys. Altarpiece of St. Anne. Central panel. 1509. Royal Museum, Brussels. (Bruck)

F. Gossaert (Mabuse). Madonna with Grapes. Kaiser Friedrich Museum.

G. Pieter Bruegel the elder (Breughel). Peasant Dance. 1568 (?). Vienna.

A. Pieter Bruegel the elder. Harvesters (August). Metropolitan Museum. (Met)

B. Bosch. Mocking of Christ. Escorial, Madrid.

C. Pieter Bruegel the elder. The Blind Beggars. 1568. National Museum, Naples. (And)

D. Antonio Moro. Alessandro Farnese. Parma.

E. Pieter Bruegel the elder. Massacre of the Innocents. Deta 1566 (?). Vienna, Gallery. (Bruck)

F. Rubens. Rape of the Daughters of Leucippus. 1619 or 162 Picture Gallery, Munich.

A. Pieter Bruegel the elder. Hunters in the Snow. 1565. Vienna.

B. Rubens. Self Portrait with Isabella Brant. 1609–10. Gallery, Munich. (Bruck)

C. Rubens. Lion Hunt. 1616–21. Gallery, Munich.

D. Rubens. Self Portrait. Detail of B.

E. Rubens. Judgment of Paris. c. 1625. National Gallery, London.

F. Rubens. Elevation of the Cross. Central panel of a Triptych. 1610–11. Antwerp.

A. Rubens. Crucifixion (Coup de Lance). 1620. Antwerp.

B. Rubens (School Work). Infants Christ, St. John and Angels. c. 1615–20. Vienna.

C. Rubens. Return of Diana from the Hunt. 1615–17. Picture Gallery, Dresden. (Al)

D. Rubens. Helena Fourment and Children. c. 1635–38. Louvre.

E. Rubens. Suzanne Fourment (The Straw Hat). c. 1620. National Gallery, London. From a wood engraving by Timothy Cole, 1905. Collection of F. J. Roos, Jr. (See p. 320 D for magnified detail.)

F. Rubens. Head of Infant St. John. Detail of a Holy Family. Pitti. (And)

G. Rubens. Head of Nicholas Rubens. Drawing. Vienna.

A. Rubens. Sir Thomas More. Detail. Prado, Madrid.

B. Rubens. Landing of Marie de' Medici at Marseilles. 1621–25. Louvre. (Al)

C. Van Dyck. Charles I of England. 1635. Louvre. (See 164 B, F)

D. Rubens. Kermess. c. 1635. Louvre.

E. Van Dyck. Children of Charles I. 1635. Picture Gallery, Turin. (L'Epi)

F. Van Dyck. Pietà, with Madonna, St. John and Angels. 1634. Royal Museum, Antwerp.

G. Van Dyck. James II, son of Charles I. Detail of E.

A. Van Dyck. Frans Snyders and His Wife. Picture Gallery Cassel. (L'Epi)

B. Van Dyck. Charles I on Horseback. c. 1636. National Gallery, London. (See 163 C)

C. Van Dyck. Pieter Bruegel the younger. Etching. Fogg Museum. (Fogg)

D. Van Dyck. Self Portrait. Uffizi. (Al)

E. David Teniers the younger. Peasant Interior. Louvre. (Al)

F. Van Dyck. Triple Portrait of Charles I. c. 1637. Windsor Castle.

G. David Teniers the younger. The Smoker. Louvre. (Bruck)

FLEMISH PAINTING · XVII CENT. · TENIERS
GERMAN ARCHITECTURE · XVII–XVIII CENT.

165

A. David Teniers the younger. Village Festival. Louvre. (A.N.)

B. David Teniers the younger. Man Lighting a Pipe. Art Institute. (Art Inst.)

C. David Teniers the younger. Barber Shop. Picture Gallery, Cassel.

D. Peller House, Nuremberg. 1605.

E. Zwinger Palace, Dresden. 1711.

F. Zwinger Palace, Dresden. 1711.

G. New Palace, Potsdam. 1763–69.

A. Brandenburg Gate, Berlin. 1788–91. Langhans, architect.

B. Peter Vischer the elder. King Arthur. XVI cent. Innsbruck. (Reiffenstein)

C. Lochner. Madonna with the Violet. Archiepiscopal Palace, Cologne. (Bruck)

D. Lochner. Altarpiece. Central panel. Cologne Cathedral. (Bruck)

E. German School. St. Christopher Bearing the Infant Christ. Woodcut. 1423. John Rylands Library, Manchester. (Fogg)

F. Schongauer. Nativity. Kaiser Friedrich Museum.

G. Schongauer. Madonna and Child in a Courtyard. Engraving. Museum of Fine Arts. (M.F.A.)

H. Schongauer. Foolish Virgin. Engraving. Fogg Museum. (Fogg)

A. Schongauer. Madonna in a Rose Hedge. 1473. Church of St. Martin, Colmar. (Bruck)

B. Grünewald. Detail of Central Panel of a Crucifixion. Virgin with St. John the Evangelist. 1510–14. Museum, Colmar.

C. Dürer. Self Portrait. 1500. Old Picture Gallery, Munich. (Bruck)

D. Dürer. Self Portrait. 1498. Prado, Madrid. (And)

E. Dürer. Heironymus Holzschuher. 1526. Kaiser Friedrich Museum.

F. Dürer. Jobst Plankfelt of Antwerp. Formerly called Hans Imhof. 1521. Prado, Madrid. (And)

G. Dürer. Portrait of a Young Woman. 1506 (?). Kaiser Friedrich Museum.

H. Dürer. Virgin with the Siskin. 1506. Kaiser Friedrich Museum.

I. Dürer. The Penitent. Woodcut. 1510. Fogg Museum. (See p. 320 A for magnified detail.) (Fogg)

A. Dürer. SS. John the Evangelist and Peter. Detail. 1526. Old Picture Gallery, Munich. (Bruck)

B. Dürer. St. Anthony. Engraving. 1519. Fogg Museum. (Fogg)

C. Dürer. St. Jerome in His Study. Engraving. 1514. Fogg Museum. (Fogg)

D. Dürer. Young Hare. Water color. 1502. Albertina, Vienna. (Wolfrum)

E. Dürer. Erasmus. Engraving. 1526. Fogg Museum. (Fogg)

F. Lucas Cranach the elder. Rest on the Flight into Egypt. Kaiser Friedrich Museum.

G. Cranach. Christ in the Garden of Gethsemane. Picture Gallery, Dresden.

H. Cranach. Madonna and Child. Frankfurt-am-Main.

A. Lucas Cranach the elder. Dr. Scheuring. Royal Museum, Brussels.

B. Cranach. Adam and Eve. Picture Gallery, Dresden.

C. Hans Holbein the younger. Madonna of the Burgomaster Meyer. Detail. 1526 (?). Ducal Palace, Darmstadt. (Bruck)

D. Holbein. Erasmus. 1523. Picture Gallery, Basel.

E. Holbein. George Gisze. Detail. 1532. Kaiser Friedrich Museum.

F. Holbein. Duchess of Suffolk. Between 1527–40. Windsor Castle.

G. Holbein. Henry VIII. c. 1537. Corsini Gallery, Rome. (And)

H. Holbein. Henry VIII. Detail of G.

I. Holbein. Jane Seymour. 1537. Imperial Museum, Vienna.

A. Holbein. Catherine Howard. 1540–41. Edward Drummond Libby Collection, Toledo Museum. (Toledo Museum)

B. Holbein. Robert Cheseman. 1533. Detail. Royal Museum, The Hague. (Bruck)

C. Prince Rupert. The Large Executioner. After 1660. Mezzotint. Museum of Fine Arts. (See p. 320 B for magnified detail.) (M.F.A.)

D. Suit of Armor, Maximilian Style. c. 1520. Cleveland Museum. (Clev. Mus.)

E. Salamanca University. Detail of portal. Plateresque. c. 1530. (See 90 H)

F. Court of the Palace of Charles V, Granada. 1527. (Gonzalez)

G. Palace of Charles V, Granada. 1527. (Gonzalez)

H. Town Hall, Seville. Plateresque. 1534–72.

A. Coello. Infanta Isabel, Daughter of Philip II. XVI cent. (Prado)

B. El Greco. Laocoön. c. 1606–10. National Gallery, London (Nat. Gall.)

C. El Greco. Christ Driving the Money Changers from the Temple. c. 1575. Minneapolis Institute of Arts. (Minn. Inst.)

D. El Greco. Christ on the Cross. 1584–90. Prado. (And)

E. El Greco. Resurrection. 1595–1603. Prado.

F. El Greco. Burial of the Count of Orgaz. c. 1584. Santo Tomé Toledo. (And)

G. El Greco. Christ with the Cross. 1587–92. Prado. (And)

H. El Greco. Don Fernando Niño de Guevara, Cardinal and Archbishop of Seville. Metropolitan Museum. (Met)

A. El Greco. St. Martin Dividing His Cloak. Collection of Joseph E. Widener, Philadelphia. (Joseph E. Widener)

B. Velásquez. Maids of Honor (Las Meninas). 1656–57. Prado. (And)

C. Velásquez. Self Portrait. Detail of B.

D. Velásquez. The Infanta. Detail of B.

E. Velásquez. Aesop. Detail. c. 1650. Prado. (And)

F. Velásquez. Man with a Wine Glass. c. 1623. Edwa Drummond Libby Collection, Toledo Museum. (Tole Museum)

G. Velásquez. The Forge of Vulcan. 1629. Prado. (And)

H. Velásquez. The Tapestry Weavers. 1656. Prado. (And)

A. Velásquez. Surrender of Breda. Detail. Between 1639–47. Prado. (And)

B. Velásquez. Philip IV of Spain. Uffizi. (And)

C. Velásquez. The Rokeby Venus. c. 1642. National Gallery, London.

D. Velásquez. The Infanta Maria Theresa. Prado. (And)

E. Ribera. Ecstasy of Mary Magdalene. Academy of St. Ferdinand, Madrid.

F. Zurbarán. Christ at Gethsemane. Collection of Eugen Boross. (Met)

G. Murillo. Detail of Madonna and Child. Pitti. (Al)

A. Murillo. The Immaculate Conception. Louvre. (Louvre)

B. Murillo. Flower Girl. Dulwich College Gallery.

C. Goya. Self Portrait. 1808–14. Collection Smith College Museum of Art. (Smith College)

D. Goya. The Shooting of a Group of Citizens by the Soldiers of Murat on the Night of May 3, 1808. Prado. (And)

E. Goya. Majas on a Balcony. Metropolitan Museum. (Met)

F. Goya. Family of Carlos IV. 1800. Prado. (And)

G. Goya. Doña Isabel Corbo de Porcel. National Gallery London.

A. Goya. La Maja Desnuda. 1795–97. Prado. (Moreno)

B. Goya. La Maja Vestida. 1797–99. Prado. (Moreno)

C. Goya. Maria Louisa of Parma, wife of Carlos IV. 1799. Taft Museum, Cincinnati. (Taft)

D. Goya. Bull Fight. Lithograph. Museum of Fine Arts. (M.F.A.)

E. Goya. Maria Louisa of Parma, wife of Carlos IV. 1799. Prado. (And)

F. Goya. Los Proverbios. The Bird-Men. Detail. Etching and Aquatint. Fogg Museum. (Fogg)

G. Goya. Old Age: Then and Now. c. 1817–19. Palace of Fine Arts, Lille. (Gir)

A. Hals. Officers of the Company of St. Adrian. 1627. Hals Museum, Haarlem.

B. Hals. Young Violin Player. Collection of Leo M. Flesh, Piqua, O. (John Levy Galleries)

C. Hals. Young Man in Fur Cap. Brooklyn Institute of Arts and Sciences. (Brooklyn Inst.)

D. Hals. Child and Nurse. 1630–35. Kaiser Friedrich Museum

E. Hals. Laughing Cavalier. 1624. Wallace Collection, London

F. Hals. Portrait of a Girl. 1630. Louvre. (L. L.)

G. Rembrandt. The Sortie of the Civic Guard (Night Watch) 1642. Rijksmuseum.

A. Rembrandt. Bathsheba. 1654. Louvre. (Al)

B. Rembrandt. The Syndics of the Cloth Guild. 1662. Rijksmuseum.

C. Rembrandt. Self Portrait. 1634. Pitti. (Brogi)

D. Rembrandt. Self Portrait. 1639. Etching. Fogg Museum. (Fogg)

E. Rembrandt. Self Portrait. 1659. National Gallery, London. (Nat. Gall.)

F. Rembrandt. Hendrickje Stoffels. 1652. Louvre. (Al)

G. Rembrandt. Dr. Tulp's Anatomy Lesson. Detail. 1632. Royal Museum, The Hague.

A. Rembrandt. Supper at Emmaus. 1648. Louvre. (Al)

B. Rembrandt. The Polish Rider (A Patrician of the Lysowski Regiment). 1655. Frick Gallery, New York. (Courtesy Trustees of the Frick Gallery)

C. Rembrandt. The Blindness of Tobit. 1651. Etching. Fogg Museum. (Fogg)

D. Rembrandt. Christ Healing the Sick (The Hundred Guilder Print). Etching. 1649. Fogg Museum. (Fogg)

E. Rembrandt. Dr. Faust in His Study. c. 1651. Etching. Fogg Museum. (Fogg)

F. Gerard Dou. Rembrandt's Mother. c. 1630. Kaiser Friedrich Museum.

G. Carel Fabritius. The Guard. 654. Museum, Schwerin.

A. De Hooch. Interior with Cardplayers. 1658. Buckingham Palace.

B. De Hooch. Mother and Child. Kaiser Friedrich Museum.

C. De Hooch. Courtyard of a Dutch House. 1672. National Gallery, London. (Nat. Gall.)

D. De Hooch. Dutch Interior. Detail. National Gallery, London. (Nat. Gall.)

E. De Hooch. The Buttery. c. 1658. Rijksmuseum.

F. Vermeer. Interior with Cavalier and Girl Drinking Wine. Kaiser Friedrich Museum. (Berlin)

G. Vermeer. Young Woman with a Water Jug. Metropolitan Museum. (Met)

A. Vermeer. The Lace Maker. Louvre. (Al)

B. Vermeer. Young Woman Reading a Letter. Rijksmuseum.

C. Vermeer. Young Girl Reading a Letter. Picture Gallery, Dresden.

D. Vermeer. Head of a Young Girl. Mauritz Haus, The Hague.

E. Vermeer. Servant Girl Pouring Milk. Rijksmuseum.

F. Terborch. Woman in a Room. Dresden. (Al)

G. Terborch. A Lesson on the Lute. Isabella Stewart Gardner Museum, Boston. (Gardner Museum)

H. Terborch. The Concert. Kaiser Friedrich Museum.

I. Terborch. The Music Lesson. National Gallery, London. (Nat. Gall.)

A. Terborch. Woman Washing Her Hands. Picture Gallery, Dresden. (Bruck)

B. Steen. The Brewery of Jan Steen. The Hague. (Bruck)

C. Ruisdael. Jewish Burial Ground. Picture Gallery, Dresden.

D. Steen. Sick Lady. Taft Museum, Cincinnati. (Taft)

E. Ruisdael. The Mill Near Wijk. Rijksmuseum. (Bruck)

F. Ruisdael. Landscape with Castle. Collection of Earl of Northbrook.

A. Ruisdael. Wheatfields. Metropolitan Museum. (Met)

B. Paul Potter. Head of a Bull. 1647. The Hague. (Bruck)

C. Potter. The Young Bull. 1645. The Hague. (Bruck)

D. A. van Ostade. Group of Peasants in an Interior. Dulwich Gallery.

E. Hobbema. Middelharnis Avenue. 1689. National Gallery London.

F. A. van Ostade. The Herring Woman. Rijksmuseum.

A. Hobbema. The Travellers. c. 1660. Collection Joseph E. Widener. (Joseph E. Widener)

B. A. van Ostade. The Golden Wedding. Art Institute. (Art Inst.)

C. Hobbema. The Mill. Gallery, Dresden. (Al)

D. A. van Ostade. Peasant at a Window. Brooklyn Institute of Arts and Sciences. (Brooklyn Inst.)

E. William van de Velde the younger. Calm Sea with Ships. Buckingham Palace.

F. William van de Velde the younger. Entrance to a Dutch Port. Metropolitan Museum. (Met)

A. Staircase, Knole House, Kent. 1570.

B. Kirby Hall, Northants. Designed by John Thorpe. 1570.

C. Kirby Hall, Northants. Designed by John Thorpe. 1570.

D. Hampton Court. Sir Christopher Wren, architect. 1689–1703.

E. Banqueting Hall, Whitehall, London. Inigo Jones, architect. 1619–22.

F. St. Paul's Cathedral, London. Sir Christopher Wren, architect. 1675–1710. (See p. 185)

A. St. Paul's Cathedral, London. Sir Christopher Wren, architect. 1675–1710. (See 184 F)

B. St. Paul's Cathedral, London. Interior.

C. St. Mary-le-Bow, London. Sir Christopher Wren, architect. 1680.

D. St. Mary-le-Bow, London. Spire.

E. St. Paul's Cathedral, London. Detail of B.

F. St. Bride's, Fleet Street, London. Sir Christopher Wren, architect. 1680–1702.

G. St. Martin's in the Fields, London. James Gibbs, architect. 1721–26.

H. St. Stephen's Walbrook, London. Interior. Sir Christopher Wren, architect. 1672–79.

I. Blenheim Palace, Oxfordshire. Sir John Vanbrugh, architect. 1705–24.

A. Kedleston. The Garden Front. Robert Adam and others, architects. c. 1760.

B. Bank of England, London. Sir John Soane, architect. 1795–1827.

C. St. George's Hall, Liverpool. H. L. Elmes, architect. 1839.

D. Eaton Hall, Cheshire. William Porden, architect.

E. Parliament Buildings, London. Sir Charles Barry, architect. 1840–68.

F. House of Parliament, London. Peers' Corridor.

A. Sir Godfrey Kneller. Sir Christopher Wren. National Gallery, London.

B. William Hogarth. Self Portrait. c. 1740. National Gallery, London.

C. Hogarth. Garrick and His Wife. 1757. Royal Collection, Windsor.

D. Hogarth. Marriage à la Mode. After Breakfast. 1745 National Gallery, London. (Berlin)

E. Hogarth. Shrimp Girl. National Gallery, London.

F. Hogarth. Marriage à la Mode. The Marriage Counter. 1745. National Gallery, London. (Berlin)

G. Hogarth. The Laughing Audience. Etching. 1733. Fogg Museum. (Fogg)

A. Reynolds. Mrs. Siddons as the Tragic Muse. 1784. Huntington Coll., San Marino, Cal.

B. Reynolds. Samuel Johnson. 1772. National Gallery, London. (Nat. Gall.)

C. Reynolds. Miss Bowles. 1776. Wallace Collection, London.

D. Reynolds. The Age of Innocence. 1788. National Gallery, London. (Berlin)

E. Reynolds. Little Samuel. 1777. Fabre Museum, Montpellier. (Gir)

F. Gainsborough. The Blue Boy. 1770. Huntington Collection, San Marino, California. (Huntington Collection)

G. Gainsborough. Skirts of the Woods. Art Institute. (Art Inst.)

H. Gainsborough. Mrs. Siddons. 1784. National Gallery, London. (Berlin)

A. Gainsborough. The Market Cart. 1767–68. National Gallery, London.

B. Gainsborough. Mrs. Graham. 1784–86. National Gallery, Edinburgh.

C. Gainsborough. Sir Benjamin Thompson, Count Rumford. Detail. Fogg Museum. (Fogg)

D. Gainsborough. Landscape with Figures and Cattle. Taft Museum, Cincinnati. (Taft)

E. Romney. Self Portrait. 1795. Metropolitan Museum. (Met)

F. Romney. Mrs. Robinson (Perdita). c. 1783. Wallace Collection, London.

G. Romney. Study of Lady Hamilton as a Bacchante. 1786. National Gallery, London.

H. Romney. Lady Hamilton. National Gallery, London.

A. Romney. Mrs. Mark Currie. 1789. National Gallery, London.

B. Raeburn. The McNab. c. 1796. Collection of John Dewar and Sons, London.

C. Raeburn. Mrs. Scott Moncriff. National Gallery, Edinburgh.

D. Turner. Dido Directing Equipment. c. 1814. National Gallery, London.

E. Hoppner. The Countess of Oxford. National Gallery, London.

F. Turner. Dido Building Carthage. 1815. National Gallery, London.

G. Lawrence. Arthur Wellesley, 1st Duke of Wellington. Copy of original in the Wellington Collection. Huntington Collection, San Marino, California. (Huntington Collection)

A. Turner. Dutch Fishing Boats. c. 1826. Art Institute. (Art Inst.)

B. Lawrence. Mrs. Siddons. National Gallery, London.

C. Turner. Bridge of Sighs. c. 1833. Art Gallery, Leicester.

D. Blake. When the Morning Stars Sang Together. From the Book of Job. 1820. Engraving. Fogg Museum. (See 192 B.) (Fogg)

E. Turner. Norham Castle on the Tweed. From the Liber Studiorum. Mezzotint. 1807–19. Fogg Museum. (Fogg)

F. Blake. Reunion of the Soul and the Body. From Blair's Grave. Engraving by Schiavonetti. Collection of F. J. Roos, Jr.

A. Turner. Rain, Steam and Speed. 1844. National Gallery, London.

B. Blake. Then the Lord Answered Job Out of a Whirlwind. From the Book of Job. 1820. Engraving. Fogg Museum. (Fogg)

C. Constable. Hay Wain. 1821. National Gallery, London.

D. Constable. The Cornfield. 1826. National Gallery, London.

E. Constable. The Glebe Farm. 1826. National Gallery, London.

F. Bonington. The Clock Tower, Evreux. Lithograph. Fogg Museum. (Fogg)

A. Watts. Hope. 1891. National Gallery, London.

B. Watts. Love and Life. 1890. National Gallery, London.

C. Rossetti. Annunciation. 1850. National Gallery, London.

D. Millais. Lorenzo at the Home of Isabella. 1849. Walker Art Gallery, Liverpool.

E. Holman Hunt. Light of the World. 1855. Keble College Chapel, Oxford.

F. Burne-Jones. The Golden Stairs. 1876–80. National Gallery, London.

G. Burne-Jones. Mirror of Venus. 1873–77. Collection Sidney Goldmann, London.

H. Burne-Jones. King Cophetua and the Beggar Maid. 1876–80. National Gallery, London.

A. Brangwyn. Unloading Oranges. Wood engraving.

B. Orpen. Sir William McCormick. 1920. National Gallery of British Art.

C. Zuloaga. The Victim of the Fête. 1910.

D. Sorolla. Valencia. 1913–19. Museum of the Hispanic Society of America. (Hispanic Society)

E. Sorolla. On the Beach. 1908. Carnegie Institute, Pittsburgh. (Carnegie Inst.)

F. Zorn. Auguste Rodin. Etching. (Fogg)

G. Zorn. Bather. (Met)

A. Armchair, Louis XIV. Louvre. (Louvre)

B. Table, Louis XIV. Louvre. (Louvre)

C. King's Study, Versailles. Louis XIV–XV. (Gir)

D. Chair, Louis XV. Fontainbleau. (L.P.)

E. Room, Versailles. Louis XV. (L.P.)

F. Chair, Louis XVI. Metropolitan Museum. (Met)

G. Chair, Louis XVI. Louvre. (Louvre)

H. Cabinet, Made by Riesener for Marie Antoinette. 1780–90. Louis XVI. (Met)

A. Cylinder Desk, Louis XVI. Style of Riesener. (Met)

B. Mirror, Empire. Metropolitan Museum. (Met)

C. Chair, Empire. Metropolitan Museum. (Met)

D. Bed, Empire. Metropolitan Museum. (Met)

E. Bed, Elizabethan. 1593. Victoria and Albert Museum. (Vict. Alb.)

F. Chairs, Jacobean, American. L., table top chair, 1625–75; R., wainscot arm chair, 1650–60. Metropolitan Museum. (Met)

G. Wainscot Chair, Jacobean, American. Late XVII cent. Metropolitan Museum. (Met)

H. Chair, Stuart. English. 1660-80. Metropolitan Museum. (Met)

A. Chest, Stuart. 1650–75. American. Metropolitan Museum. (Met)

B. Chair, Stuart. English. 1680–85. Metropolitan Museum. (Met)

C. Chair, Stuart. English. 1660–75. Metropolitan Museum. (Met)

D. Cabinet, Restoration. English. c. 1680. Victoria and Albert Museum. (Vict. Alb.)

E. Cabinet, William and Mary. English. 1688–1702. Metropolitan Museum. (Met)

F. Chair, Queen Anne. English. 1720–30. Metropolitan Museum. (Met)

G. Mirror, Early Georgian. English. Metropolitan Museum. (Met)

H. Highboy, Early Georgian. American. 1725–50. Metropolitan Museum. (Met)

I. Lowboy, Early Georgian. American. 1700–25. Metropolitan Museum. (Met)

A. Chair, Chippendale. English. 1750–95. Metropolitan Museum. (Met)

B. Chair, Chippendale. Gothic Influence. English. 1700–70. Metropolitan Museum. (Met)

C. Chair, Chippendale. Chinese Influence. English. 1755–60. Metropolitan Museum. (Met)

D. Chair, Ladder Back, Chippendale. English. 1765–75. Metropolitan Museum. (Met)

E. Chair, Chippendale. English. 1740–50. Metropolitan Museum. (Met)

F. Bed, Chippendale. Chinese Influence. English. 1760. Metropolitan Museum. (Met)

G. Card Table, Chippendale. English. 1760. Metropolitan Museum. (Met)

H. Desk, American. XVIII cent. Metropolitan Museum. (Met)

I. Chair, Sheraton. American. 1790–1800. Metropolitan Museum. (Met)

A. Table, Sheraton. American. 1800–10. Metropolitan Museum. (Met)

B. Chair, Heppelwhite. American. 1785–95. Metropolitan Museum. (Met)

C. Mirror, Heppelwhite. English. 1775–85. Metropolitan Museum. (Met)

D. Chair, Adam Style. English. 1760–70. Metropolitan Museum. (Met)

E. Settee, Adam Style. English. 1778–80. Metropolitan Museum. (Met)

F. Drop Leaf Table, Phyfe. American. 1810–15. Metropolitan Museum. (Met)

G. Chair Back, Phyfe. American. 1800–10. Taft Museum. (Roos)

H. Ceiling Detail of 15 Hanover Sq., London. Adam. Late XVIII cent. Victoria and Albert Museum. (Vict. Alb.)

I. Mantel and Grate, Adam. English. Late XVIII cent. Metropolitan Museum. (Met)

A. House of Diane de Poitiers, Rouen. XVI cent. (N.D.)

B. Château of Chaumont. XV–XVI cent.

C. Château of Chenonceaux. 1515–23. (N.D.)

D. Château of Chenonceaux 1515–23. (N.D.)

E. Château of Azay-le-Rideau. 1521.

F. Château of Chambord. The Lantern. 1526–44. (See 201 C.)

A. Château of Blois. Wing of Louis XII. c. 1200.

B. Château of Blois. Stairway, Wing of Francis I. 1520–30.

C. Château of Chambord. 1526–44. (See 200 F.) (N.D.)

D. Château of Blois. Detail of B.

E. Versailles. XVII–XVIII cent.

F. Versailles. Hall of Mirrors. 1680. Mansard, architect; Le Brun, decorator.

A. Versailles. The Park. By Le Notre. An engraving by Perelle.

B. Versailles. Court of the Statues. 1665–70. Louis le Vau, architect. (Gir)

C. Versailles. Hall of the Oval Window. (Gir)

D. Versailles. The Petit Trianon. 1762–68. Gabriel, architect. (X)

E. Louvre, Paris. Court of Lescot and Goujon. 1546–76.

F. Louvre, Paris. Detail of E.

A. Louvre, Paris. W. façade of Pavilion Sully. Lescot, architect. XVI cent. (X)

B. Louvre, Paris. Detail of A.

C. Louvre, Paris. Colonnade by Perrault. 1665.

D. Hôtel des Invalides Chapel, Paris. Mansard, architect. 1699–1704.

E. Panthéon, Paris. Soufflot, architect. 1755–80. (X)

F. Arc de l'Etoile, Paris. Chalgrin, architect. 1806–36.

A. The Madeleine, Paris. Vignon, architect. 1807–42.

B. The Opéra, Paris. Interior. Charles Garnier, architect. 1861–74. (X)

C. The Opéra, Paris. Charles Garnier, architect. 1861–74. (X)

D. Goujon. Water Nymph from Fountain of the Innocents. 1547–49. Paris.

E. Coysevox. Portrait of the Artist. Early XVIII cent. Louvre.

F. Goujon, attributed to. Diane de Poitiers as Diana. From Château d'Anet. XVI cent. Louvre. (Al)

G. Coysevox. Louis XIV. Before 1715. Versailles. (Gir)

A. Coysevox. River God of the Rhône. Early XVIII cent. Versailles.

B. Coustou. The Horses of Marly. XVIII cent. Place de la Concorde, Paris.

C. Clodion. The Intoxication of Wine. XVIII cent. Metropolitan Museum. (Met)

D. Canova. Pauline Borghese as Venus Victrix. Early XIX cent. Borghese Gallery, Rome. (Al)

E. Canova. Detail of D.

F. Houdon. George Washington. 1785. Mount Vernon, Virginia. (Courtesy of Mount Vernon Ladies' Association)

A. Houdon. Benjamin Franklin. 1778. Louvre.

B. Houdon. Voltaire. 1781. Louvre. (Gir)

C. Carpeaux. The Dance. Façade of the Opéra, Paris.

D. Barye. Theseus Slaying the Minotaur. 1848. Metropolitan Museum. (Met)

E. Barye. Tiger Walking. Louvre.

F. Chapu. Joan of Arc. Luxembourg. (Lux)

G. Rodin. St. John the Baptist. 1878. (Arch. Photo.)

H. Rodin. Eve. 1881. Rodin Museum, Paris. (Rodin Museum)

I. Rodin. The Kiss. 1886. Rodin Museum, Paris.

J. Rodin. The Thinker. 1889. Rodin Museum, Paris.

A. Bibliothèque Sainte Geneviève, Paris. Interior, Second Floor. Henri Labrouste, architect. 1843–50. (U. of Ill.)

B. Eiffel Tower, Paris. Gustave Eiffel, engineer. 1889. (U. of Ill.)

C. Bibliothèque Nationale, Paris, Reading Room. Henri Labrouste, architect. 1858–68.

D. Arcade, Victoria Buildings, Manchester. c. 1873. (U. of Ill.)

E. Crystal Palace, London. Joseph Paxton, architect. 1851. (U. of Ill.)

F. Iron Column and Staircase, 12 Rue de Turin, Brussels, Victor Horta, architect. (U. of Ill.)

A. Workers' Houses, Hook of Holland. J. J. P. Oud, architect. 1924–26. (U. of Ill.)

B. Church of St. Therese, Montmagny, France. Auguste and Gustave Perret, architects. 1925. (U. of Ill.)

C. Bath House, Hilversum, Holland. Willem Dudok, architect. 1921. (U. of Ill.)

D. Interior of B. (U. of Ill.)

E. Stoclet Palace, Brussels. Josef Hoffmann, architect. 1905–11. (U. of Ill.)

F. Dirigible Hangar, Orly, France. Eugene Freyssinet, architect. 1916. (U. of Ill.)

A. Schocken Department Store, Chemnitz, Germany. Eric Mendelsohn, architect. 1928. (U. of Ill.)

B. Einstein Tower, Potsdam, Germany. Eric Mendelsohn, architect. 1921. (U. of Ill.)

C. Model Factory, Exhibition Building, Cologne, Germany. Walter Gropius, architect. 1914. (U. of Ill.)

D. Fagus Factory, Alfeld-an-der-Leine, Germany. Walter Gropius and Adolph Meyer, architects. 1911. (U. of Ill.)

E. Bauhaus, Dessau, Germany. Walter Gropius, architect. 1925. (U. of Ill.)

F. Bauhaus, Student's Studio Building, Dessau. Walter Gropius, architect. 1926. (U. of Ill.)

A. Savoye House, Poissy-sur-Seine, France. Le Corbusier, architect. 1929–30. (U. of Ill.)

B. St. Wenceslas, Prague. Josef Gocar, architect. c. 1930. (Arch. Record)

C. Gertrude Stein House, Garches, France. Le Corbusier, architect. 1927–28. (U. of Ill.)

D. German Pavilion, International Exposition, Barcelona. Plan. Miës van der Rohe, architect. 1929. (U. of Ill.)

E. German Pavilion, International Exposition, Barcelona. Miës van der Rohe, architect. 1929. (U. of Ill.)

F. Bergpolder Apartments, Rotterdam. J. Brinkman and Van der Vlugt, architects. 1934. (U. of Ill.)

A. Franco-Italian Pieta. XV cent. Frick Collection, New York. (Courtesy of the Trustees of the Frick Collection)

B. J. Fouquet. Guillaume Jouvenal des Ursins. 1461–75. Louvre. (Bruck)

C. Pietà from Avignon. Late XV cent. Louvre. (Gir)

D. Detail of C. Head of Donor.

E. Man with a Glass of Wine. c. 1475. Louvre. (Arch. Photo.)

F. J. Clouet, attributed to. François, Dauphin of France. Royal Museum, Antwerp.

G. J. Clouet, attributed to. Francis I. After 1518. Louvre.

A. Clouet, attributed to. Francis I. c. 1540. Louvre. (Louvre)

B. Poussin. Triumph of David. Gallery, Dulwich.

C. François Clouet, attributed to. Henry II of France. Collection of A. M. Lawrie, London. (Gir)

D. Poussin. Rape of Sabine Women. c. 1637. Metropolitan Museum. (Met)

E. Poussin. Orpheus Asking the Way to Hades. Metropolitan Museum. (Met)

F. Claude Mellan. The Veronica. Engraving. 1649. Fogg Museum. (See p. 320 C for magnified detail.) (Fogg)

POUSSIN · MELLAN · CLAUDE LORRAIN · NANTEUIL · RIGAUD

A. Poussin. Shepherds of Arcadia. Louvre. (Gir)

B. Claude Mellan. Fabri de Peyresc. Engraving. Fogg Museum (Fogg)

C. Claude Lorrain. Seaport at Sunset. c.1644. National Gallery, London.

D. Nanteuil. Louis XIV. Engraving. 1669. Fogg Museum. (Fogg)

E. Claude Lorrain. Landscape with Mill. Doria Palace, Rome. (Al)

F. Rigaud. Louis XIV. 1701. Louvre. (Gir)

A. Watteau. Embarkation for Cythera. c. 1717. Louvre.

B. Rigaud. Jacques Bossuet, Bishop of Meaux. 1693. Uffizi. (Al)

C. Charles Le Brun. Portrait of the Cologne Banker Eberhard Jabach and His Family. Kaiser Friedrich Museum. (Berlin)

D. Watteau. Picnic in the Woods. Kaiser Friedrich Museum. (Berlin)

E. Lancret. Mlle. Camargo. c.1742. Wallace Collection, London.

F. Watteau. Gilles. Detail. c. 1719–21. Louvre. (Gir)

A. Watteau. L'Indifferent. c. 1710–16. Louvre. (Gir)

B. Lancret. L'Été. 1738. Louvre.

C. Lancret. The Music Lesson. Louvre.

D. Lancret. Pastoral. Kaiser Friedrich Museum. (Berlin)

E. Chardin. Self Portrait. 1775. Louvre.

F. Chardin. Corner of the Kitchen Table. Collection of Dr. Bredius, The Hague.

A. Chardin. The Blessing. 1740. Louvre. (Gir)

B. Chardin. Housewife. 1739. Louvre. (Al)

C. Chardin. The Cook. Old Gallery, Munich.

D. Boucher. Mme. Pompadour. National Gallery, Edinburgh.

E. Boucher. Toilet of Venus. 1751. Metropolitan Museum. (Met)

F. Boucher. The Judgment of Paris. Wallace Collection, London.

G. Boucher. Pastoral. Louvre.

H. Nattier. Princesse de Condé as Diana. 1756. Metropolitan Museum. (Met)

A. Nattier. Mme. Henriette as Flora. Uffizi. (Al)

B. Fragonard. The Rendezvous. 1773. Frick Collection, New York. (Courtesy of the Trustees of the Frick Collection)

C. Fragonard. The Schoolmistress. c. 1780. Wallace Collection, London.

D. Fragonard. The Swing. Wallace Collection, London.

E. Greuze. Milkmaid. Louvre. (Al)

F. Prud'hon. Psyche. 1808. Louvre. (Gir)

G. Prud'hon. Josephine, Empress of the French. Detail. 1805. Louvre. (Al)

A. Vigée Le Brun. Self Portrait with Her Daughter. c. 1787.
Louvre. (Al)

B. J. L. David. Coronation of Napoleon and Josephine. Detail.
1806. Louvre.

C. David. Mme. Récamier. c. 1809. Louvre. (Louvre)

D. David. Death of Marat. Brussels Museum. (Al)

E. David. Oath of the Horatii. 1784. Louvre. (Gir)

F. Constance Charpentier. Mlle. Charlotte du Val d'Ogne
c. 1801. Formerly attributed to David. Metropolitan Mu
seum. (Met)

A. David. Paris and Helen. Detail. 1788. Louvre. (Al)

B. David. Mme. Tangry and Daughters. Louvre.

C. Ingres. Mme. Rivière. 1805. Louvre. (Gir)

D. Ingres. Apotheosis of Homer. 1827. Louvre. (Louvre)

E. Ingres. Cherubini. 1841. Cincinnati Museum. (Cincinnati Mus.)

F. Ingres. Oedipus and the Sphinx. 1808. Louvre. (Gir)

G. Ingres. Comtesse d'Haussonville. 1842–45. Frick Collection, New York. (Courtesy of the Trustees of the Frick Collection)

H. Ingres. M. Bertin. 1832. Louvre.

A. Ingres. The Source 1856. Louvre. (Gir)

B. Ingres. Joan of Arc at the Coronation of Charles VII. 1854. Louvre.

C. Ingres. Turkish Bath. 1859–1863. Louvre. (Gir)

D. Ingres. The Bather. 1808. Louvre. (Gir)

E. Gerard. Mme. Récamier. Petit Palais, Paris. (Gir)

F. Gros. Bonaparte on the Bridge at Arcola. Detail. Louvre. (Louvre)

G. Gros. Napoleon Among the Plague-Stricken at Jaffe. Study for the original in the Louvre. 1804. Musée Condé. Chantilly. (Gir)

H. Bouguereau. Birth of Venus. Luxembourg.

A. Gérôme. Cock Fight. Louvre. (Louvre)

B. Géricault. Officer of the Guard. 1812. Louvre. (Gir)

C. Géricault. Raft of the Medusa. 1819. Louvre. (Gir)

D. Delacroix. Self Portrait. 1837. Louvre.

E. Géricault. The Derby at Epsom. 1821. Louvre. (Gir)

F. Delacroix. The Massacre of Scio. 1824. Louvre. (Al)

A. Delacroix. Dante and Virgil in Hell. 1822. Louvre. (Gir)

B. Millet. The Cooper. Museum of Fine Arts. (M.F.A.)

C. Delacroix. Liberty on the Barricade (July 28, 1830). 1830. Louvre. (Louvre)

D. Millet. The Sower. 1850. Museum of Fine Arts. (M.F.A

E. Delacroix. Death of Sardanapalus. 1822–27. Louvre (Louvre)

F. Millet. The Knitting Lesson. Museum of Fine Art (M.F.A.)

A. Millet. The Angelus. Louvre. (Louvre)

B. Millet. Autumn. Metropolitan Museum. (Met)

C. Millet. The Gleaners. 1856. Louvre. (Gir)

D. Millet. Maternity. Collection of Grenville Winthrop, New York. (Grenville Winthrop)

E. Corot. Spring. Detail. Louvre.

F. Corot. Bacchante by the Sea. 1865. Metropolitan Museum. (Met)

A. Corot. View of the Colosseum. Louvre.

B. Corot. Woman with the Pearl. Louvre. (Louvre)

C. Théodore Rousseau. The Oaks. Louvre.

D. Breton. Song of the Lark. 1884. Art Institute. (Art Inst.)

E. Meissonier. Campaign of France, 1814. Louvre. (Louvre)

F. Meissonier. Cavalier. 1861. Wallace Collection, London.

A. Courbet. Deer in Wood. 1863. Louvre. (Louvre)

B. Courbet. Man with a Pipe. 1847. Museum, Montpellier. (Gir)

C. Courbet. Deer in Forest. Louvre. (Louvre)

D. Courbet. The Woman with the Mirror. 1886. Metropolitan Museum. (Met)

E. Courbet. The Source. 1868. Louvre. (Louvre)

F. Puvis de Chavannes. Summer. Detail. 1873. Museum, Chartres.

A. Puvis de Chavannes. Pro Patria Ludus. 1881. Picardy Museum, Amiens.

B. Puvis de Chavannes. Fisherman's Family. 1887. Art Institute. (Art Inst.)

C. Daumier. The Drinkers. Collection of Adolph Lewisohn, New York. (Met)

D. Daumier. The Uprising. Phillips Memorial Gallery. (Phillips Gall.)

E. Daumier. The Rue Transnonain, April 13, 1834. Lithograph. Museum of Fine Arts. (M.F.A.)

F. Daumier. Peace. Bibliothèque Nationale. (Bib. Nat.)

FRENCH PAINTING · XIX CENT. · DAUMIER
FRENCH MINOR ARTS · XVI–XVII CENT.

227

A. Daumier. Crispin and Scapin. Louvre. (Louvre)

B. Daumier. Salle des Pas-Perdus. Bibliothèque Nationale. (Bib. Nat.)

C. Daumier. The Third Class Carriage. Metropolitan Museum. (Met)

D. Chair, Henry II. XVI cent. Museum of Decorative Arts, Paris.

E. Daumier. Soup. Drawing. Louvre. (Louvre)

F. Chair, Louis XIV. Metropolitan Museum. (Met)

A. Edouard Manet. Bar at the Folies Bergère. 1882. Courtauld Collection, London. (Gir)

B. Edouard Manet. Berthe Morisot. Collection M. and Mme. Rouart. (Gir)

C. Edouard Manet. Bon Bock. 1873. Collection Carroll S. Tyson, Philadelphia. (Carroll S. Tyson)

D. Edouard Manet. Olympia. 1863. Louvre, Paris. (Louvre)

E. Edouard Manet. Dinner Under the Trees. 1863. Louvre, Paris. (Louvre)

F. Edouard Manet. Boy with a Fife. 1866. Louvre, Paris. (Louvre)

A. Edouard Manet. The Balcony. 1868. Louvre, Paris. (Louvre)

B. Claude Monet. The Japanese Fan. 1876. Collection Lord Duveen. (Duveen Bros.)

C. Edouard Manet. Alabama and Kearsarge. c. 1864. Philadelphia Museum of Art. (Phila. Mus.)

D. Claude Monet. Bridge at Argenteuil. 1874. New Staats Gallery, Munich, Germany.

E. Claude Monet. Detail of D.

F. Claude Monet. Rouen Cathedral. c. 1894. Louvre, Paris. (Louvre)

G. Claude Monet. Haystacks in Snow. 1891. Metropolitan Museum, New York. (Met)

A. Claude Monet. Old St. Lazare Station, Paris. 1877. Ryerson Collection, Art Institute. (Art Inst.)

B. Claude Monet. Self Portrait. Unfinished. Louvre, Paris. (Louvre)

C. Claude Monet. Waterlilies. 1908. Worcester Art Museum. (Worcester Mus.)

D. Edgar Degas. Bather. Lithograph. Fogg Museum, Harvard University. (See 320 E for detail.) (Fogg)

E. Edgar Degas. Absinthe Drinkers. 1876–77. Louvre, Paris. (Gir)

F. Edgar Degas. The Ironers. c. 1884. Louvre, Paris. (Louvre)

A. Edgar Degas. Le Foyer de la Danse à l'Opéra de la Rue Le Peletier. 1872. Louvre, Paris. (Arch. Photo)

B. Edgar Degas. Detail of A.

C. Edgar Degas. Carriage at the Races. 1873. Museum of Fine Arts. (M.F.A.)

D. Toulouse-Lautrec. The Moulin Rouge. 1892. Art Institute. (Art Inst.)

E. Toulouse-Lautrec. Woman Seated. Detail. Collection John T. Spaulding, Boston. (Fogg)

F. Toulouse-Lautrec. The Moorish Dance. Louvre, Paris. (Louvre)

A. Marie Laurencin. Two Girls. Collection O. von V., Dusseldorf, Germany.

B. Amadeo Modigliani. Maternity. Chester Dale Collection. (U. S. Nat. Gall.)

C. Odilon Redon. The Closed Eyes. Luxembourg, Germany. (Gir)

D. Camille Pissarro. Place du Havre. 1893. Art Institute. (Art Inst.)

E. Alfred Sisley. Snow at Louveciennes. Phillips Collection, Washington, D. C. (Phillips Coll.)

F. Pierre Renoir. Luncheon of the Boating Party. 1881. Phillips Collection, Washington, D. C. (Phillips Coll.)

G. Pierre Renoir. Woman with a Parasol. 1877. Collection John T. Spaulding, Boston. (John T. Spaulding)

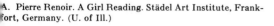

A. Pierre Renoir. A Girl Reading. Städel Art Institute, Frankfort, Germany. (U. of Ill.)

B. Pierre Renoir. Detail of A.

C. Pierre Renoir. Girls at the Piano. Louvre, Paris. (Louvre)

D. Pierre Renoir. Bathers. Drawing. Detail. 1885. Laroche Collection. (Librarie de France)

E. Pierre Renoir. Two Little Circus Girls. 1875–76. Potter Palmer Collection, Art Institute. (Art Inst.)

F. Pierre Renoir. Portrait of Mme. Charpentier and Her Children. 1878. Metropolitan Museum of Art, New York. (Met)

A. Pierre Renoir. The Dancer. 1874. U. S. National Gallery of Art, Washington. (U. S. Nat. Gall.)

B. André de Segonzac. Landscape. Luxembourg. (Gir)

C. Georges Seurat. Models. 1888. Barnes Collection, Merion, Pa. (Barnes Coll.)

D. Pierre Renoir. By the Seashore. 1883. Metropolitan Museum of Art, New York. (Met)

E. Georges Seurat. The Circus. Louvre, Paris. (Louvre)

F. Georges Seurat. Sunday on the Island of La Grand Jatte. 1884–86. Art Institute. (Art Inst.)

A. Henri Rousseau. The Dream. 1910. Sidney Janis Gallery, N. Y. (Sidney Janis Gall.)

B. Vincent Van Gogh. La Berceuse. 1889. Collection John T. Spaulding, Boston. (Fogg)

C. Henri Rousseau. The Sleeping Gypsy. 1897. Museum of Modern Art, New York. (Mus. Mod. Art)

D. Vincent Van Gogh. The Postman. 1888. Museum of Fine Arts. (M.F.A.)

E. Paul Cézanne. Bathers. 1895–1905. Pellerin Collection, Paris.

F. Van Gogh. Detail of B.

A. Vincent Van Gogh. Pére Tanguy. 1886–88. Edward G. Robinson Collection. (Ed. G. Robinson)

B. Paul Cézanne. Mont Ste. Victoire. c. 1885. Phillips Collection, Washington, D. C. (Phillips Coll.)

C. Vincent Van Gogh. Cypresses. Drawing, 1889. Brooklyn Museum, New York. (Brooklyn Mus.)

D. Paul Cézanne. Card Players. 1892. Barnes Collection, Merion, Pa. (Barnes Coll.)

E. Vincent Van Gogh. Street of Auvers. 1890. Collection John T. Spaulding, Boston. (Fogg)

F. Paul Cézanne. Still Life. Collection John T. Spaulding, Boston. (Fogg)

A. Paul Gauguin. Seated Woman (La Faaturuma). 1891.
Worcester Art Museum. (Worcester Mus.)

B. Paul Gauguin. The Day of the God (Mahara no Atua).
1894. Art Institute. (Art Inst.)

C. Paul Gauguin. Oh, You're Jealous (No Te Aha Oe Riri).
1896. Art Institute. (Art Inst.)

D. Paul Gauguin. The White Horse. Luxembourg, Paris. (Gir)

E. Paul Gauguin. Tahitian Women. 1891. Luxembourg, Paris.
(Gir)

F. Vincent Van Gogh. Sun Flowers. 1888. Carroll S. Tyson
Collection, Philadelphia. (Carroll S. Tyson)

A. Vincent Van Gogh. Starry Night. Museum of Modern Art, New York (Mus. Mod. Art)

B. Paul Gauguin. The Yellow Calvary. 1889. Albright Art Gallery, Buffalo, N. Y. (Albright Art Gall.)

C. Pablo Picasso. Guitar Player. 1903. Art Institute. (Art Inst.)

D. Pablo Picasso. The Frugal Repast. Etching, second state. 1904. (Univ. of Ill.)

E. Pablo Picasso. Mme. Picasso. 1923. Coll. Mr. and Mrs. Chester Dale. (Mr. and Mrs. Chester Dale)

F. Pablo Picasso. Les Demoiselles d'Avignon. 1907. Museum of Modern Art, New York. (Mus. Mod. Art)

G. Pablo Picasso. Still Life: Vive la . . . 1914–15. Sidney Janis Gallery, New York. (Sidney Janis Gall.)

A. Pablo Picasso. Abstraction. 1916. Columbus Gallery of Fine Art, Columbus, Ohio. (Col. Gall.)

B. Pablo Picasso. Harlequin. 1928. Reber Collection, Lugano.

C. Pablo Picasso. Combat of Perseus and Phineus over Andromeda. Etching, 1930. (U. of Ill.)

D. Pablo Picasso. Seated Woman. 1927. James Thrall Soby Collection, Farmington, Conn. (J. T. Soby)

E. Pablo Picasso. The Painter and His Model. 1928. Sidney Janis Gallery, New York. (Sidney Janis Gall.)

F. Pablo Picasso. Girl Before a Mirror. 1932. Museum of Modern Art, New York. (Mus. Mod. Art)

G. Pablo Picasso. Figure in a Red Chair. 1932. Collection of the Artist. (U. of Ill.)

H. Pablo Picasso. Guernica. Detail. 1937. Collection of the Artist. (Mus. Mod. Art)

A. Marcel Duchamp. Nude Descending the Stairs. 1912. Arensberg Collection, Philadelphia Museum of Art. (Phila. Mus.)

B. Fernand Léger. Three Women. 1921. Museum of Modern Art, New York. (Mus. Mod. Art)

C. Andre L'Hote. The Judgment of Paris. 1912. Collection Georges Pauli, Stockholm. (U. of Ill.)

D. Fernand Léger. The City. 1919. Philadelphia Museum of Art. (Phila. Mus.)

E. Georges Braque. Still Life with Grapes. 1927. Phillips Collection, Washington, D. C. (Phillips Coll.)

F. Georges Braque. Woman Combing her Hair. 1936. (U. of Ill.)

A. Georges Braque. Still Life with Playing Cards. 1914. (U. of Ill.)

B. Georges Braque. Oval Still Life. 1914. Museum of Modern Art, New York. (Mus. Mod. Art)

C. Juan Gris. Fruit Dish, Glass and Newspaper. 1916. Museum of Modern Art, New York. (Mus. Mod. Art)

D. Juan Gris. Bottle and Fruit Dish. 1915. Museum of Modern Art, New York. (Mus. Mod. Art)

E. Andre Derain. Three Trees. Lewisohn Collection, Museum of Modern Art, New York. (U. of Ill.)

F. Andre Derain. Window on a Park. 1912. Collection Mrs. Cornelius J. Sullivan, New York. (Mrs. Cornelius J. Sullivan)

G. Georges Rouault. Christ Mocked by Soldiers. 1932. Museum of Modern Art, New York. (Mus. Mod. Art)

H. Georges Rouault. The Old King. Carnegie Institution, Pittsburgh, Pa. (Carnegie Inst.)

I. Georges Rouault. Detail of H.

A. Edvard Munch. The Scream. 1893. National Gallery, Oslo. (U. of Ill.)

B. Henri Matisse. Odalisque. Luxembourg, Paris. (Gir)

C. Henri Matisse. Hindu Pose. 1923. Ex. S.C.C. Collection, New York. (U. of Ill.)

D. Henri Matisse. The Dance. 1909. Museum of Western Art, Moscow. (U. of Ill.)

E. Henri Matisse. Girl Looking at a Fishbowl. Art Institute. (Art Inst.)

F. Ernst Kirchner. Street Scene. 1913. National Gallery, Berlin. (U. of Ill.)

A. Max Beckmann. Young Men by the Sea. 1943. St. Louis City Art Museum. (St. Louis C.A.M.)

B. Käthe Kollwitz (Schmidt). Never Again War. Lithograph. 1924. (U. of Ill.)

C. Käthe Kollwitz (Schmidt). Self Portrait. Etching. 1910. (U. of Ill.)

D. Karl Hofer. Girls Throwing Flowers. c. 1926. Art Institute. (Art Inst.)

E. Franz Marc. Red Horses. 1909. Essen Museum. (U. of Ill.)

F. Wassily Kandinsky. Improvisation No. 30. 1913. Art Institute. (Art Inst.)

G. Paul Klee. Jörg. Arensberg Collection, Philadelphia Museum of Art. (Phila. Mus.)

A. Otto Dix. Dr. Meyer-Hermann. 1926. Museum of Modern Art, New York. (Mus. Mod. Art)

B. Marc Chagall. I and the Village. 1911. Museum of Modern Art, New York. (Mus. Mod. Art)

C. Marc Chagall. The Fiddler. 1913–20. Solomon R. Guggenheim Museum, New York. (S. R. Guggenheim Mus.)

D. Marc Chagall. The Soldier Drinks. 1913. Solomon R. Guggenheim Museum, New York. (S. R. Guggenheim Mus.)

E. Marc Chagall. The Birthday. 1915–23. Solomon R. Guggenheim Museum, New York. (S. R. Guggenheim Mus.)

F. George Grosz. Couple. 1934. Whitney Museum of American Art, New York. (Whitney Mus.)

G. Salvador Dali. The Persistence of Memory. 1931. Museum of Modern Art, New York. (Mus. Mod. Art)

DALI · GUGLIELMI · DE CHIRICO · BLUME · ROY

A. Salvador Dali. Visage of War. 1949. Carstairs Gallery, New York. (Carstairs Gall.)

B. Louis Guglielmi. Terror in Brooklyn. 1941. Whitney Museum of American Art, New York. (Whitney Mus.)

C. Giorgio de Chirico. Toys of a Prince. c. 1914. Museum of Modern Art, New York. (Mus. Mod. Art)

D. Detail of A.

E. Peter Blume. Parade. 1930. Museum of Modern Art, New York. (Mus. Mod. Art)

F. Pierre Roy. The Electrification of the Country. c. 1929. Wadsworth Atheneum, Hartford, Conn. (Wadsworth Atheneum)

A. Roberto Matta Echaurren. Three Men Crying. Pierre Matisse Gallery, New York. (Pierre Matisse Gall.)

B. Joan Miro. Dog Barking at the Moon. 1926. Philadelphia Museum of Art. (Phila. Mus.)

C. Joan Miro. Person Throwing a Stone at a Bird. 1926. Museum of Modern Art, New York. (Mus. Mod. Art)

D. Piet Mondrian. Broadway Boogie-Woogie. 1942–43. Museum of Modern Art, New York. (Mus. Mod. Art)

E. Joan Miro. Carnival of Harlequin. 1924–25. Albright Art Gallery, Buffalo, N. Y. (Albright Art Gall.)

F. Pierre Roy. Daylight Saving. 1930. Museum of Modern Art, New York. (Mus. Mod. Art)

A. Karl Zerbe. Melancholia. c. 1946. Art Institute. (Art Inst.)

B. Pavel Tchelitchew. Twilight Head. 1948. Durlacher Brothers, New York. (Durlacher Bros.)

C. Jack Levine. The Feast of Pure Reason. 1937. (W.P.A. Art Program)

D. Karl Priebe. The Fronfroneur. c. 1947. Collection of the artist. (Karl Priebe)

E. Nahum Tschacbasov. The Clown. Perls Galleries, New York. (Perls Galls.)

F. Adolph Gottlieb. Spectre of the Sea. c. 1947. Kootz Gallery, New York. (Kootz Gall.)

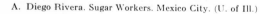

A. Diego Rivera. Sugar Workers. Mexico City. (U. of Ill.)

B. Diego Rivera. The Reconstruction. The School Teacher. Mexico City. (Met)

C. David Siqueiros. Ethnography. 1939. Museum of Modern Art, New York. (Mus. Mod. Art)

D. Diego Rivera. Vaccination Panel. 1933. Detroit Institute of Arts. (Detroit Inst.)

E. José Orozco. Migration of the Spirit. 1932–34. Dartmouth College, Hanover, N. H. (Dartmouth Coll.)

F. José Orozco. Golden Age of Aztec Civilization. 1931. Dartmouth College, Hanover, N. H. (Dartmouth Coll.)

G. Diego Rivera. The Flower Vendor. 1935. San Francisco Museum of Art, Cal. (S. F. Mus.)

MEXICAN ARCHITECTURE · XVI–XVIII CENT.
AMERICAN ARCHITECTURE · MISSIONS · XVIII CENT.

249

A. Cathedral, Mexico City. Completed 1667.

B. Church of San Sebastián and Santa Prisca, Taxco, Mexico. XVIII century.

C. Detail of B.

D. Cathedral, Puebla, Mexico. Begun 1552, consecrated 1649.

E. Church of San Martin. Tepotzotlán, Mexico. XVIII century.

F. Mission of San Antonio de Valero (The Alamo), San Antonio, Texas. 1774. (H. L. Summerville from San Antonio C. of C.)

G. Mission, Santa Barbara, Cal. 1787–1800. (Karl Obert from Santa Barbara C. of C.)

A. Church of La Santísima Trinidad, Mexico City. 1755–83. Façade. (Monumentos Coloniales)

B. Church of Santo Domingo, Mexico City. c. 1736. Altar. (Monumentos Coloniales)

C. Mission San José, San Antonio, Texas. Started 1720. Baptistry Window. (Wayne Andrews)

D. Convent of La Merced, Mexico City. c. 1700. Patio. (Monumentos Coloniales)

E. Mission St. Francis of Assisi, Ranchos de Taos, New Mexico. Rebuilt 1772. (Wayne Andrews)

F. Mission St. Francis of Assisi, Ranchos de Taos, New Mexico. (Wayne Andrews)

G. Mission San Xavier del Bac, Tucson, Arizona. 1784–97. (Wayne Andrews)

A. Capen House, Topsfield, Mass. 1683. (Roos)

B. Paul Revere House, Boston, Mass. 1680. (Roos)

C. Whitman House, Farmington, Conn. c. 1660. (Roos)

D. Bacon's Castle, near Smithfield, Va. 1655. (Turpin Bannister)

E. McPhedris-Warner House, Portsmouth, N. H. c. 1720. (Roos)

F. Moffatt-Ladd House, Portsmouth, N. H. 1763. (Roos)

G. Usher-Royall House, Medford, Mass. Stairway. c. 1737. (Roos)

A. McPhedris-Warner House. Door. Detail of 251 E. (Roos)

B. Jones House, Hatfield, Mass. Door. c. 1730. (Roos)

C. Old North Church, Boston, Mass. 1723. Spire by Bulfinch, 1807. (Roos)

D. Craigie (Longfellow) House, Cambridge, Mass. 1759. (Roos)

E. King's Chapel, Boston, Mass. 1753. (Roos)

F. Church, Acworth, N. H. c. 1825. (Roos)

G. Old City Hall, Newport, R. I. Peter Harrison, architect. 1761. (Wayne Andrews)

A. Old State House, Boston, Mass. 1748. (Roos)

B. Moffatt-Ladd House. Interior. (See 251 F.) (Roos)

C. Meeting House, Rockingham, Vt. 1787. (Roos)

D. Detail of C. (Roos)

E. Governor Hancock House, Boston, Mass. 1737–40. **A** replica at Ticonderoga, N. Y. Original destroyed. (Roos)

F. Wentworth-Gardner House, Portsmouth, N. H. **Door.** 1760. (Roos)

A. Redwood Library, Newport, R. I. Peter Harrison, architect. c. 1798. (U. of Ill.)

B. Christ Church, Philadelphia, Pa. Detail. 1727. (Roos)

C. St. Paul's Chapel, New York, N. Y. 1756–94. (Essex Inst.)

D. Dyckman House, New York, N. Y. 1798. (Roos)

E. Federal Hall, New York, N. Y. As remodeled by P. C. L'Enfant, 1788. Destroyed 1830's. (U. of Ill.)

F. Room from the Powell House, Philadelphia, Pa. c. 1768. Metropolitan Museum. (Met)

A. Hammond-Harwood House. Door. Detail of B. (Roos)

B. Hammond-Harwood House, Annapolis, Md. 1774. (Roos)

C. Westover, Charles City Co., Va. c. 1726. (H. P. Cook)

D. Bruton Parish Church, Williamsburg, Va. 1710–15. (Roos)

E. Mt. Pleasant, Philadelphia, Pa. After 1761. (Roos)

F. President's House, College of William and Mary, Williamsburg, Va. 1732. (Roos)

A. The Capitol, Williamsburg, Va. 1705. (Roos)

B. Wythe House, Williamsburg, Va. 1755. (Roos)

C. St. Michael's Church, Charleston, S. C. 1752–61. (Wayne Andrews)

D. William Gibbes House, Charleston, S. C. c. 1779. (Wayne Andrews)

E. The Cabildo, New Orleans, La. 1795. (U. of Ill.)

F. Parlange Plantation, near New Roads, La. c. 1750. (U. of Ill.)

A. John Pierce House, Portsmouth, N. H. 1799. Sometimes attributed to Bulfinch. (Roos)

B. First Church, Lancaster, Mass. Charles Bulfinch, architect. 1818. (Roos)

C. Detail of B. Tower. (Roos)

D. Assembly Hall, Salem, Mass. Remodeled by Samuel McIntire, 1793. (Roos)

E. Church, Fitzwilliam, N. H. 1817. (Roos)

F. Park Street Church, Boston, Mass. Peter Banner, architect. 1819. (Roos)

G. State House, Boston, Mass. Charles Bulfinch, architect. 1790–98. (Roos)

H. Church, Bennington, Vt. Tower. Asher Benjamin, architect. 1806. (Roos)

A. Center Congregational Church, New Haven, Conn. Ithiel Town, architect. 1812–15. (Roos)

B. Detail of A. Tower. (Roos)

C. Harrison Gray Otis House, Boston, Mass. Detail. Charles Bulfinch, architect. 1800–01. (Roos)

D. Gardner-White-Pingree House, Salem, Mass. Samuel McIntire, architect. 1805–10. (Roos)

E. Room from the Derby House, Salem, Mass. Samuel McIntire, architect. Philadelphia Museum. (Phila. Mus.)

F. Faneuil Hall, Boston, Mass. Built 1742, Rebuilt 1764, Remodeled by Charles Bulfinch, 1805. (Roos)

G. United Church, New Haven, Conn. Tower. David Hoadley, architect. 1813–15. (Roos)

H. Merchant's Exchange, Philadelphia, Pa. Tower. William Strickland, architect. 1834. (Roos)

A. City Hall, New York, N. Y. Detail of E. (Roos)

B. Bank of the United States (Assay Office), New York, N. Y. 1822–24. Martin Thompson, architect. Removed 1922 to Metropolitan Museum. (Essex Inst.)

C. Old Customs House (U. S. Sub-Treasury), New York, N. Y. Ithiel Town and A. J. Davis, architects. 1834–41. (See 280 D.) (Roos)

D. Portico, Number 12, Washington Square, New York, N. Y. c. 1835. (Roos)

E. City Hall, New York, N. Y. McComb and Mangin, architects. 1803–12. (Roos)

F. Independence Hall, Philadelphia, Pa. Spire. Remodeled 1828. William Strickland, architect. (Roos)

A. Homewood, Baltimore, Md. 1798–1800. (Roos)

B. Original Design for Washington Monument, Washington, D. C. Robert Mills, architect. Started 1848. (U. of Ill.)

C. Capitol, Washington, D. C. Central Pavilion, W. facade. Detail of D. (Roos)

D. Capitol, Washington, D. C. Begun 1793. Thornton, Latrobe, Bulfinch and others, architects. Dome designed by T. U. Walter, finished 1865. (Roos)

E. Capitol, Washington, D. C. Exterior from S.E. As was in 1840.

F. Tobacco Capital, designed by B. H. Latrobe for National Capitol. Model at Monticello. c. 1817. (Roos)

A. Corn Order, designed by B. H. Latrobe for National Capitol. c. 1809.

B. White House, Washington, D. C. James Hoban, architect. 1792–1829. Portico by B. H. Latrobe, 1818. (Roos)

C. Detail of B. (Roos)

D. City Plan, Washington, D. C. P. C. L'Enfant, architect. 1791.

E. Monticello, near Charlottesville, Va. Detail of the Portico. (See 262 A.) (Roos)

F. University of Virginia, Charlottesville, Va. Thomas Jefferson, architect. 1817–24. (Roos)

G. Pavilion VII, University of Virginia. 1817. (Roos)

A. Monticello, near Charlottesville, Va. Thomas Jefferson, architect. 1796–1808. (See 261 E.) (Roos)

B. Capitol, Richmond, Va. Design influenced by Thomas Jefferson, 1785–98. (Roos)

C. Labranche Building, New Orleans, La. c. 1835. (Wayne Andrews)

D. Design for a Country Villa, from Minard Lafever, *Modern Builder's Guide*, 1833.

E. Moravian Village reconstruction, Schoenbrunn, Ohio. Settled 1772. (Roos)

F. Taft House, Cincinnati, Ohio. c. 1820. B. H. Latrobe (?) architect. (Roos)

G. Avery-Downer House, Granville, Ohio. 1842. (Roos)

A. D'Evereaux Plantation, Natchez, Miss. 1840. (Wayne Andrews)

B. Grace Church, New York, N. Y. James Renwick, architect. 1843–46. (Roos)

C. Evergreen Plantation, near Edgard, La. c. 1840. (U. of Ill.)

D. Trinity Church, New York, N. Y. Richard Upjohn, architect. 1839–46. (Wurts Bros.)

E. Rotch House, New Bedford, Mass. A. J. Davis, architect. 1845. (Wayne Andrews)

F. State Capitol, Baton Rouge, La. 1847–50. Reconstructed 1882. (Wayne Andrews)

A. Schoolcraft House, Guilderland, N. Y. (Roos)

B. Wedding Cake House, Kennebunk, Me. c. 1850. Original house, c. 1800. (Wayne Andrews)

C. Longwood Plantation, Natchez, Miss. Started c. 1858. (U. of Ill.)

D. Carson House, Eureka, Cal. c. 1885. (U. of Ill.)

E. Museum of Fine Arts, Boston, Mass. Sturgis and Brigham, architects. 1871–76. (U. of Ill.)

F. Provident Trust Co., Philadelphia, Pa. c. 1878. (Wayne Andrews)

A. Court of Honor, World's Columbian Exposition, Chicago. 1893. Burnham, Root, R. M. Hunt and others, architects. (See 281 C.) (Met)

B. Biltmore, Ashville, N. C. R. M. Hunt, architect. 1890–95. (Wayne Andrews)

C. New York University Library. McKim, Mead and White, architects. 1899. (Roos)

D. W. K. Vanderbilt House, New York, N. Y. R. M. Hunt, architect. 1879–81. Destroyed c. 1926. (U. of Ill.)

E. Washington Square Arch, New York, N. Y. Stanford White, architect. 1892. (Roos)

F. Marshall Field Wholesale Building, Chicago. H. H. Richardson, architect. 1885–87. (U. of Ill.)

A. Trinity Church, Boston, Mass. H. H. Richardson, chief architect. Mostly 1872–77. Porch and turrets, 1894–98. (U. of Ill.)

B. Detail of A. Interior. Decoration by John La Farge. (Met)

C. Glessner House, Chicago. H. H. Richardson, architect. 1885–87. (U. of Ill.)

D. A. T. Stewart Store, New York, N. Y. 1862. (Wayne Andrews)

E. Design for the Bogardus Factory showing the strength of cast iron construction. James Bogardus, architect. 1856. (U. of Ill.)

F. Brooklyn Bridge, New York, N. Y. John and W. A. Roebling, architects. 1883. (U. of Ill.)

A. Transportation Building, Chicago. Louis Sullivan, architect. 1893. (Ralph Line)

B. Carson Pirie Scott Store, Chicago. Louis Sullivan, architect. 1899. (Chgo. Architectural Photo. Co.)

C. Prudential Building, Buffalo, N. Y. Louis Sullivan, architect. 1894–95. (Ralph Line)

D. Detail of C. (Ralph Line)

E. Auditorium Building, Chicago. Louis Sullivan, architect. 1887–89. (Ralph Line)

F. Josephine Bradley House, Madison, Wis. Louis Sullivan, architect. 1909. (Ralph Line)

A. Monadnock Block, Chicago. J. W. Root, architect. 1891. (U. of Ill.)

B. Woolworth Building, New York. Cass Gilbert, architect. 1913. (U. of Ill.)

C. Metropolitan Life Insurance Co., New York. N. le Brun and Sons, architects. 1909. (U. of Ill.)

D. State Capitol, Lincoln, Neb. Bertram Goodhue, architect. 1922–26. (U. of Ill.)

E. American Radiator Building, New York. Raymond Hood, architect. 1924. (U. of Ill.)

F. State Capitol, Lincoln, Neb. Detail of D. Lee Lawrie, sculptor. (Winston Weisman)

G. Application of Building Zone Law to a Block 200′ x 800′, New York. H. W. Corbett, architect. Drawing by Hugh Ferriss.

H. Fourth State of G.

I. Barclay-Vesey Telephone Building, New York. McKenzie, Voorhees and Gmelin, architects. 1925–26. (U. of Ill.)

A. Charlotte Wainright Tomb, St. Louis, Mo. Louis Sullivan, architect. 1892. (Ralph Line)

B. National Farmer's Bank, Owatonna, Minn. Louis Sullivan, architect. 1907–08. (Ralph Line)

C. Unity Temple, Oak Park, Ill. Frank Lloyd Wright, architect. 1906. (U. of Ill.)

D. Larkin Building, Buffalo, N. Y. Interior. Destroyed 1947. (F. L. Wright)

E. Larkin Building, Buffalo, N. Y. Frank Lloyd Wright, architect. 1903–05. (F. L. Wright)

F. Robie House, Chicago. Frank Lloyd Wright, architect. 1909. (F. L. Wright)

A. Barnsdall House, Los Angeles, Cal. Frank Lloyd Wright, architect. 1917. (F. L. Wright)

B. Johnson Wax Co., Administration Building. Racine, Wis. Frank Lloyd Wright, architect. 1936–39. (Wayne Andrews)

C. Falling Water, Bear Run, Pa. Frank Lloyd Wright, architect. 1937–39. (Mus. Mod. Art)

D. Wertheim Department Store, Berlin. Alfred Messel, architect. 1897–1904. (U. of Ill.)

E. Johnson Wax Co., Administration Building, Tower. Racine, Wis. Frank Lloyd Wright, architect. 1949. (U. of Ill.)

F. R. R. Station, Helsingfors, Finland. Eliel Saarinen, architect. 1906–14. (U. of Ill.)

A. Tribune Tower, Chicago. Raymond Hood, architect. 1922. (Chgo. Trib.)

B. Tribune Building Competition. Second Prize. Eliel Saarinen. (Chgo. Trib.)

C. Tribune Building Competition. Design by Walter Gropius. (Chgo. Trib.)

D. Tribune Building Competition. Design by Adolph Loos, (Chgo. Trib.)

E. Tribune Building Competition. Design by Frank Fort. (Chgo. Trib.)

F. Travel and Transport Building, Century of Progress Exposition, Chicago. Bennett, Burnham, Holabird and Skidmore, architects. 1933. (Roos)

G. Electrical Building, Century of Progress Exposition, Chicago. Raymond Hood, architect. 1933. (Roos)

H. McGraw-Hill Building, New York. Raymond Hood, architect. 1930. (Roos)

I. Empire State Building, New York. Shreve, Lamb and Harmon, architects. 1931. (U. of Ill.)

A. Tabernacle Church of Christ, Columbus, Ind. Eliel and Eero Saarinen, architects. 1941. (Arch. Forum, Hedrich-Blessing)

B. Generator Hall, Pickwick Landing Dam, Savannah, Tenn. (T.V.A.)

C. Rockefeller Center, New York. Associated architects. 1937–40. (Thomas Airviews)

D. Tuberculosis Clinic, Alexandria, Egypt. I. Gardella and L. Martini, architects. 1938. (Arch. Forum)

E. Loggia, Cranbrook Academy of Art, Bloomfield Hills, Mich. Eliel Saarinen, architect. 1941. (Cranbrook Acad.)

F. Museum of Modern Art, New York. Philip L. Goodwin and Edward Stone, architects. 1939. (Mus. Mod. Art)

A. Philip Johnson House, Cambridge, Mass. Philip Johnson, architect. 1942. (Mus. Mod. Art)

B. Columbia Broadcasting Studios, Hollywood, Cal. William Lescaze, architect. 1938. (Arch. Forum)

C. Welfare Building, Naval Training Station, Great Lakes, Ill. Skidmore, Owings and Merrill, architects. 1942. (Arch. Forum, Hedrich-Blessing)

D. Breuer House, Lincoln, Mass. Marcel Breuer, architect. 1939. (Wayne Andrews)

E. Normal School, Mexico City. Mario Pani, architect. 1946. (Arch. Record)

F. Lake County Tuberculosis Sanatorium, Waukegan, Ill. W. A. Ganster and W. L. Pereira, architects. 1939. (Arch. Forum, Hedrich-Blessing)

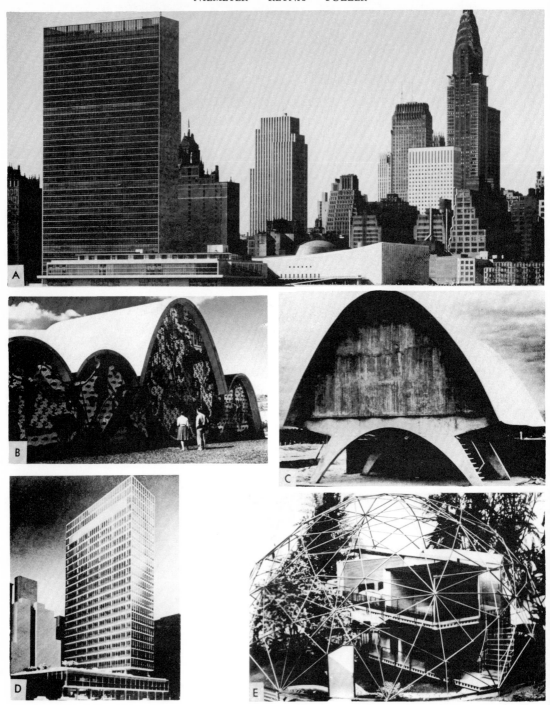

A. United Nations Secretariat, New York. Wallace K. Harrison, Director of Planning. 1952. (UNations)

B. St. Francis of Assisi, Pampulha, Minas Gerais, Brazil. Oscar Niemeyer, architect. Ceramic tile mural by Portinari. 1942. (Three Lions)

C. Nuclear Physics Laboratory, University of Mexico, Mexico City. 1951. J. G. Reyna, architect. (Erwin G. Lang)

D. Lever House, New York. Model. Skidmore, Owings and Merrill, architects. 1951. (Arch. Forum)

E. Geodesic Dome House. Model. Buckminster Fuller, architect. 1950. (Buckminster Fuller)

A. Chicago Circle Campus, University of Illinois, Chicago, Illinois. Lower Level. Skidmore, Owings and Merrill, architects. 1960. (University of Illinois)

B. Dulles International Airport, Chantilly, Virginia. Eero Saarinen, architect. 1962. (Wayne Andrews)

C. Chicago Circle Campus, University of Illinois, Chicago, Illinois. Upper level. Skidmore, Owings and Merrill, architects. 1960. (University of Illinois)

D. Deere Implement Company, Moline, Illinois. Eero Saarinen, architect. (Wayne Andrews)

E. United States Air Force Academy, Colorado Springs, Colorado. General view. Skidmore, Owings and Merrill, architects.

F. United States Air Force Academy, Colorado Springs, Colorado. Chapel. Skidmore, Owings and Merrill, architects.

A. Solomon R. Guggenheim Museum, New York. Exterior. Frank Lloyd Wright, architect. 1957–1959. (Guggenheim Museum)

B. Solomon R. Guggenheim Museum, New York. Interior. Frank Lloyd Wright, architect. 1957–1959. (Guggenheim Museum)

C. Assembly Hall, University of Illinois, Urbana, Illinois. Harris and Abramowitz, architects. 1963. (University of Illinois)

D. Gateway Arch, St. Louis, Missouri. Eero Saarinen, architect. 1964–1966. (Arthur Witman, St. Louis Post-Dispatch)

E. Hockey Rink, Yale University, New Haven, Connecticut. Eero Saarinen, architect. 1960. (Wayne Andrews)

A. Reston, Planned Community (now Gulf Reston), Fairfax County, Virginia. Robert E. Simon, Jr., Enterprises, Planning. Architects, Whittlesey and Conklin (now Conklin and Rossant); Goodman Associates; Chlothiel W. Smith and Associates; additional architects. (Reston photo by Blue Ridge.)

B. Ford Foundation Building, New York City. Kevin Roche and John Dinkeloo and Associates, architects. 1967. (Courtesy ESTO for the Ford Foundation.)

C. John Hancock Center. Chicago, Illinois. Skidmore, Owings and Merrill, Architects. Bruce Graham, Chief Designer. 1968. (John Hancock)

D. Arena Stage. Washington, D. C. Harry Weese and Associates, Architects. 1961. (Arena Stage.)

A. Notre-Dame-du-Haut, Ronchamp, France. Le Corbusier, architect. 1950–1955. (Wayne Andrews)

B. Marina City Towers, Chicago. Illinois. Bertrand Goldberg Associates, architects. 1963. (Wayne Andrews)

C. S. R. Crown Hall, Illinois Institute of Technology, Chicago, Illinois. Mies van der Rohe, architect. 1956. (Illinois Institute of Technology)

D. Wishnick Hall, Illinois Institute of Technology, Chicago, Illinois. Mies van der Rohe, architect. 1945. (Illinois Institute of Technology)

A. William Rush. Eagle. 1808–10. Pennsylvania Academy of the Fine Arts, Philadelphia. (Pa. Acad.)

B. William Rush. Tragedy. 1808. Philadelphia Museum of Art. (Phila. Mus.)

C. William Rush. Water Nymph and Bittern. c. 1809. Philadelphia Museum of Art. (Phila. Mus.)

D. William Rush. Dr. Caspar Wistar. c. 1813. Pennsylvania Academy of the Fine Arts,.Philadelphia. (Pa. Acad.)

E. John Browere. Thomas Jefferson, age 82. Life mask. 1825. New York State Historical Assoc., Cooperstown, N. Y. (N.Y.S.H.A.)

F. John Browere. Henry Clay, age 48. Life mask. 1825. New York State Historical Assoc., Cooperstown, N. Y. (N.Y.S.H.A.)

G. John Browere. John Adams, age 90. Life mask. 1825. New York State Historical Assoc., Cooperstown, N. Y. (N.Y.S.H.A.)

H. Hiram Powers. Greek Slave. 1846. Corcoran Collection, Washington, D. C. (Corcoran Coll.)

A. Hiram Powers. Andrew Jackson. Metropolitan Museum, New York. (Met)

B. H. K. Brown and J. Q. A. Ward. George Washington. 1856. Union Square, New York, N. Y. (Roos)

C. Horatio Greenough. George Washington. 1832–41. Smithsonian Institution, Washington, D. C. (Met)

D. J. Q. A. Ward. George Washington. 1883. Wall St., New York, N. Y. (See 259 C.) (Roos)

E. Frederick Macmonnies. Nathan Hale. 1890. New York, N. Y. (Roos)

F. Frederick Macmonnies. Horse Tamers. 1898. New York, N. Y. (Met)

G. Frederick Macmonnies. Civic Virtue. 1922. New York, N. Y. (Roos)

H. Frederick Macmonnies. Diana. 1890. Metropolitan Museum, New York. (Met)

I. William Rimmer. Falling Gladiator. Museum of Fine Arts, Boston. (M.F.A.)

A. George Gray Barnard. The Burden of Life and Relief in Labor. 1917. Capitol, Harrisburg, Pa. (Roos)

B. Detail of A. (Roos)

C. Daniel Chester French. The Republic. 1893. Jackson Park, Chicago. (See 265 A.) (Winston Weisman)

D. Daniel Chester French. Abraham Lincoln. 1923. Lincoln Memorial, Washington, D. C. (Roos)

E. Daniel Chester French. Death Staying the Hand of the Sculptor. c. 1883. Replica in the Metropolitan Museum. (Met)

F. Daniel Chester French. Alma Mater. 1902–03. Columbia University, New York. (Courtesy Mrs. William Penn Cresson)

G. Augustus Saint-Gaudens. The Sherman Monument. 1887–1903. New York. (Roos)

H. Detail of G. (Roos)

A. Augustus Saint-Gaudens. Robert Louis Stevenson. 1887. Metropolitan Museum. (Met)

B. Augustus Saint-Gaudens. The Shaw Memorial. 1884–97. Boston Common. (Lorado Taft)

C. Augustus Saint-Gaudens. The Farragut Monument. 1875. New York, N. Y. (Roos)

D. Augustus Saint-Gaudens. Diana. 1888. Philadelphia Museum of Art. (Phila. Mus.)

E. H. K. Brown. Abraham Lincoln. 1868. Union Square, New York, N. Y. (Roos)

F. George Gray Barnard. Head of Abraham Lincoln. Metropolitan Museum. New York. (Met)

G. Cyrus Dallin. Appeal to the Great Spirit. 1909. Museum of Fine Arts. (M.F.A.)

H. Martin Milmore. Sphinx. 1872. Mt. Auburn Cemetery, Cambridge, Mass. (Roos)

A. Paul Manship. Prometheus. Rockefeller Plaza, New York. (See 278 A.) (Roos)

B. Paul Manship. Diana. 1920. (DeWitt Ward)

C. Paul Manship. Detail of A. (Roos)

D. Anna Hyatt Huntington. Joan of Arc. c. 1924. New York, N. Y. (Roos)

E. Paul Manship. Dancer and Gazelles. 1916. Art Institute. (Art Inst.)

F. Lorado Taft. Abraham Lincoln. 1926–27. Urbana, Ill. (Lorado Taft)

A. The Mason Limner. Alice Mason. 1670. Adams National Historic Site, Quincy, Mass. (Dept. of Interior)

B. John Smibert. Dean Berkeley and His Entourage. 1729. Yale University Art Gallery. (Yale Univ.)

C. John Smibert. Detail of B. Self Portrait.

D. Robert Feke. Gen. Samuel Waldo. c. 1748–50. Bowdoin College, Brunswick, Me. (Bowdoin Coll.)

E. Robert Feke. Gov. James Bowdoin II. 1748. Bowdoin College, Brunswick, Me. (Bowdoin Coll.)

F. Ralph Earl, Maj. Gen. William Augustin, Baron von Steuben. c. 1786. Yale University Art Gallery. (Yale Univ.)

G. Gustavus Hesselius. Self Portrait. c. 1740. Historical Society of Pennsylvania, Philadelphia. (Hist. Soc. Pa.)

A. John Smibert. Nathaniel Byfield. 1730. Metropolitan Museum, New York. (Met)

B. John Hesselius. Mrs. Richard Galloway, Jr. 1764. Metropolitan Museum, New York. (Met)

C. John Hesselius. Charles Calvert and Colored Slave. 1761. Baltimore Museum of Art. (Balt. Mus.)

D. John Singleton Copley. Watson and the Shark. 1782. Detroit Institute of Arts. (Det. Inst.)

E. John Singleton Copley. John Quincy Adams. 1795. Museum of Fine Arts. (M.F.A.)

F. John Singleton Copley. Gov. and Mrs. Thomas Mifflin. 1773. Historical Society of Pennsylvania, Philadelphia. (Hist. Soc. Pa.)

G. John Singleton Copley. John Adams. 1783. Harvard University. (Fogg)

H. John Singleton Copley. Nicholas Boylston. Museum of Fine Arts. (M.F.A.)

I. John Singleton Copley. John Hancock. 1765. Courtesy City of Boston through the Museum of Fine Arts. (M.F.A.)

A. Gilbert Stuart. Portrait of Elizabeth Boardley. Pennsylvania Academy of the Fine Arts, Philadelphia. (Pa. Acad.)

B. Gilbert Stuart. George Washington. Gibbs-Channing-Avery Portrait. 1795. Metropolitan Museum, New York. (Met)

C. Gilbert Stuart. George Washington. Unfinished. 1796. Deposited in the Museum of Fine Arts by the Boston Atheneum. (M.F.A.)

D. Gilbert Stuart. William Redwood. c. 1774. Redwood Library and Atheneum, Newport, R. I. (Redwood Lib.)

E. Gilbert Stuart. Benjamin West. National Portrait Gallery, London. (Nat. Port. Gall.)

F. Gilbert Stuart. Mrs. Pérez Morton. After 1802. Worcester Art Museum. (Worcester Mus.)

G. Gilbert Stuart. James Ward. Minneapolis Institute of Art. (Minn. Inst.)

H. Matthew Pratt. The American School. 1765. Metropolitan Museum, New York. (Met)

A. Charles Willson Peale. The Peale Family. New-York Historical Society, New York. (N. Y. Hist. Soc.)

B. Charles Willson Peale. General Washington. 1779. Pennsylvania Academy of the Fine Arts, Philadelphia. (Pa. Acad.)

C. Charles Willson Peale. Exhuming of the First American Mastodon. 1806–10. The Peale Museum, Baltimore, Md. (Peale Mus.)

D. Charles Willson Peale. Staircase Group—Portrait of the Sons of the Artist. 1795. Philadelphia Museum of Art. (Phila. Mus.)

E. Charles Willson Peale. Gen. Washington, Lafayette and Tench Tilghman. 1786. State House, Annapolis, Md. (State Ho.)

F. Charles Willson Peale. Portrait of the Artist in his Museum. 1824. Pennsylvania Academy of the Fine Arts, Philadelphia. (Pa. Acad.)

G. Charles Willson Peale. Self Portrait. Pennsylvania Academy of the Fine Arts, Philadelphia. (Pa. Acad.)

A. Charles Willson Peale. Worthy of Liberty, Mr. Pitt scorns to invade the liberties of other people. 1768. (U. of Ill.)

B. Rembrandt Peale. Thomas Jefferson. 1805. New-York Historical Society, New York. (N. Y. Hist. Soc.)

C. Raphaelle Peale. After the Bath. 1823. Nelson-Atkins Gallery of Art, Kansas City, Mo. (Nelson-Atkins Gall.)

D. Charles Willson Peale. Benjamin Franklin. 1787. Pennsylvania Academy of the Fine Arts, Philadelphia. (Pa. Acad.)

E. Benjamin West. Penn's Treaty with the Indians. 1771. Pennsylvania Academy of the Fine Arts, Philadelphia. (Pa. Acad.)

F. Benjamin West. Charles Willson Peale. 1767–69. New-York Historical Society, New York. (N. Y. Hist. Soc.)

G. Raphaelle Peale. Still Life with Vegetables. c. 1823. Wadsworth Atheneum, Hartford, Conn. (Wadsworth Atheneum)

A. John Vanderlyn. Ariadne. c. 1812. Pennsylvania Academy of the Fine Arts, Philadelphia. (Pa. Acad.)

B. John Vanderlyn. Portrait of the Artist. c. 1815. Metropolitan Museum, New York. (Met)

C. Washington Allston. Moonlit Landscape. 1819. Museum of Fine Arts. (M.F.A.)

D. Washington Allston. The Dead Man Restored to Life by Touching the Bones of the Prophet Elisha. 1811–13. Pennsylvania Academy of the Fine Arts, Philadelphia. (Pa. Acad.)

E. Washington Allston. Belshazzar's Feast. Begun 1817. Washington Allston Trust, Boston. (Wash. Allston Trust)

F. Washington Allston. Italian Landscape. c. 1830. Detroit Institute of Arts. (Det. Inst.)

A. Thomas Sully. The Torn Hat. 1820. Museum of Fine Arts. (M.F.A.)

B. John Trumbull. The Death of General Mercer at the Battle of Princeton. 1777. Yale University Art Gallery. (Yale Univ.)

C. Thomas Sully. Portrait of the Artist. 1860. Historical Society of Pennsylvania, Philadelphia. (Hist. Soc. Pa.)

D. Samuel F. B. Morse. Old House of Representatives. 1882. Corcoran Collection, Washington, D. C. (Corcoran Coll.)

E. John Neagle. Pat Lyon at his Forge. 1829. Pennsylvania Academy of the Fine Arts, Philadelphia. (Pa. Acad.)

F. Samuel F. B. Morse. The Gallery of the Louvre. 1832. Syracuse University. (Syracuse Univ.)

A. John Trumbull. Battle of Bunker Hill. 1786. Yale University Art Gallery. (Yale Univ.)

B. Asher Durand. Kindred Spirits, William C. Bryant and Thomas Cole. 1849. New York Public Library. (N.Y.P.L.)

C. Thomas Cole. Destruction of the Empire. 1836. New-York Historical Society, New York. (N. Y. Hist. Soc.)

D. Gustavus Hesselius. Lapowinsa. 1735. Historical Society of Pennsylvania, Philadelphia. (Hist. Soc. Pa.)

E. Thomas Doughty. In Nature's Wonderland. 1835. Detroit Institute of Arts. (Det. Inst.)

F. John Mix Stanley. Ko-kak-koo-kiss, a Towoccono Warrior. 1844. U. S. National Museum, Washington. (Smithsonian Institution.)

A. George Catlin. Osceola. Before 1838. American Museum of Natural History, New York. (Am. Mus. Nat. Hist.)

B. Charles Wimar. The Captive Charger. 1854. St. Louis City Art Museum. (St. Louis C. A. M.)

C. Anonymous American. Henry Ward Beecher. 1850–60? Metropolitan Museum of Art, New York. (Met)

D. Anonymous American. Cigar Store Indian. XIX century. Index of American Design, U. S. National Gallery of Art, Washington. (Index of Am. Des.)

E. Albert Bierstadt. Starr King Mountain, California. 1866. Cleveland Museum of Art, The Hinman B. Hurlbut Coll. (Clev. Mus. Art)

F. George Catlin. Ha-won-je-tah, the One Horn; First Chief of the Tribe, Sioux, (Dak-co-ta). c. 1832. U. S. National Museum, Washington. (Smithsonian Institution)

G. Anonymous American. Samuel Houston as Marius. 1831. From a copy, 1912. State Capitol, Austin, Texas. (Texas State Lib.)

H. Anonymous American. Baby in Red High Chair. c. 1790. Metropolitan Museum of Art, New York. (Met)

A. Edmond Brown. Carrousel Rooster. 19th c. Index of American Design, U. S. National Gallery of Art, Washington. (Index of Am. Des.)

B. Joseph Pickett. Manchester Valley. c. 1916. Museum of Modern Art, New York. (Mus. Mod. Art)

C. "Deacon" Shem Drowne. Weathervane, Indian Archer. c. 1716. Massachusetts Historical Society, Boston. (Mass. Hist. Soc.)

D. John James Audubon. Virginia Deer. Brooklyn Museum. (Brooklyn Mus.)

E. William Harnett. Old Models. 1892. Museum of Fine Arts, Boston. (M.F.A.)

F. John Quidor. Wolfert's Will. 1856. Brooklyn Museum. (Brooklyn Mus.)

A. Erastus Field. Historical Monument of the American Republic. c. 1876. Springfield Museum of Fine Arts, Mass. (Spr. Mus.)

B. Richard C. Woodville. Politics in an Oyster House. 1848. Walters Art Gallery, Baltimore, Md. (Walters Art Gall.)

C. Eastman Johnson. Family Group. 1871. Metropolitan Museum, New York. (Met)

D. Henry Sargent. The Tea Party. c. 1825. Museum of Fine Arts. (M.F.A.)

E. William S. Mount. The Banjo Player. Detail. c. 1858. Detroit Institute of Arts. (Det. Inst.)

F. Eastman Johnson. Old Kentucky Home—Life in the South. 1859. New York Public Library. (N.Y.P.L.)

A. George Caleb Bingham. Figure of an Elderly Gentleman Smoking a Long Pipe. c. 1850. St. Louis Mercantile Library Association. (St. Louis M.L.A.)

B. George Caleb Bingham. Raftsmen Playing Cards. 1847. St. Louis City Art Museum. (St. Louis C.A.M.)

C. George Caleb Bingham. Senile Old Man Tottering Down Steps. c. 1850. St. Louis Mercantile Library Association. (St. Louis M.L.A.)

D. Winslow Homer. Sloop, Bermuda. 1899. Metropolitan Museum, New York. (Met)

E. George Caleb Bingham. Two Citizens Engaged in a Conversation. c. 1850. St. Louis Mercantile Library Association. (St. Louis M.L.A.)

F. Winslow Homer. Detail of D.

A. Winslow Homer. All's Well. 1896. Museum of Fine Arts. (M.F.A.)

B. Winslow Homer. The Herring Net. 1885. Art Institute. (Art Inst.)

C. Winslow Homer. Breezing Up. 1876. U. S. National Gallery of Art, Washington. (U. S. Nat. Gall.)

D. Thomas Eakins. Walt Whitman. 1887. Pennsylvania Academy of the Fine Arts, Philadelphia. (Pa. Acad.)

E. Thomas Eakins. The Agnew Clinic. University of Pennsylvania, Philadelphia. (Univ. of Pa.)

F. Thomas Eakins. The Gross Clinic. 1875. Jefferson Medical College, Philadelphia. (Jeff. Med. Coll.)

A. Thomas Eakins. Salutat. 1898. Addison Gallery, Phillips Academy, Andover, Mass. (Addison Gall.)

B. Thomas Eakins. Max Schmidt in a Single Scull. 1871. Metropolitan Museum, New York. (Met)

C. A. P. Ryder. The Temple of the Mind. c. 1888. Albright Art Gallery, Buffalo, N. Y. (Albright Art Gall.)

D. A. P. Ryder. Death on a Pale Horse. c. 1910. Cleveland Museum of Art, The J. H. Wade Collection. (Clev. Mus.)

E. A. P. Ryder. Siegfried and the Rhine Maidens. U. S. National Gallery of Art, Washington. (U. S. Nat. Gall.)

F. A. P. Ryder. Toilers of the Sea. c. 1900. Addison Gallery, Phillips Academy, Andover, Mass. (Addison Gall.)

A. James M. Whistler. Thomas Carlyle. Glasgow Corporation Gallery. (Glasgow Corp.)

B. James M. Whistler. Black Lion Wharf. Etching. 1859. (See 320 F for detail.) (Fogg)

C. John S. Sargent. Robert Louis Stevenson. 1885. Taft Museum, Cincinnati, Ohio. (Taft Mus.)

D. James M. Whistler. Portrait of the Artist's Mother. 1871. Louvre.

E. James M. Whistler. Old Battersea Bridge. Tate Gallery, London. (Nat. Gall.)

F. James M. Whistler. Nocturne in Black and Gold (The Fire Wheel). Collection Mr. A. H. Studd. (Met)

A. W. M. Hunt. Flight of Night. Pennsylvania Academy of the Fine Arts, Philadelphia. (Pa. Acad.)

B. W. M. Hunt. The Bathers. 1887. Worcester Art Museum. (Worcester Mus.)

C. George de Forest Brush. Mother and Child. 1895. Museum of Fine Arts. (M.F.A.)

D. George Inness. Peace and Plenty. Metropolitan Museum, New York. (Met)

E. Frank Duveneck. Whistling Boy. 1872. Taft Museum, Cincinnati, Ohio. (Taft Mus.)

F. Homer Martin. Harp of the Winds; a View of the Seine. 1895. Metropolitan Museum, New York. (Met)

A. George Bellows. Dempsey, Firpo. 1924. Whitney Museum of American Art, New York. (Whitney Mus.)

B. George Bellows. Eleanor, Jean and Anna. 1920. Albright Art Gallery, Buffalo, N. Y. (Albright Gall.)

C. Arthur B. Davies. Maya, Mirror of Illusions. Before 1910. Art Institute. (Art Inst.)

D. Robert Henri. Dutch Joe. 1910. Milwaukee Art Institute. (Met)

E. George Luks. The Spielers. 1905. Addison Gallery, Phillips Academy, Andover, Mass. (Addison Gall.)

F. George Bellows. Forty-Two Kids. Detail. 1907. Corcoran Collection, Washington, D. C. (Corcoran Coll.)

A. George Luks. Portrait of Mrs. Gamley. Whitney Museum of American Art, New York. (Whitney Mus.)

B. William J. Glackens. Chez Mouquin. 1905. Art Institute. (Art Inst.)

C. Childe Hassam. Church at Old Lyme, Connecticut. 1905. Albright Art Gallery, Buffalo, N. Y. (Albright Gall.)

D. Maurice Prendergast. Ponte della Paglia. Phillips Collection, Washington, D. C. (Phillips Coll.)

E. Frank W. Benson. My Daughters. 1907. Worcester Art Museum. (Worcester Mus.)

F. Mary Cassatt. Mother and Child. 1903. Worcester Art Museum. (Worcester Mus.)

A. Thomas Benton. The Art of Building. 1930. New School for Social Research, New York. (New School)

B. John Taylor Arms. Mont St Michel. Aquatint. Collection Frank J. Roos, Jr. (See 320 G for detail.)

C. Bernard Karfiol. Bathers. 1917–18. (Bernard Karfiol)

D. Eugene Speicher. Portrait of a Girl. Whitney Museum of American Art, New York. (Whitney Mus.)

E. John Steuart Curry. The Tornado. Hackley Art Gallery, Muskegon, Mich. (Hackley Gall.)

F. Reginald Marsh. High Yaller. 1934. Collection Mr. and Mrs. Alfred Easton Poor. (Mr. and Mrs. Alfred Easton Poor

A. Grant Wood. American Gothic. 1930. Art Institute. (Art Inst.)

B. Thomas Benton. The Jealous Lover of Lone Green Valley. 1931. Collection of the artist. (Thomas Benton)

C. Charles Burchfield. Winter Solstice. Columbus Gallery of Fine Arts, Ohio. (Col. Gall.)

D. Preston Dickinson. Industry. Whitney Museum of American Art, New York. (Whitney Mus.)

E. Charles Burchfield. Winter Twilight. Whitney Museum of American Art, New York. (Whitney Mus.)

F. Charles Demuth. My Egypt. 1925. Whitney Museum of American Art, New York. (Whitney Mus.)

A. Lyonel Feininger. Glorious Victory of the Sloop Maria. 1926. City Art Museum, St. Louis (Mus. Mod. Art)

B. Charles Demuth. Modern Conveniences. 1922. Columbus Gallery of Fine Arts, Ohio. (Col. Gall.)

C. John Marin. Maine Islands. 1922. Phillips Collection, Washington, D. C. (Phillips Coll.)

D. Charles Sheeler. Still Life Number One. Columbus Gallery of Fine Arts, Ohio. (Col. Gall.)

E. John Marin. The Cove. 1917. Columbus Gallery of Fine Arts, Ohio. (Col. Gall.)

F. Charles Sheeler. Interior. 1926. Whitney Museum of American Art, New York. (Whitney Mus.)

A. Ben Shahn. Handball. 1939. Museum of Modern Art, New York. (Mus. Mod. Art)

B. Karl Knaths. Cock and Glove. 1927–28. Phillips Collection, Washington, D. C. (Phillips Coll.)

C. Yasuo Kuniyoshi. Self Portrait as a Golf Player. 1927. Museum of Modern Art, New York. (Mus. Mod. Art)

D. Marsden Hartley. Mt. Katahdin, Autumn, No. 1. 1939–40. Hall Collection, University of Nebraska Art Gall. (Hall Coll.)

E. Max Weber. Flute Soloist. 1945. Collection Paul Rosenberg and Co., New York. (Paul Rosenberg and Co.)

F. Stuart Davis. Red Cart. 1932. Addision Gallery, Phillips Academy, Andover, Mass. (Addison Gall.)

A. Max Weber. Detail of 305 E.

B. John Carroll. The White Flower. 1951. Collection of the artist. (John Carroll)

C. William Gropper. Time. Associated American Artists Galleries, New York. (A. A. A. Galls.)

D. Peter Blume. Crucifixion. Detail. c. 1950. Durlacher Bros., New York. (Durlacher Bros.)

E. Philip Guston. Martial Memory. 1941. St. Louis City Art Museum. (St. Louis C.A.M.)

F. Richard Koppe. A Collection of Things. c. 1948. Collection of the artist. (Richard Koppe)

G. I. Rice Pereira. Receding Red. c. 1948. Collection of the artist. (I. R. Pereira)

A. Abraham Rattner. Sodom and Gomorrah. 1965. The Downtown Gallery, New York. (The Downtown Gallery)

B. Robert Motherwell. The Easel. 1954. Marlborough-Gerson Gallery, New York. (Marlborough-Gerson Gallery)

C. Loren MacIver. Paris Roofs. 1962. University of Illinois,

Krannert Art Museum. (Krannert Art Museum)

D. Mark Tobey. Allegro. 1954. Willard Gallery, New York. (Willard Gallery)

E. Edward Hopper. Solitude. 1947. Frank K. M. Rehn Gallery, New York.

A. Morris Graves. Guardian. 1955. University of Illinois, Krannert Art Museum. (University of Illinois, Krannert Art Museum)

B. Hans Hofmann. Scattered Sunset. 1961. Samuel Kootz Gallery, New York. (Samuel Kootz Gallery)

C. Jackson Pollock. "#5". 1952. Sidney Janis Gallery, New York. (Sidney Janis Gallery)

D. Andrew Wyeth. Back Apartment. 1961. Collection Mr. and Mrs. Donald Gilmore. (Knoedler and Company, New York)

E. Jasper Johns. 0 through 9. 1962.

F. Milton Avery. Spring in France. 1953. Grace Borgenicht Gallery, New York. (Grace Borgenicht Gallery)

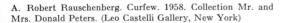

A. Robert Rauschenberg. Curfew. 1958. Collection Mr. and Mrs. Donald Peters. (Leo Castelli Gallery, New York)

B. Larry Rivers. Don't Fall. 1966. Marlborough-Gerson Gallery, New York. (Marlborough-Gerson Gallery)

C. Franz Kline. White Forms. 1955. Collection Philip Johnson, New York.

D. Philip Guston. Heir. 1964. Marlborough-Gerson, Gallery, New York. (Marlborough-Gerson Gallery)

E. Kenneth Noland. Drive. 1964. André Emmerich Gallery, New York.

F. Andy Warhol. Jackie. 1964. Leo Castelli Gallery, New York. (Leo Castelli Gallery)

A. Robert Indiana. The Figure 5. 1963.

B. Theodoros Stamos. Red Sun Box. 1965. Courtesy André Emmerich Gallery. Collection of Mr. and Mrs. Leonard Bocour, New York. (Photograph, Eric Pollitzer)

C. Paul Jenkins. Phenomena Point Swing and Flank. 1964. Krannert Art Museum, University of Illinois. (Krannert Art Museum.)

D. Sam Francis. Untitled. 1960.

A. Frank Gallo. Man in Rocker. 1967. Courtesy of the artist. Edition in various collections.

B. Pablo Picasso. Construction, 1967. Chicago Civic Center Plaza, Chicago, Illinois. (Charles Scott, Chicago Daily News and Sun-Times)

C. Philip Evergood. The Future. 1954. Gallery 63, New York. (Gallery 63)

D. Richard Diebenkorn. Yellow Seascape. 1958. Poindexter Gallery, New York. (Poindexter Gallery)

E. Willem de Kooning. Woman. 1949. Sidney Janis Gallery, New York. (Sidney Janis Gallery)

A. Edgar Degas. Ballet Dancer, Dressed. Bronze. 1880. (U. of Ill.)

B. Ernst Barlach. Monks Reading. Art Institute. (Art Inst.)

C. Charles Despiau. Standing Nude. Luxembourg (Librarie de France)

D. Ernst Barlach. Singing Man. 1928. Museum of Modern Art, New York. (Mus. Mod. Art)

E. Émile Bourdelle. Centaur. One of several copies. (U. of Ill.)

F. Eric Gill. Mater Amabalis. 1923. (Met)

G. Aristide Maillol. Torso. Metropolitan Museum, New York. (Met)

H. Ivan Meštrović. Archangel Gabriel. Brooklyn Museum. (Brooklyn Mus.)

I. Leo Friedlander. Spirit of Radio. 1932–33. R.C.A. Building, Rockefeller Center, New York. (Roos)

A. Lee Lawrie. Architectural Figure. R.C.A. Building, Rockefeller Center, New York. (See 283 A.) (Roos)

B. Carl Milles. Europa and the Bull. Gothenburg Museum, Sweden. (U. of Ill.)

C. Carl Milles. Fountain Detail. 1930. Gothenburg, Sweden. (U. of Ill.)

D. Leo Friedlander. Valor, for Arlington Memorial Bridge, Washington, D. C. 1916. (Leo Friedlander)

E. Wilhelm Lehmbruck. Kneeling Woman. 1911. Museum of Modern Art, New York. (Mus. Mod. Art)

F. Carl Milles. Orpheus. Fountain. Stockholm, Sweden. (U. of Ill.)

G. Raymond Duchamp-Villon. Baudelaire. 1911. Louvre, Paris. (U. of Ill.)

A. William Zorach. Child and Cat. 1926. Museum of Modern Art, New York. (Mus. Mod. Art)

B. Jacob Epstein. Night. 1929. London Underground Railway Offices, London. (U. of Ill.)

C. Alexander Archipenko. Flat Torso. 1914. Collection Dr. Ruth Morris Bakwin. (R. M. Bakwin)

D. Jacob Epstein. Primavera God. (Met)

E. Constantin Brancusi. Mlle. Pogany. Philadelphia Museum of Art. (Phila. Mus.)

F. Constantin Brancusi. The Bird. c. 1925. Philadelphia Museum of Art. (Phila. Mus.)

G. Alexander Archipenko. Glorification of Beauty. Berlin. (U. of Ill.)

H. Jacob Epstein. John Dewey. 1928. Columbia University. (John Dewey)

I. Jacob Epstein. Madonna and Child. 1927. (Met)

J. Gaston Lachaise. Woman. 1912–27. Albright Art Gallery, Buffalo, N. Y. (U. of Ill.)

A. Henry Moore. Reclining Figure. 1935. Albright Art Gallery, Buffalo, N. Y. (Albright Art Gall.)

B. Henry Laurens. Dance. 1915. (U. of Ill.)

C. John Storrs. Ceres. Board of Trade Building, Chicago. (John Storrs)

D. Jacques Lipchitz. Figure. 1926–30. Museum of Modern Art, New York. (Mus. Mod. Art)

E. Umberto Boccioni. Unique Forms of Continuity in Space. 1913. Museum of Modern Art, New York. (Mus. Mod. Art)

F. Umberto Boccioni. Muscles in Action. 1911. Gallery of Modern Art, Milan, Italy. (U. of Ill.)

G. Pablo Picasso. Head. Bronze. 1909. Museum of Modern Art, New York. (Mus. Mod. Art)

H. Raymond Duchamp-Villon. The Horse. 1914. Museum of Modern Art, New York. (Mus. Mod. Art)

A. Naum Gabo. Head of a Woman. Before 1926. Museum of Modern Art, New York. (Mus. Mod. Art)

B. Meret Oppenheim. Still Life: Fur-Lined Tea Cup. 1936. Museum of Modern Art, New York. (Mus. Mod. Art)

C. Max Ernst. Two Children are Menaced by a Nightingale. 1924. Museum of Modern Art, New York. (Mus. Mod. Art)

D. Hans Arp. Individuals. 1931. (U. of Ill.)

E. Rudolph Belling. Head. 1923. Weyhe Collection, New York. (Weyhe Coll.)

F. Jacques Lipchitz. Composition. 1927. (U. of Ill.)

G. Oskar Schlemmer. Rotund Plastic. 1921. (U. of Ill.)

H. Antoine Pevsner. Developable Column. 1942. Museum of Modern Art, New York. (Mus. Mod. Art)

A. Alberto Giacometti. The Palace at 4 A.M., III. 1934. Paris. (U. of Ill.)

B. Ladislaus Moholy-Nagy. Plexiglas and Chromium Construction. 1940. (Sibyl Moholy-Nagy)

C. Naum Gabo. Column. 1923. Collection of the artist. (U. of Ill.)

D. Alberto Giacometti. The Palace at 4 A.M. 1933. Museum of Modern Art, New York. (Mus. Mod. Art)

E. Isamu Noguchi. Kouros. 1945. Collection of the artist. (I. Noguchi)

F. Henry Moore. The Bride. 1940. Museum of Modern Art, New York. (Mus. Mod. Art)

G. Alexander Calder. Mobile: Red Petals. 1942. The Arts Club, Chicago. (Arts Club)

H. Isamu Noguchi. Table. c. 1947. (Herman Miller Furniture Co.)

A. Ibram Lassaw. Parade. 1962. Samuel Kootz Gallery, New York. (Samuel Kootz Gallery)

B. Theodore Rozak. Golden Hawk. 1961–1962. Pierre Matisse Gallery, New York. (Pierre Matisse Gallery)

C. Harry Bertoia. Untitled. 1960.

D. David Smith. Hudson River Landscape. 1951. Whitney Museum of American Art, New York. (Whitney Museum)

E. Mirko (Basaldello). Motivo Alato. 1964. Courtesy of the artist.

F. Claes Oldenberg. Dormeyer Mixer. 1965. Whitney Museum of American Art. (Whitney Museum)

A. Jacob Epstein. Head of Wynne Godley. 1956. University of Illinois, Krannert Art Museum. (Krannert Art Museum)

B. Jacques Lipchitz. Hagar. 1948. Marlborough-Gerson Gallery, New York. (Marlborough-Gerson)

C. Leonard Baskin. Poet Laureate. 1956. Boris Mirsky Gallery, Boston. (Boris Mirsky)

D. Seymour Lipton. Storm Bird. 1953. Marlborough-Gerson Gallery, New York. (Marlborough-Gerson)

E. William Zorach. The Family. 1957. The Downtown Gallery, New York. (Downtown Gallery)

F. Charles Umlauf. Reclining Mother and Child. 1956. University of Illinois, Krannert Art Museum. (Krannert Art Museum)

A. Woodcut. Dürer. (See 167 I)

B. Mezzotint. Prince Rupert. (See 170 C)

C. Engraving. Claude Mellan. (See 212 F)

D. Wood Engraving. Timothy Cole. (See 162 E)

E. Lithograph. Degas. (See 230 D)

F. Etching. Whistler. (See 298 B)

G. Aquatint and Etching. John Taylor Arms. (See 302 B)

CHART A

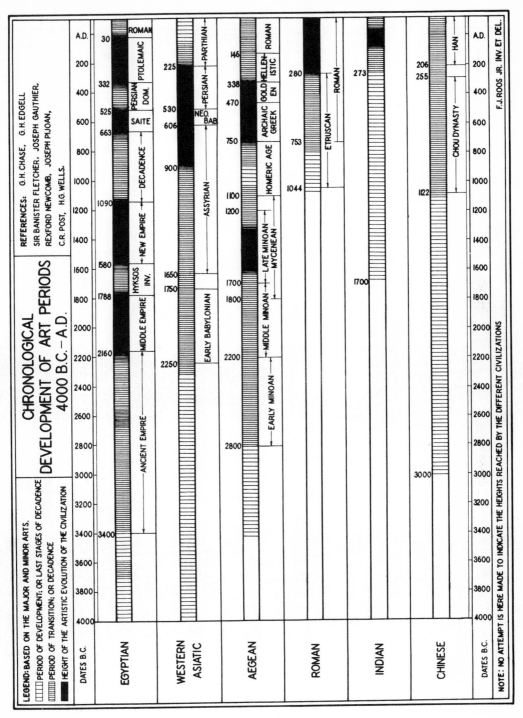

CHRONOLOGICAL DEVELOPMENT OF ART PERIODS 4000 B.C. – A.D.

REFERENCES: G.H. CHASE, G.H. EDGELL
SIR BANISTER FLETCHER, JOSEPH GAUTHIER,
REXFORD NEWCOMB, JOSEPH PIJOAN,
C.R. POST, H.G. WELLS.

LEGEND: BASED ON THE MAJOR AND MINOR ARTS.
PERIOD OF DEVELOPMENT; OR LAST STAGES OF DECADENCE
PERIOD OF TRANSITION; OR DECADENCE
HEIGHT OF THE ARTISTIC EVOLUTION OF THE CIVILIZATION

NOTE: NO ATTEMPT IS HERE MADE TO INDICATE THE HEIGHTS REACHED BY THE DIFFERENT CIVILIZATIONS

F.J. ROOS JR. INV. ET DEL.

321

CHART B

CHRONOLOGICAL DEVELOPMENT OF ART PERIODS
I A.D.—DATE

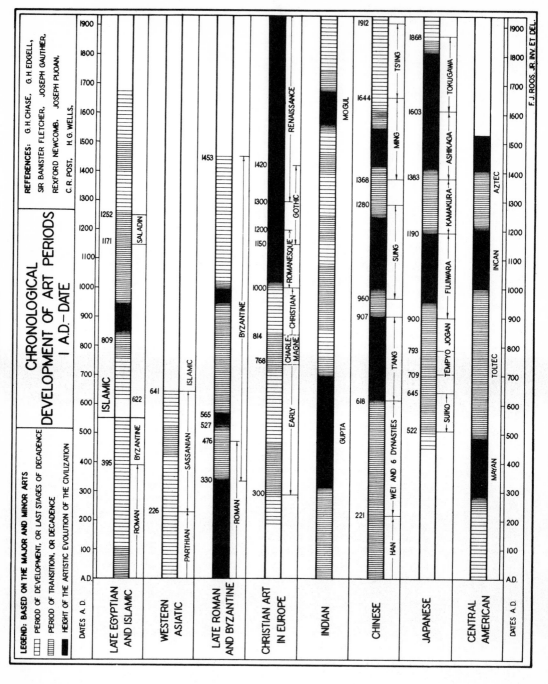

LEGEND: BASED ON THE MAJOR AND MINOR ARTS

PERIOD OF DEVELOPMENT, OR LAST STAGES OF DECADENCE

PERIOD OF TRANSITION, OR DECADENCE

HEIGHT OF THE ARTISTIC EVOLUTION OF THE CIVILIZATION

REFERENCES: G.H.CHASE, G.H.EDGELL, SIR BANISTER FLETCHER, JOSEPH GAUTHIER, REXFORD NEWCOMB, JOSEPH PIJOAN, C.R. POST, H.G. WELLS,

F.J. ROOS JR. INV. ET DEL.

322

CHART C

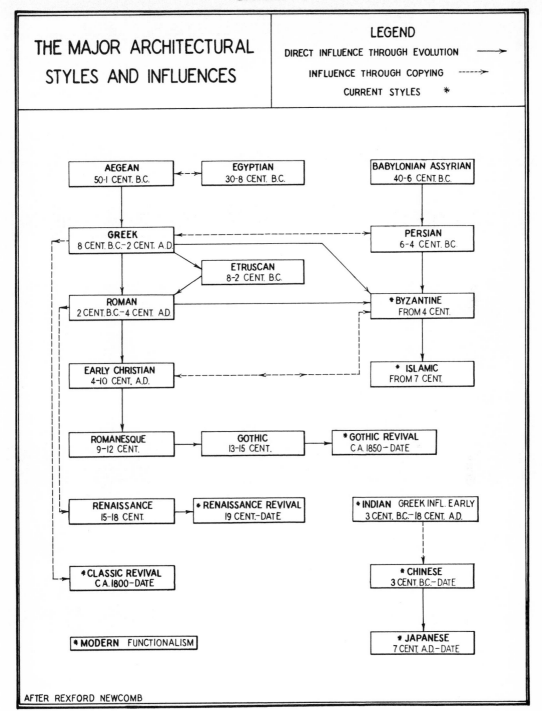

THE MAJOR ARCHITECTURAL STYLES AND INFLUENCES

LEGEND

DIRECT INFLUENCE THROUGH EVOLUTION ⟶

INFLUENCE THROUGH COPYING ----⟶

CURRENT STYLES *

AEGEAN
50-1 CENT. B.C.

EGYPTIAN
30-8 CENT. B.C.

BABYLONIAN ASSYRIAN
40-6 CENT. B.C.

GREEK
8 CENT. B.C.–2 CENT. A.D.

PERSIAN
6-4 CENT. B.C.

ETRUSCAN
8-2 CENT. B.C.

ROMAN
2 CENT. B.C.–4 CENT. A.D.

* BYZANTINE
FROM 4 CENT.

EARLY CHRISTIAN
4-10 CENT. A.D.

* ISLAMIC
FROM 7 CENT.

ROMANESQUE
9-12 CENT.

GOTHIC
13-15 CENT.

* GOTHIC REVIVAL
C.A. 1850–DATE

RENAISSANCE
15-18 CENT.

* RENAISSANCE REVIVAL
19 CENT.–DATE

* INDIAN GREEK INFL. EARLY
3 CENT. B.C.–18 CENT. A.D.

* CLASSIC REVIVAL
C.A. 1800–DATE

* CHINESE
3 CENT. B.C.–DATE

* MODERN FUNCTIONALISM

* JAPANESE
7 CENT. A.D.–DATE

AFTER REXFORD NEWCOMB

323

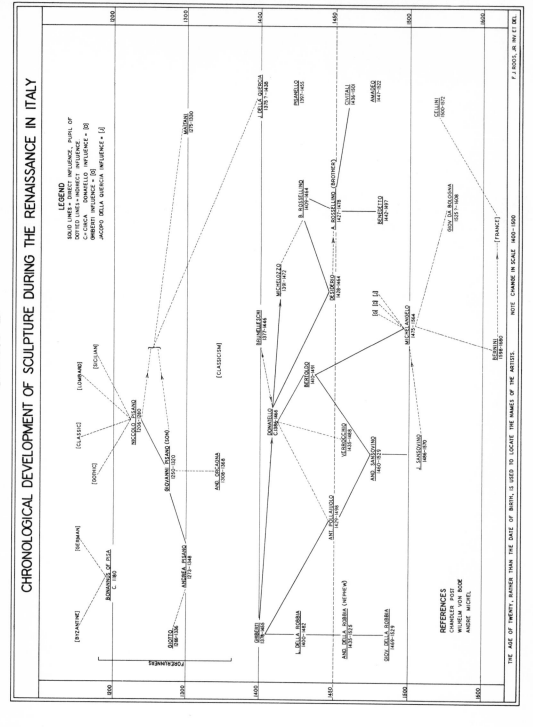

CHART D

CHRONOLOGICAL DEVELOPMENT OF SCULPTURE DURING THE RENAISSANCE IN ITALY

LEGEND
SOLID LINES = DIRECT INFLUENCE, PUPIL OF
DOTTED LINES = INDIRECT INFLUENCE.
C= CIRCA   DONATELLO INFLUENCE = [D]
GHIBERTI INFLUENCE = [G]
JACOPO DELLA QUERCIA INFLUENCE = [J]

[BYZANTINE]   [GERMAN]

BONANNUS OF PISA
C. 1180

[GOTHIC]   [CLASSIC]   [LOMBARD]

[SICILIAN]

NICCOLO PISANO
1206-1280

GIOVANNI PISANO (SON)
1250-1320

MAITANI
1275-1330

GIOTTO
1266-1336

ANDREA PISANO
1273-1348

AND. ORCAGNA
1308-1368

[CLASSICISM]

J. DELLA QUERCIA
1375-1438

GHIBERTI
1378-1455

BRUNELLESCHI
1377-1446

PISANELLO
1397-1455

L. DELLA ROBBIA
1400-1482

DONATELLO
C.1386-1466

MICHELOZZO
1391-1472

B. ROSSELLINO
1409-1464

CIVITALI
1436-1501

AND. DELLA ROBBIA (NEPHEW)
1435-1525

VERROCCHIO
1435-1488

BERTOLDO
1400-1491

DESIDERIO
1428-1464

A. ROSSELLINO (BROTHER)
1427-1478

AMADEO
1447-1522

GIOV. DELLA ROBBIA
1469-1529

ANT. POLLAIUOLO
1429-1498

AND. SANSOVINO
1460-1529

BENEDETTO
1442-1497

J. SANSOVINO
1486-1570

MICHELANGELO
1475-1564

[G] [D] [J]

CELLINI
1500-1572

GIOV. DA BOLOGNA
1525?-1608

BERNINI
1598-1680

[FRANCE]

REFERENCES
CHANDLER POST
WILHELM VON BODE
ANDRE MICHEL

FORERUNNERS

THE AGE OF TWENTY, RATHER THAN THE DATE OF BIRTH, IS USED TO LOCATE THE NAMES OF THE ARTISTS.   NOTE CHANGE IN SCALE 1400-1500

F J ROOS, JR INV ET DEL

1200   1300   1400   1450   1500   1600

CHART E

CHRONOLOGICAL DEVELOPMENT OF PAINTING DURING THE RENAISSANCE IN ITALY

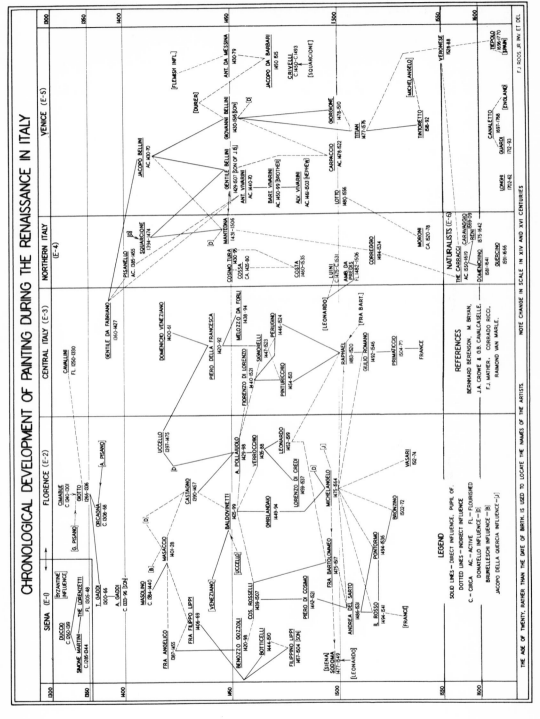

F J ROOS JR INV ET DEL

SIENA (E-1) · FLORENCE (E-2) · CENTRAL ITALY (E-3) · NORTHERN ITALY (E-4) · VENICE (E-5)

LEGEND

SOLID LINES = DIRECT INFLUENCE, PUPIL OF.
DOTTED LINES = INDIRECT INFLUENCE
C = CIRCA   AC = ACTIVE   FL = FLOURISHED
DONATELLO INFLUENCE = [D].
BRUNELLESCHI INFLUENCE = [B].
JACOPO DELLA QUERCIA INFLUENCE = [J].

REFERENCES

Bernhard Berenson,   M. Bryan,
J.A. Crowe & G.B. Cavalcaselle,
F.J. Mather,   Corrado Ricci,
Raimond Van Marle.

THE AGE OF TWENTY, RATHER THAN THE DATE OF BIRTH, IS USED TO LOCATE THE NAMES OF THE ARTISTS.   NOTE CHANGE IN SCALE IN XIV AND XVI CENTURIES

CHART F

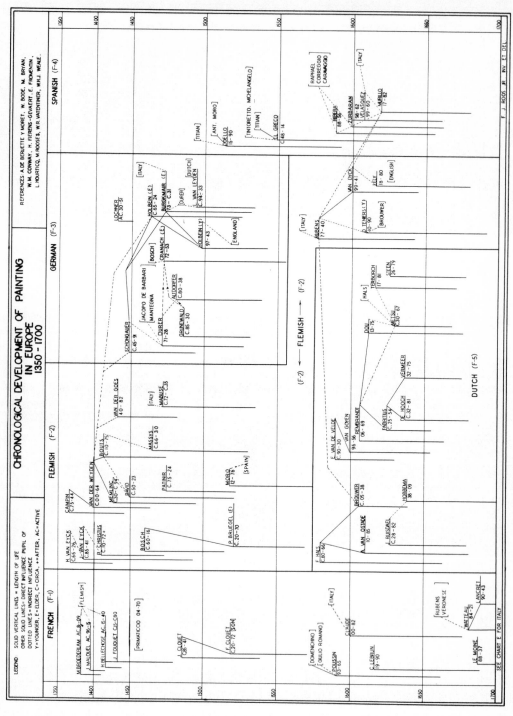

CHRONOLOGICAL DEVELOPMENT OF PAINTING IN EUROPE 1350-1700

LEGEND: SOLID VERTICAL LINES = LENGTH OF LIFE. OTHER SOLID LINES = DIRECT INFLUENCE. DOTTED LINES = INDIRECT INFLUENCE. PUPIL OF. Y = YOUNGER, E = ELDER, C = CIRCA, + = AFTER, AC = ACTIVE

REFERENCES: A. DE BÉRUÈTTE Y MORET, W. BODE, M. BRYAN, W. M. CONWAY, H. FIERENS-GEVAERT, E. FROMENTIN, L. HOURTICQ, M. ROOSES, W. R. VAETENTINER, W.H.J. WEALE.

FRENCH (F-1) FLEMISH (F-2) GERMAN (F-3) SPANISH (F-4) DUTCH (F-5)

SEE CHART E FOR ITALY

F J ROOS JR INV ET DEL

326

CHART G

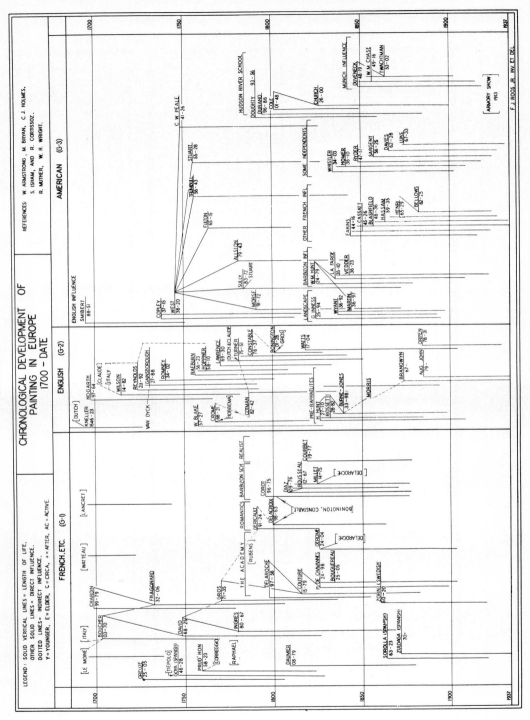

CHRONOLOGICAL DEVELOPMENT OF PAINTING IN EUROPE 1700 – DATE

LEGEND: SOLID VERTICAL LINES = LENGTH OF LIFE.
OTHER SOLID LINES = DIRECT INFLUENCE.
DOTTED LINES = INDIRECT INFLUENCE.
Y = YOUNGER, E = ELDER, C = CIRCA, + = AFTER, AC = ACTIVE.

REFERENCES: W. ARMSTRONG., M. BRYAN., C. J. HOLMES,
S. ISHAM, AND R. CORTISSOZ.
R. MUTHER., W. H. WRIGHT.

FRENCH. ETC. (G-1)

ENGLISH (G-2)

AMERICAN (G-3)

F. J. ROOS, JR. INV. ET DEL.

327

CHART H

BASIC EUROPEAN FURNITURE STYLES

DATES — 1500 | 1600 | 1700 | 1800

FRANCE

PERIOD	GOTHIC	RENAISSANCE			ROCOCO		CLASSIC	
STYLE	GOTHIC FROM AB. 1150	FRANCIS I	HENRY II	HENRY IV	LOUIS XIV / TRANSITION	LOUIS XV	LOUIS XVI	DIRECTORY / EM-PIRE
SOVE-REIGN		FRANCIS I	HENRY II to 1559 / FRANCIS II 1560 / CHARLES IX 1574 / HENRY III	HENRY IV	LOUIS XIV / REGENCY	LOUIS XV	LOUIS XVI	NAPOLEON
DATE	1515	1547	1589	1610	06 1643 50 / 1715 1723	1774	1793 1804 1815

ENGLAND

PERIOD	GOTHIC	EARLY RENAISSANCE		LATE					GEORGIAN		CLASSIC
STYLE	GOTHIC FROM AB. 1150	TUDOR	ELIZABETHAN	JACOBEAN	[STUART] REST. LATE	WM. & MARY	QUEEN ANNE		CHIPP-ENDALE 1710-79	SHERATON 1751-1806 / R.& J. ADAM 1760-92 / HEPPLEWHITE 1765-95	
SOVE-REIGN		HENRY VIII	ELIZABETH FROM 1558	EARLY JAMES I TO 1625 / CHARLES I	MID CROMWELL / CHARLES II TO 1685 / JAMES II	WM. & MARY	ANNE	GEORGE I	GEORGE II	GEORGE III	
DATE	1509	1557	1603	1649 1660	1688 1702	1714 1727	1760	1820

ITALY

PERIOD	RENAISSANCE	
	LOW FROM 1400	HIGH
	FLORENCE 1475	ROME

NOTE: ALL EUROPE TOOK ITS INSPIRATION FROM THE RENAISSANCE IN ITALY

AMERICA

EARLY COLONIAL	LATE COLONIAL	FEDERAL
		DUNCAN PHYFE AC.1795-1818
1725		1790

NOTE: AMERICAN COLONIAL STYLES FOLLOW THE ENGLISH ONE TO TWO DECADES LATER

AGES OF WOODS

OAK	OAK & WALNUT	WALNUT	COLOR WOODS	INLAY	MAHO-GANY
12th 13th 14th CENTS.	2nd HALF 14 - END 15	16 &17 CENTURIES			
EBONY			PEAR ROSEWOOD OLIVE		

F J ROOS, JR. INV ET DEL

328

INDEX

Aachen (see Aix-la-Chapelle)
Abbeville, St. Vulfrand, 82
Abraham Avenging Lot, 71
Abraham Entertains the Three Angels, Ghiberti, 108
Absinthe Drinkers, Degas, 230
Abstraction, Picasso, 230
Abu Simbel, Temple of Ramses II, 7
Abydos, Temple of Seti I, 6, 8
Academy, The, 327(G-1)
Achilles, 25
Acropolis, The: Athens, 19; Pergamon, 22
Acropolis, Ladies, 26
Acworth, N. H., 252
Adam, Creation of, Michelangelo, 139
Adam and Eve: Cranach, 169, Titian, 148
Adam and Eve, Expulsion of: Masaccio, 123, Quercia, 108
Adam and Eve, Temptation and Expulsion of, Michelangelo, 140
Adam style furniture, 199
Adam, Robert H., 186
Adams, John: Browere, 279; Copley, 285
Adams, John Quincy, Copley, 285
Adoration (see *Magi*)
Adoration of the Lamb, Van Eyck, 155
Aegean: architecture, 14; art, 321, 323; minor arts, 15, 16; painting, 15; sculpture, 14
Aegina, Temple of, 28
Aemilia, Basilica, 42
Aesop, Velásquez, 172
Age of Innocence, Reynolds, 188
Agnew Clinic, Eakins, 296
Agony in the Garden (see *Christ*)
Aix-la-Chapelle Cathedral, 89: chapel, 56, 89
Alabama and Kearsarge, Manet, 229
Alamo, The, 249
Alberti, Leon Battista, 93, 100
Albi Cathedral, 82
Aldobrandini Marriage, 52
Alexander the Great, Battle of, 50, 51
Alexander Sarcophagus, 38
Alexander Tapestry, 84
Alexandria, Egypt, 272
Alfeld-an-der-Leine, Germany, 209
Alhambra, Granada, 91
Alice Mason, Mason Limner, 284
Allegro, Tobey, 307
All's Well, Homer, 296
Allston, Washington, 289, 327(G-3)
Alma Mater, D. C. French, 281
Alpera, painting, 1
Alpheios, 29
Altamira, painting, 1
Altar, Gertrudis, 72
Altarpiece: Benedetto, 112; Campin, 156; Lochner, 166; Memlinc, 158; Robbia, 111
Amadeo, Giovanni Antonio, 114, 324
Amazon, Hercules and an, 28
Amazons, Polyclitus, School of, 35
Amazons and Greeks, Battle of, 24, 37
Ambrogio di Predis, 133, 325(E-4)
Amenophis III, court of, 5
American: architecture, 249–278; folk art, 292–293; furniture, 196–199; painting, 284–311, 327; sculpture, 279–283, 292–293, 312–319
American Gothic, Wood, 303
American Radiator Building, N.Y.C., 268
American School, The, Pratt, 286
Amiens Cathedral, 79–80
Amon, Temples of: Karnak, 5; Luxor, 6
Amorino in Breeches, Donatello, 109
Amphitheatres, 45, 46
Amphitrite, 25
Amphora, 16, 23, 24
Anatomy Lesson, Dr. Tulp's, Rembrandt, 177
Ancient Empire, 321
Andrea da Firenze, 122

Andrea del Sarto, 133, 134, 325(E-2)
Angel with Tambourine, Melozzo da Forli, 135
Angelico, Fra, 122, 123, 325(E-2)
Angelico Fra, Signorelli, 136
Angels Appearing to Joshua Before the Walls of Jericho, 61
Angelus, The, Millet, 223
Anglo-Saxon architecture, 69
Angoulême Cathedral, 67
Annapolis, Md., 255
Annunciation (see *Virgin*)
Antaeus, 25, 113, 127
Anti-Christ, Overthrow of the, Signorelli, 136
Antonello da Messina, 143, 325(E-5)
Antonio da Sangallo, 101, 102
Apelles, Calumny of, Botticelli, 131
Aphrodite, 30, 36, 38, 40
Apocalypse, Christ of, 75
Apollo, 26, 35, 41, 48
Apollo and Daphne: Bernini, 116; Pollaiuolo, 127
Apollo and Diana, Jacopo da Barbari, 144
Apollo, Temple of, 16, 17
Apollo Epicurius, Temple of, 18
Apollonius, 39
Apoxyomenos, Lysippus, 36
Appeal to the Great Spirit, Dallin, 282
Apse, Monreale Cathedral, 64
Apulia, Niccolo d' (see Pisano, Niccolo)
Aquatint, 175, 302, 320
Aqueduct, Segovia, 47
Aquitaine, 66, 67
Ara Pacis, 49, 50
Arc de l'Etoile, Paris, 203
Arcade, Victoria Buildings, Manchester, 207
Arch: of Constantine, 46, 49; at Orange, 47; of Septimius Severus, 42, 43, 47; of Titus, 46, 48, 49
Archaic Head, 27, 28
Archaic Period, Greek, 17, 18, 25–28, 321
Archaistic Athena, 41
Archangel Gabriel, Meštrovič, 321
Archangel Michael, Reni, 152
Archers of Darius, 12
Archipenko, Alexander, 314
Architectural styles, 323
Architecture: Aegean, 14; American, 249–278; Anglo-Saxon, 69; Assyrian, 12; Byzantine, 55–57; Dutch, 208–210; Early Christian, 53, 54; Egyptian, 2, 3, 5–7, 10, 272; English, 69–71, 85–88, 184–186, 207; Finnish, 270; Flemish, 82; French, 66–69, 74–83, 200–204, 207–208, 210, 278; German, 72, 89, 165, 166, 209, 270; Gothic, 74–95; Greek, 16–22; Italian, 62–64, 92–95, 98–106; Mexican, 249, 250, 274; Missions, 249, 250; Moorish, 90, 91; Norman, 70; Persian, 13; Roman, 42–47; Spanish, 71, 90, 170
Arena Chapel, Padua, 120, 121
Arena State, Washington, D.C., 277
Ares Ludovisi, 37
Argonauts, 24
Ariadne, Vanderlyn, 289
Aristion, Stele of, Aristocles, 26, 27
Aristocles, 26, 27
Aristogeiton, 29
Aristotle, Raphael, 138
Arizona, Tucson, 250
Arkesilaos, 34
Arles, St. Trophîme, 67
Armor: German, 170; Italian, 154
Arms, John Taylor, 302, 320
Arnolfini, Jan, and His Wife, Van Eyck, 156
Arnolfo di Cambio, 92–94
Arp, Hans, 316

Art of Building, The, Benton, 302
Artaxerxes, Palace of, 13
Artemis: of Delos, 25; of Gabii, 36; of Versailles, 40
Arundel Psalter, 88
Ashika period, 322
Ashurbanipal Hunting, 11
Ashurnasirpal, Palace of, 11
Ashville, N.C., 265
Assembly Hall, Salem, Mass., 257
Assisi, San Francesco, 92, 118, 120
Assumption (see *Virgin*)
Assyrian: architecture, 12; period, 321, 323; sculpture, 11–13
Athena, 25, 30, 33, 34, 41: Myron, 30
Athena and Hercules, 24
Athena Lemnia, Phidias, 33
Athena and Marsyas, 30
Athena, Mourning, 30
Athena Nike, Temple of, 19, 34
Athena, Temple of, 19
Athens: Acropolis Temples, 19, 32–34; Choragic Monument, 22; Dipylon Cemetery (Ceramicus), 23, 38; Parthenon, 16, 18, 19, 31–34; Propylaea, 17, 20; Temple of Athena Nike, 20; Temple of Jupiter Olympus, 22; Theseum, 21; Tower of the Winds, 22
Atreus, Treasury of, 14
Atrium, the: Pompeii, 45; Sant' Ambrogio, 62
Auditorium Building, Chicago, 267
Audubon, John J., 293
Augean Stable, 29
Augusta, Temple of Fortuna, 43
Augustin, Maj. Gen. William, Earl, 284
Augustus, 48
Aurora, Reni, 152
Autumn: Cossa, 143; Millet, 223
Autun Cathedral, 68
Auvers, Street of, Van Gogh, 236
Avenue of Sphinxes, Karnak, 5
Avery, Milton, 308
Avery-Downer House, Granville, Ohio, 262
Avignon, Papal Palace, 82, 211
Azay-le-Rideau, Château, 200
Aztec period, 322

Baalbek, 43
Baby in Red High Chair, 292
Babylonian: period, 321, 323; sculpture, 11
Bacchante by the Sea, Corot, 223
Bacchus, 36: Michelangelo, 115; Sansovino, 114
Back Apartment, A. Wyeth, 308
Bacon's Castle, Smithfield, Va., 251
Balcony, The, Manet, 229
Baldovinetti, Alesso, 125, 325(E-2)
Ballet Dancer, Degas, 312
Baltimore, Maryland, 260
Banjo Player, The, Mount, 294
Bank of England. London, 186
Bank of U.S., N.Y.C., 259
Banker and Wife, Massys, 159
Banner, Peter, 257
Banquet Scene, 8
Banqueting Hall, Whitehall, 184
Baptism (see *Christ*)
Baptistry, Florence, 64, 65: East doors, 107, 108; North doors, 107; South doors, 97
Baptistry: Parma, 63; Pisa, 63, 96; San Satiro, Milan, 101
Bar at the Folies Bergère, Manet, 228
Barbari (see Jacopo)
Barbarians and Romans, 50
Barber Shop, Teniers, 165
Barberini Faun, 41
Barbizon School, 327(G-1)

Barcelona, Spain, 210
Barclay-Vesey Telephone Building, N.Y.C., 268
Bari, San Niccolo, 64
Barlach, Ernst, 312
Barnard, George Grav, 281, 282
Barnsdall House, Los Angeles, 270
Baroncelli Chapel, 121
Barry, Sir Charles, 186
Bartolommeo, Fra, 133, 325(E-2)
Barye, Antoine Louis, 206
Basilica: Aemilia, 42; Constantine, 45; Julia, 42; Maxentius, 45; Paestum, 18; St. Paul's outside the walls, 53; St. Peter, 53; San Clemente, 53; San Stefano Rotondo, 53; Tourmanin, 54; Vincenza, 103 (see also St.; San; Santa)
Baskin, Leonard, 319
Bassae, Temple of Apollo, 18
Bath, After the, Raphaelle Peale, 288
Bath House, Hilversum, Neth., 208
Bather: Degas, 230; Ingres, 220; Zorn, 194
Bathers: Cézanne, 235; W. M. Hunt, 299; Karfiol, 302; Renoir, 233
Baths: of Diana, 43; of Diocletian, 44
Bathsheba, Rembrandt, 177
Baton Rouge, La., 263
Battersea Bridge, Old, Whistler, 298
Battle of Bunker Hill, Trumbull, 291
Battle of Issus, 50, 51
Battle of the Nudes, Pollaiuolo, 127
Battle of Pisa, Michelangelo, 141
Baudelaire, Duchamp-Villon, 313
Bauhaus, Dessau, 209
Bayeux Tapestry, 69
Beach, On the, Sorolla, 194
Bead and reel motif, 20
Bear Run, Pa., 270
Beau Dieu, Le, Amiens, 79
Beauvais Cathedral, 80
Beckmann, Max, 243
Bed: Chinese Chippendale, 198; Elizabethan, 196; Empire, 196
Beecher, Henry Ward, 292
Bellechose, Henri, 155, 326(F-1)
Belling, Rudolph, 316
Bellini, Gentile, 144, 325(E-5)
Bellini, Giovanni, 144, 145, 325(E-5)
Bellini, Jacopo, 325(E-5)
Bellows, George, 300
Belshazzar's Feast, Allston, 289
Belvedere, Apollo, 41
Bench, church, 85
Benedetto da Maiano, 99, 100, 112, 113, 324
Benihassan tombs, 5
Benjamin, Asher, 257
Benjamin's Sack, Finding of the Cup in, Ghiberti, 108
Bennett, Burnham, Holabird, and Skidmore, architects, 271
Bennington, Vt., 257
Benozzo Gozzoli (see Gozzoli)
Benson, Frank W., 301
Benton, Thomas, 302, 303
Berceuse, La, Van Gogh, 235
Bergpolder Apartments, Rotterdam, 210
Berlin: Brandenburg Gate, 166; Wertheim Department Store, 270
Bernini, Giovanni Lorenzo, 102, 116, 324
Bertin, M., Ingres, 219
Bertoia, Harry, 318
Bertoldo di Giovanni, 324
Bibliothèque: Nationale, Paris, 207; Sainte Geneviève, Paris, 207
Bierstadt, Albert, 292
Biltmore, Ashville, N.C., 205
Bingham, George C., 295
Bird, The, Brancusi, 314
Birthday, The, Chagall, 244
Bison, prehistoric, 2

Black Lion Wharf, Whistler, 298
Blake, William, 191, 192, 327(G-2)
Blashfield, Edwin H., 327(G-3)
Blenheim Palace, 185
Blessing, The, Chardin, 216
Blind Beggars, Bruegel, 160
Blois, Château, 201
Blue Boy, Gainsborough, 188
Blume, Peter, 245, 306
Boardley, Elizabeth, Stuart, 286
Boccioni, Umberto, 315
Boethos, 38
Bogardus, James, 266
Bologna: San Petronio, sculpture, 108, 109
Bon Bock, The, Manet, 288
Bonaiuti, Andrea, 122
Bonannus of Pisa, 65, 324
Bonaparte on the Bridge at Arcola, Gross, 220 (see also Napoleon)
Bonington, Richard Parkes, 192, 327(G-1, 2)
Book cover: Byzantine, 59; French, 59
Borghese Mars, 34
Borghese, Pauline, Canova, 205
Bosch, Jerome, 160, 326(F-2)
Boscoreale, mural from, 51
Bossuet, Jacques, Rigaud, 214
Boston, Mass., 251–253, 257–258, 264, 266, 282
Botticelli, 129–131, 325(E-2)
Bottle and Fruit Dish, Gris, 241
Boucher, François, 216, 327(G-1)
Bouguereau, William, 220, 327(G-1)
Bourdelle, Émile Antoine, 312
Bourges, House of Jacques Coeur, 82
Bouts, Dierick, 326(F-2)
Bowdoin, Gov. James, Feke, 284
Bowles, Miss, Reynolds, 188
Boxer, 39, 40
Boy with a Dolphin, 48
Boy with a Fife, Manet, 228
Boy with a Goose, 38
Boylston, Nicholas, Copley, 285
Bradley House, Madison, Wis., 267
Bramante, Donato, 101, 102
Brancacci Chapel, 123, 124, 131
Branchidae, seated figure from, 25
Brancusi, Constantin, 314
Brandenburg Gate, Berlin, 166
Brangwyn, Frank, 194, 327(G-2)
Brant, Isabella, Rubens, 161
Braque, Georges, 240, 241
Brazilian architecture, 274
Breda, Surrender of, Velásquez, 173
Breezing Up, Homer, 296
Breton, Jules, 224
Breuer House, Lincoln, Mass., 273
Breuer, Marcel, 273
Breughel (see Bruegel)
Brewery of Jan Steen, Steen, 181
Bride, The, Moore, 317
Bridge at Argenteuil, Monet, 229
Bridge, Brooklyn, N.Y., 266
Bridge of Sighs, Turner, 191
Brinkman, J., 210
Broadway Boogie-Woogie, Mondrian, 246
Broederlam, Melchior, 326(F-1)
Bronze doors: Baptistry, Florence, 97, 107, 108 (see also Hildesheim; Pisa; Monreale)
Bronzino, 134, 325(E-2)
Brooklyn Bridge, N.Y., 266
Brouwer, Adriaen, 326(F-2)
Browere, John, 279
Brown, Edmond, 293
Brown, H. K., 280, 282
Bruegel, Pieter, the Elder, 159–161, 326 (F-2)
Bruegel, Pieter, the Younger, Van Dyck, 164
Bruges, Madonna of, Michelangelo, 114

Brunelleschi, Filippo of, 93, 98, 100, 107, 324, 325(E-2)
Bruni, Leonardo, Tomb of, 111
Brush, George de Forest, 299
Brussels, 207: Hôtel de Ville, 82; Stoclet Palace, 208
Bruton Parish Church, Williamsburg, Va., 255
Bryant, William C., Durand, 291
Buffalo, N.Y., 267, 269
Bulfinch, Charles, 252, 257, 258, 260
Bull, Farnese, 41
Bull Fight, Goya, 175
Bull, Head of a, Potter, 182
Bull, Winged Man-Headed, 11
Bull, Young, Potter, 182
Bulls, Parthenon, 32
Bunker Hill, Battle of, Trumbull, 291
Buon, 105
Burchfield, Charles, 303
Burden of Life and Relief in Labor, Barnard, 281
Burgos Cathedral, 90
Burgundy, 67, 68
Burne-Jones, Sir Edward, 193, 327(G-2)
Burnham, Daniel, 265
Bury, Church, 69
Butter Tower, Rouen, 81
Buttery, The, de Hooch, 179
Buttresses: Chartres, 74; Exeter, 87; Reims, 78
Byfield, Nathaniel, Smibert, 285
Byzantine: architecture, 55–57; period, 322–324, 325(E-1); sculpture, 57–60

Cabildo, The, New Orleans, 256
Cabinets: Louis XVI, 195; Restoration, 197; William and Mary, 197
Caen: La Trinité, 69; St. Etienne, 68, 69
Caesar, Augustus, 48
Caesar, Triumph of, Mantegna, 143
Calder, Alexander, 317
Calf Bearer, 28
California: Eureka, 264; Hollywood, 273; Los Angeles, 270; Santa Barbara, 249
Callicrates, 18, 19
Calvert, Charles, and Colored Slave, John Hesselius, 285
Camargo, Mlle., Lancret, 214
Cambio, Arnolfo di, 92–94
Cambridge, Mass., 252, 273, 282
Campaign of France, Meissonier, 224
Campanile: Florence, 93, 97, 100; Pisa, 63; Venice, 104 (see also Cathedrals)
Campin, Robert, 156, 326(F-2)
Campo Santo, 119
Cana, Marriage at, Veronese, 151
Canaletto, 153, 325(E-5)
Canon and Saints, G. David, 159
Canon van der Paele, Van Eyck, 156
Canova, Antonio, 205
Canterbury, 70: Cathedral, 85, 86
Cantoria (see Singing Gallery)
Capen House, Topsfield, Mass., 251
Capitals: Corinthian, 21; Egyptian, 6, 10; Gondi Palace, 99; Ionic, 20; Persian, 13; Reims Cathedral, 78; St. Mark's, Venice, 56; San Vitale, 57; tobacco, 260 (see also Orders)
Capitols: Baton Rouge, La., 263; Lincoln, Neb., 268; Richmond, Va., 262; Washington, D.C., 260, 261; Williamsburg, Va., 256
Capra (Villa Rotonda), 103
Captive Charger, Wimar, 292
Capua, Aphrodite, 40
Caracalla, 50
Caravaggio, 151, 152, 325(E-6), 326(F-4)
Carcassonne: Château, The, 83
Card Players: Cézanne, 236; de Hooch, 179

Carlos IV, Family of, Goya, 174
Carlos IV, Wife of, Goya, 175
Carlyle, Thomas, Whistler, 298
Carnival of Harlequin, Miró, 246
Carpaccio, Vittore, 145, 146, 325(E-5)
Carpeaux, Jean Baptiste, 206
Carracci, Ludovico, 152, 325(E-6)
Carrey, Jacques, 31
Carriage at the Races, Degas, 231
Carroll, John, 306
Carrousel Rooster, Brown, 293
Carson Pirie Scott Building, Chicago, 267
Carson House, Eureka, Cal., 264
Caryatid Porch, 34
Casket, ivory, 84
Cassatt, Mary, 301, 327(G-3)
Cassone, 153
Cast iron construction, 266
Castagno, Andrea del, 125, 325(E-2)
Castel San Angelo, 47
Castor and Pollux, Temple of, 42
Catalonia, 71
Cathedrals: Aix-la-Chapelle, 56, 89; Albi, 82; Amiens, 79; Angoulême, 67; Autun, 68; Beauvais, 80; Burgos, 90; Canterbury, 85, 86; Chartres, 74–76, 84; Cologne, 89; Durham, 70, 85; Ely, 70, 86; Exeter, 87; Florence, 93; Freiberg, 89; Gloucester, 87, 88; Lincoln, 86; London, 184, 185; Lucca, 108; Mainz, 72; Mexico City, 249; Milan, 95; Modena, 62; Monreale, 61, 64, 65; Orvieto, 92, 93, 97, 135, 136; Paris, 74, 76–77; Parma, 63; Pisa, 63; Puebla, 249; Reims, 77, 78; Rouen, 81; Salisbury, 86, 87; Santiago, 71; Seville, 90; Siena, 92, 96; Speyer, 72; Toledo, 90; Wells, 85, 86; Worms, 72 (see also St.; San, Santa)
Catlin, George, 292
Cattle, Egyptian, 4
Cavalier, Meissonier, 224
Cavalier and Girl Drinking Wine, Vermeer, 179
Cavallini, Pietro, 325(E-3)
Ceiling, Adam style, 199
Cellini, Benvenuto, 116, 324
Celtic art, 70
Cenci, Beatrice, Reni, 152
Centaur, Bourdelle, 312
Centaur Biting a Boy, 29
Centaur and Lapith, 29, 31
Centaur, Lapith Conquering a, 31
Centaur, Pirithous Rescuing Ippotamia from the, 51
Center Congregational Church, New Haven, Conn., 258
Central Italian painting, 325(E-3)
Century of Progress Exposition, Chicago, 271
Ceramicus, Athens, 38
Ceres, Storrs, 315
Certosa of Pavia, 114
Cézanne, Paul, 235, 236
Chagall, Marc, 244
Chairs: Adam, 199; Chippendale, 198; Egyptian, 9; Empire, 196; German, 73; Gothic, 85; Henry II, 227; Hepplewhite, 199; Italian, 154; Jacobean, 196; Louis XIV, 195, 227; Louis XV, XVI, 195; Norwegian, 73; Phyfe, 199; Queen Anne, 197; Sheraton, 198; Stuart, 196, 197
Chalgrin, J. F., 203
Chambord, Château, 200, 201
Chapel of Henry VII, Westminster Abbey, 88
Chapu, Henri, 206
Chardin, J. B., 215, 216, 327(G-1); Self portrait, 215
Chares, 25
Chariot Scene, Knossus, 15

Charioteer of Delphi, 30
Charity, Sarto, 134
Charlemagne, 322
Charles I, Van Dyck, 164
Charles I, Children of, Van Dyck, 163
Charleston, S.C., 256
Charlotte du Val D'Ognes, Mlle., Charpentier, 218
Charlottesville, Va., 261, 262
Charpentier, Constance, 218
Charpentier, Mme., and Her Children, Renoir, 233
Chartres Cathedral, 74–76, 84
Chase, W. M., 327(G-3)
Châteaux: Azay-le-Rideau, 200; Blois, 201; Carcassonne, 83; Chambord, 200, 201; Chaumont, 200; Chenonceaux, 200
Chaumont, Château, 200
Chavannes, Puvis de, 225, 226, 327(G-1)
Chemnitz, Germany, 209
Chenonceaux, Château, 200
Cherubini, Ingres, 219
Cheseman, Robert, Holbein, 170
Chest: Stuart, 197; Venetian, 154
Chez Mouquin, Glackens, 301
Chicago Circle campus, University of Illinois, 275
Chicago, Ill., 265–269, 271, 275, 277, 278, 281, 311, 315
Child and Cat, Zorach, 314
Child and Nurse, Hals, 176
Chinese Chippendale, 198
Chinese periods, 321–323
Chippendale furniture, 198, 328
Chirico, Giorgio de, 245
Choir, Chartres, 74
Choir stalls, Italian, 154
Choragic Monument of Lysicrates, Athens, 22
Chou Dynasty, 321
Christ, 73: Amiens, 79; G. David, 159; Leonardo, 133; Michelangelo, 141; Veronese, 151
Christ, Agony in the Garden, Giovanni Bellini, 145; Cranach, 168; Mantegna, 143; Zurbarán, 173
Christ of Apocalypse, 75
Christ, Baptism of, Verrocchio, 132
Christ Before Pilate, Ghiberti, 107
Christ Blessing Romanus IV, 60
Christ Borne by St. Christopher, 166
Christ, Crucifixion of, 65: Blume, 306; El Greco, 171; Grünewald, 167; Italian School, 117; Perugino, 137; Pisano, 96; Rubens, 161, 162; Tintoretto, 150
Christ Delivering the Keys to St. Peter, Perugino, 136
Christ, Deposition of: Van der Weyden, 156; Van der Goes, 158; Duccio, 117
Christ Driving the Money Changers from the Temple: El Greco, 171; Ghiberti, 107
Christ Entering Jerusalem, 61
Christ Enthroned, Orcagna, 122
Christ, Entombment of: Caravaggio, 152; Michelangelo, 141
Christ, Flagellation of: Duccio, 117; Ghiberti, 107
Christ Healing the Sick, Rembrandt, 178
Christ, Miracles of, 57
Christ Mocked by Soldiers, Rouault, 241
Christ, Mocking of, Bosch, 160
Christ, Nativity of, 59: Schongauer, 166
Christ, Presentation in the Temple, 59: Carpaccio, 146; Mantegna, 142
Christ and Peter on the Water, Ghiberti, 107
Christ, Resurrection of: El Greco, 171; Signorelli, 136
Christ, Supper at Emmaus, Rembrandt, 178
Christ with the Cross, El Greco, 171

Christ, with the Infant St. John, Rubens, 162
Christ (see also Flight into Egypt; Last Supper; Madonna and Child; Virgin)
Christus, Petrus, 157, 326(F-2)
Church Fathers, Signorelli, 135
Church, Frederick, 327(G-3)
Church Militant and Triumphant, Bonaiuti, 122
Church at Old Lyme, Hassam, 301
Churches: Acworth, N.H., 252; Bennington, Vt., 257; Boston, Mass., 252, 257, 266; Charleston, S.C., 256; Columbus, Ind., 272; Fitzwilliam, N.H., 257; Lancaster, Mass., 257; New Haven, Conn., 258; New York City, 263; Philadelphia, Pa., 254; Williamsburg, Va., 255 (see also Basilica; Cathedral; St.; San; Santa)
Cigar Store Indian, 292
Cimabue, 119, 325(E-2)
Cincinnati, Ohio, 263
Circus, The, Seurat, 234
Circus Girls, Two Little, Renoir, 233
Circus Maximus, 45
City, The, Léger, 240
City Hall, New York, 259
Civic Virtue, Macmonnies, 280
Civitale, Matteo, 324
Claude Lorrain, 213, 326(F-1), 327(G-2)
Claus de Werve, 83
Clay, Henry, Browere, 279
Clock Tower, Evreaux, Bonington, 192
Clodion, 205
Cloisonné Medallion, 73
Cloisters: Monreale, 64; Mont St. Michel, 81; St. Paul's Outside the Walls, 64
Closed Eyes, The, Redon, 232
Clouet, François, 212, 326(F-1)
Clouet, Jean, 211, 212, 326(F-1)
Clown, The, Tschacbasov, 247
Cnidos, Venus of, 36
Cock and Glove, Knaths, 305
Cock Fight, Gérôme, 221
Codex: Ecternach, 72; Egberti, 73
Coello, Sánchez, 171, 326(F-4)
Coffee Shop, Longhi, 153
Coffer, Byzantine, 59
Cole, Thomas, 291, 327(G-3)
Cole, Thomas, Durand, 291
Cole, Timothy, 162, 320
Collection of Things, Koppe, 306
Colleoni, Verrocchio, 113
Cologne: Cathedral, 89; factory, 209
Colorado Springs, Colo., 275
Colossi: of Memnon, 7; of Ramses II, 7
Colosseum, Rome, 45
Colosseum, View of, Corot, 224
Columbaria, 47
Columbia Broadcasting Studios, Hollywood, Cal., 273
Columbus, Indiana, 272
Column, Gabo, 317
Column of Trajan, 49
Comb, Egyptian, 9
Combat of Perseus and Phineus . . . , Picasso, 239
Competition panel, North Baptistry Doors, Florence, 107
Compiègne, House at, 83
Composition, Lipchitz, 316
Compton Wynates, 88
Concert, The: Giorgione, 147; Terborch, 180
Concord, Temple of, 42
Condé, Princesse de, Nattier, 216
Condottière, Il, Antonello da Messina, 143
Connecticut: Farmington, 251; New Haven, 258, 276
Constable, John, 192, 327(G-1,2)
Constantine: Arch of, 46, 49; Basilica of, 45

Constantinople, 55
Construction: Moholy-Nagy, 317; Picasso, 311
Consular diptychs, 58
Convent of La Merced, Mexico City, 250
Cook, The, Chardin, 216
Cooper, The, Millet, 222
Cophetua, King, and the Beggar Maid, Burne-Jones, 193
Copley, John Singleton, 285, 327(G-3)
Corbel arch, Tiryns, 14
Corbett, H. W., 268
Córdova, Mosque, 91
Corinth, Temple at, 16, 17
Corinthian capital, 21, 43
Corinthian order: Greek, 16; Choragic Monument, 22
Corner of the Kitchen Table, Chardin, 215
"Corner" Palace, Venice, 105
Cornfield, Constable, 192
Cornices: Temple of Vespasian, 42; Strozzi Palace, 99
Coronation (see *Virgin*)
Coronation of Napoleon and Josephine, David, 218
Corot, J. B. C., 223, 224, 327(G-1)
Corpus Christi Procession, Gentile Bellini, 144
Correggio, Antonio, 148, 149, 325(E-4), 326(F-4), 327(G-1)
Cosimo, Piero di, 132, 325(E-2)
Cosmati work, 65
Cossa, Francesco, 143, 325(E-4)
Costa, Lorenzo, 325(E-4)
Cotman, John Sell, 327(G-2)
Couple, Grosz, 244
Courbet, Gustave, 225, 327(G-1)
Courts: Palace of Sargon, 12; of the Lions, 91
Courtyard of a Dutch House, de Hooch, 179
Coustou, Guillaume, 205
Couture, Thomas, 327(G-1)
Cove, The, Marin, 304
Coysevox, Antoine, 204, 205; *Self portrait,* 204
Craigie House, Cambridge, Mass., 252
Cranach, Lucas, the Elder, 168, 169, 326(F-3)
Cranbrook Academy of Art, Bloomfield Hills, Mich., 272
Creation (see *Adam*)
Credence, 85
Credi, Lorenzo di, 132, 325(E-2)
Crispin and Scapin, Daumier, 227
Critius, 29
Crivelli, Carlo, 142, 325(E-5)
Crome, John, 327(G-2)
Cronaca, Il, 99
Cross, Story of the True, A. Gaddi, 122 (see also *Christ, Crucifixion*)
Crosses: Celtic, 70; Gertrudis, 73
Crown Hall, Illinois Institute of Technology, Chicago, 278
Crozier, 85
Crucifixion (see *Christ*)
Crypt, 80
Crystal Palace, London, 207
Cumaean Sibyl, Michelangelo, 140
Cup, Rospigliosi, Cellini, 116
Cupbearer, Knossus, 15
Cupboard, English, 88
Cupid Riding a Crab, 51 (see also *Amorino*)
Cupola (see Cathedrals; St. Peter's, Rome)
Cups, gold, 15
Curfew, Rauschenberg, 309
Currie, Mrs. Mark, Romney, 190
Curry, John Steuart, 302
Customs House, N.Y.C., 259
Cypresses, Van Gogh, 236
Cypriote stele, 17
Cyrene, Aphrodite of, 36

Cythera, Watteau, 214

Dagobert, Throne of, 73
Dali, Salvador, 244, 245
Dallin, Cyrus, 282
Damned, The, Signorelli, 136
Dance, The: Carpeaux, 206; Laurens, 315; Matisse, 242
Dancer, The, Renoir, 234
Dancer and Gazelles, Manship, 283
Dante, Giotto, 120
Dante and Virgil in Hell, Delacroix, 222
Daphne (see *Apollo*)
Darius, King, Archers of, 12
Darius, Tomb of, 13
Daumier, Honoré, 226, 227, 327(G-1)
David: Donatello, 109; Michelangelo, 114; Verrocchio, 113
David, Triumph of, Poussin, 212
David, Gheeraert, 159, 326(F-2)
David, J. L., 218, 219, 327(G-1)
Davies, Arthur B., 300, 327(G-3)
Davis, A. J., 259, 263
Davis, Stuart, 305
Dawn, Michelangelo, 115
Day, Michelangelo, 115
Day of the God, Gauguin, 237
Daylight Saving, Roy, 246
Dead Man Restored to Life . . . , Allston, 289
Dean Berkeley and His Entourage, Smibert, 284
Death on a Pale Horse, Ryder, 297
Death Staying the Hand of the Sculptor, D. C. French, 281
Deer in Forest, Courbet, 225
Deer in Wood, Courbet, 225
Deere Implement Company, Moline, Ill., 275
Degas, Edgar, 230, 231, 312, 320
De Hooch, Pieter, 179, 326(F-5)
Deir el-Bahri, Temple at, 5
De Kooning, William, 311
Delacroix, Eugène, 221, 222, 327(G-1); *Self portrait,* 221
Delaroche, Paul, 327(G-1)
Della Robbia, Andrea, 110, 111, 324
Della Robbia, Luca, 110, 111, 324
Delos, Artemis of, 25
Delos, Temple of, 16
Delos, Winged Figure from, 25
Delphi, Treasuries at, 17, 27
Delphic Sibyl, Michelangelo, 141
Demeter, 32, 34
Demeter: Precinct of Eleusis, 21; Temple of, Paestum, 17
Demoiselles d'Avignon, Picasso, 238
Demosthenes, 41
Dempsey and Firpo, Bellows, 300
Demuth, Charles, 303, 304
Denderah, Temple of, capital from, 6
Deposition (see *Christ*)
Derain, André, 241
Derby at Epsom, Géricault, 221
Derby House, Salem, Mass., 258
Dermys, 25
Desiderio da Settignano, 111, 112, 324
Desk: American, 198; Louis XVI, 196
Despiau, Charles, 312
Dessau, Germany, 209
Destruction of the Empire, Thomas Cole, 291
Detroit, Mich., 248
Developable Column, Pevsner, 316
Development of Art, 321–328
D'Evereaux Plantation, Natchez, Miss., 263
Devil, 61
Dewey, John, Epstein, 314
Dexileos, Grave Relief, 38
Diadoumenos, Polyclitus, 34

Diana: Goujon, 204; Jacopo da Barbari, 144; Macmonnies, 280; Manship, 283; Nattier, 216; Saint-Gaudens, 282
Diana, Baths of, 43
Diana, Return of, from the Hunt, Rubens, 162
Diane de Poitiers as Diana, Goujon, 204
Diane de Poitiers, house of, Rouen, 200
Diaz de la Peña, 327(G-1)
Dickinson, Preston, 303
Dido Building Carthage, Turner, 190
Dido Directing Equipment, Turner, 190
Diebenkorn, Richard, 311
Dijon, 83
Dinner Under the Trees, Manet, 228
Diocletian, Baths of, 44
Dionysius the Carthusian, Christus, 157
Dionysus, 24, 32, 35
Diptych, 58, 84: of Martin van Nieuwenhoven, Memlinc, 157
Dipylon Cemetery, amphora from, 23
Directoire furniture, 328
Discobolus, Myron, 35
Dispute of the Sacrament, Raphael, 139
District of Columbia (see Washington, D.C.)
Dix, Otto, 244
Dr. Faust in His Study, Rembrandt, 178
Dr. Meyer-Hermann, Dix, 244
Dr. Tulp's Anatomy Lesson, Rembrandt, 177
Dog Barking at the Moon, Miró, 246
Dolphin, Boy with a, 48
Dolphins, Knossus, 15
Domenichino, 325(E-6), 326(F-1)
Donatello, 109, 110, 112, 324, 325(E-2,4)
Doni, Maddalena, Raphael, 137
Don't Fall, Rivers, 309
Doors: Hildesheim, 73; Monreale, Pisa, 65 (see also Bronze doors)
Doric Order, Greek, 16, 17
Dormeyer Mixer, Oldenberg, 318
Doryphorus, Polyclitus school, 35
Dou, Gerard, 178, 326(F-5)
Doughty, Thomas, 291, 327(G-3)
Doves, mosaic, 52
Dream, The, H. Rousseau, 235
Dresden, Germany, 165
Drinkers, The, Daumier, 226
Drive, Noland, 309
Drowne, Shem, 293
Duc de Berri, manuscript of, 85
Ducal Palace, Venice, 95, 104, 105
Duccio, 117, 119, 325(E-1)
Duchamp, Marcel, 240
Duchamp-Villon, Raymond, 313, 315
Duchess of Suffolk, Holbein, 169
Dudok, Willem, 208
Duke of Norfolk, Titian, 148
Dulles International Airport, Chantilly, Va., 275
Durand, Asher B., 291, 327(G-3)
Dürer, Albrecht, 167, 168, 320, 325(E-5); *Self portrait,* 167
Durham Cathedral, 70, 85
Dutch: architecture, 208, 210; painting, 176–183, 235–238, 326(F-5)
Dutch Fishing Boats, Turner, 191
Dutch Interior, de Hooch, 179
Dutch Joe, Henri, 300
Dutch Port, Van de Velde, 183
Duveneck, Frank, 299, 327(G-3)
Dyck (see Van Dyck)
Dyckman House, N.Y.C., 254
Dying Gaul, 39

Eagle, Rush, 279
Eagle-Headed Winged Being, 11
Eakins, Thomas, 296, 297, 327(G-3)
Earl, Ralph, 284
Earl's Barton, 69

Early Christian: architecture, 53, 54; period, 322–323; sculpture, 57
Easel, The, Motherwell, 307
Eaton Hall, Cheshire, 186
Echaurren, Roberto Matta, 246
Echternach codex, 72
Edfu, Temple of Horus, 6, 10
Edgard, La., 263
Egberti codex, 73
Egg and dart motif, 20
Egyptian: architecture, 2, 3, 5–7, 10, 272; art, 2–10, 321, 322; painting, 8, 9, 52; sculpture, 2–5, 7–10
Eiffel, Gustave, 207
Eiffel Tower, 207
Einstein Tower, Potsdam, 209
Eirene and Ploutos, Kephisodotus, 37
Elderly Gentleman Smoking a Long Pipe, Bingham, 295
Eleanor, Jean and Anna, Bellows, 300
Electra, 41
Electrical Building, Chicago, 271
Electrification of the Country, Roy, 245
Eleusis, Precinct of Demeter at, 21
El Greco, 171, 172, 326(F-4)
Elizabethan furniture, 196, 328
Elmes, H. L., 186
Ely Cathedral, 70, 86
Embarkation for Cythera, Watteau, 214
Empire furniture, 196, 328
Empire State Building, N.Y.C., 271
English: architecture, 69–71, 85–88, 184–186, 207; furniture, 88, 196–199; painting, 187–194, 327; sculpture, 312–315, 317, 319
Engraving, 102, 103, 127, 141, 143, 144, 166, 168, 191, 212, 213, 320
Entombment (see *Christ*)
Ephesus, drum from, 37
Epictetus, 23
Epidaurus, theatre, 21
Epstein, Jacob, 314, 319
Erasmo da Narni, 110
Erasmus: Dürer, 168; Holbein, 169
Erechtheum, 19, 20, 34
Ergotimus, 23
Eriphyle, 24
Ernst, Max, 316
Erythraean Sibyl, Michelangelo, 140
Esneh, capitals from, 10
Etching, 164, 175, 177, 178, 187, 194, 238, 243, 298, 320
Ethnography, Siqueiros, 248
Etruscan art, 321, 323
Eudosia, Empress, 58, 60
Euphronius, 25
Eureka, Cal., 264
Europa and the Bull, Milles, 313
Europa, Rape of, Veronese, 150
Eve, Rodin, 206
Eve, Creation of, Quercia, 109 (see also *Adam*)
Evergood, Philip, 311
Evergreen Plantation, Edgard, La., 263
Evreux, Clock Tower of, Bonington, 192
Executioner, Large, Prince Rupert, 170
Exeter Cathedral, 87
Expositions: Barcelona, 210; Chicago, 265, 267, 271; Cologne, 209; London, 207
Expulsion (see *Adam*)
Eyck (see Van Eyck)
Ezekiel, Michelangelo, 140

Fabri de Peyrese, Mellan, 213
Fabriano, Gentile da, 135, 325(E-3)
Fabritius, Carel, 178, 326(F-5)
Factories: Alfeld-an-der-Leine, 209; Cologne, 209
Fall of Man, Quercia, 108 (see also *Adam and Eve*)

Falling Gladiator, Rimmer, 280
Falling Water, Bear Run, Pa., 270
Family, The, Zorach, 319
Family Group, Johnson, 294
Faneuil Hall, Boston, Mass., 258
Farmington, Conn., 251
Farnese: *Athena,* 33; *Bull,* 41; *Hercules,* Glycon, 36
Farnese, Alessandro, Moro, 160
Farnese Palace, Rome, 101
Farragut Monument, Saint-Gaudens, 282
Fates, Three, Phidias, 31
Faun, 35
Faun, Dancing, 48
Feast in the House of Levi, Veronese, 151
Feast of Pure Reason, Levine, 247
Federal Hall, N.Y.C., 254
Federigo da Montefeltro, Piero della Francesco, 128
Feininger, Lyonel, 304
Feke, Robert, 284
Fernando Niño de Guevara, El Greco, 171
Ferriss, Hugh, 268
Festival of Roses, tapestry, 84
Fiddler, The, Chagall, 244
Field, Erastus, 294
Figure 5, The, Indiana, 310
Figure in a Red Chair, Picasso, 239
Filippo Lippi Fra (see Lippi)
Filippino Lippi (see Lippi)
Fiorenzo di Lorenzo, 128, 325 (E-3)
Fire in the Borgo, Raphael, 139
Fire Wheel, The, Whistler, 298
First Church, Lancaster, Mass., 257
Fisherman, Old, 41
Fisherman's Family, The, Puvis de Chavannes, 226
#5, Pollock, 308
Flagellation (see *Christ*)
Flat Torso, Archipenko, 314
Flemish: architecture, 82; painting, 155–165, 326; tapestry, 84
Flight into Egypt: Cranach, 168; Fra Angelico, 123; Giotto, 120
Flight of Night, W. M. Hunt, 299
Flora, Nattier, 217.
Florence, The Arno in, Canaletto, 153
Florence, Italy: Baptistry, 64, 65, 97, 107, 108; Campanile, 93, 97, 109; Cathedral, 93; Foundling's Hospital, 98, 111; Gondi Palace, 99; Medici-Riccardi Palace, 98, 126; Or San Michele, 97; Palazzo Vecchio, 94, 100; Pazzi Chapel, 98; Pitti Palace, 100; Quaratesi Palace, 100; Rucellai Palace, 100; San Lorenzo, 98, 115; San Marco, 122, 123; San Miniato, 63, 64, 65; Santa Croce, 109, 111, 121, 122; Santa Maria del Carmine, 123, 124, 131; Santa Maria Maddalena dei Pazzi, 137; Santa Maria Novella, 93, 100, 122; Santo Spirito, 98; Strozzi Palace, 99; Uffizi, 94 (see also Italian: architecture; painting; sculpture)
Florentine painting, 325(E-2)
Flower Girl, Murillo, 174
Flower Vendor, Rivera, 248
Flute Soloist, Weber, 305, 306
Flying Buttresses (see Buttresses)
Folk art, American, 292, 293
Font-de-Gaume cave, 1
Fontana, Giovanni, 106
Foolish Virgin, Schongauer, 166
Ford Foundation Building, N.Y.C., 277
Forli, Melozzo da, 135, 325(E-3)
Fort Frank, 271
Fortuna Augustus, Temple of, 43
Fortuna Virilis, Temple of, 44
Forty-Two Kids, Bellows, 300
Forum Romanum, 42, 43
Foundling, Andrea della Robbia, 111
Foundling's Hospital, Florence, 98, 111
Fountain of the Innocents, Paris, 204

Fountains: Paolo, Rome, 106; Trevi, Rome, 106; Orpheus, Stockholm, 313
Fouquet, Jean, 211, 326(F-1)
Fourment, Helena, and Children, Rubens, 162
Fourment, Suzanne, Rubens, 162
Fourth century Greek sculpture, 35–38
Foyer de la Danse . . . , Degas, 231
Fra Angelico, 122, 123, 325(E-2)
Fra Bartolommeo, 133, 325(E-2)
Fra Filippo Lippi (see Lippi)
Fragonard, Jean-Honoré, 217, 327(G-1)
Francesca, Piero della, 128, 325(E-3)
Francis, Sam, 310
Francis I, J. Clouet, 211, 212
Francis I: furniture, 328; saltcellar of, Cellini, 116
François, Dauphin of France, J. Clouet. 211
François vase, 23
Frankish art, 73
Franklin, Benjamin: Houdon, 206; C. W. Peale, 288
Frari, Church of the, woodcarving, 95
Frauenkirche, Nuremberg, 89
Freiberg, Cathedral of, door, 89
French: architecture, 66–69, 74–83, 200–204, 207–208, 210, 278; furniture, 84, 85, 195, 196, 227; painting, 211–242, 246, 326, 327; sculpture, 67, 68, 75–79, 83, 204–206, 312–316
French, Daniel Chester, 281
Fresco, 14, 15, 51, 52, 71 (see Florentine painting; individual artists)
Freyssinet, Eugene, 208
Friedlander, Leo, 312, 313
Frieze: Erechtheum, 20, Mausoleum, Halicarnassus, 37; Parthenon, 32, 33; Pergamon, 39; Treasury of Siphnians, 27; Youths, 27
Fronfroneur, The, Priebe, 247
Frugal Repast, Picasso, 238
Fruit Dish, Glass, and Newspaper, Gris, 241
Fuga, Ferdinando, 106
Fujiwara period, 322
Fuller, Buckminster, 274
Fulton, Robert, 327(G-3)
Functionalism, 323
Fur-Lined Tea Cup, Oppenheim, 316
Furniture: American, 196–199; English, 88, 196–199; French, 84, 85, 195–196, 227; styles, 328
Future, The, Evergood, 311

Gabii, Artemis of, 36
Gabo, Naum, 316, 317
Gaddi, Agnolo, 122, 325(E-2)
Gaddi, Taddeo, 121, 325(E-2)
Gainsborough, Sir Thomas, 188, 189, 327(G-2)
Galilee, The, Durham, 70
Galilei, Alessandro, 106
Galla Placidia, Tomb of, 54
Gallo, Frank, 311
Galloway, Mrs. Richard, Jr., J. Hesselius, 285
Gamley, Mrs., Luks, 301
Ganster, W. A., 273
Garches, France, 210
Gardella, I., and Martini, L., architects, 272
Gardner-White-Pingree House, Salem, Mass., 258
Gargoyle, 77
Garnier, Charles, 204
Garrick and His Wife, Hogarth, 187
Gates of Paradise (see Florence, Baptistry)
Gateway Arch, St. Louis, Mo., 276
Gateway of Palace of Sargon II, 12

Gattamelata, Donatello, 110
Gauguin, Paul, 237, 238
Gaul, Dying, 39
Gaul and His Wife, 39
Gazelles and Ostriches, Egyptian, 2
Generator Hall, Savannah, Tenn., 272
Gentile da Fabriano, 135, 325(E-3)
Geodesic dome house, 274
Georgian furniture, 197
Gérard, François, 220
Géricault, Théodore, 221, 327(G-1)
German: architecture, 72, 89, 165, 166,
     209, 270; painting, 166–170, 242–244,
     326; sculpture, 166, 312, 313, 316
German Pavilion, Barcelona, 210
Germiny-les-Prés, 66
Gérôme, Jean Léon, 221, 327(G-1)
Gertrudis: Altar, 72; Cross, 73
Gesù, Church of the, Rome, 106
Gethsemane (see *Christ, Agony in the
     Garden*)
Ghent, Altarpiece, Van Eyck, 155
Ghiberti, Lorenzo, 107, 324
Ghirlandaio, Domenico, 128, 129,
     325(E-2)
Giacometti, Alberto, 317
Giacomo della Porta, 102, 106
Gibbes House, Charleston, S.C., 256
Gibbs, James, 185
Gibbs-Channing-Avery Portrait, Stuart,
     286
Gilbert, Cass, 268
Gill, Eric, 321
Gilles, Watteau, 214
Giorgione, 146, 147, 325(E-5)
Giotto, 93, 119–121, 324, 325(E-2)
Giovanni da Bologna, 116, 324
Giralda, Seville, 60
Girl Before a Mirror, Picasso, 239
Girl Looking at a Fishbowl, Matisse, 242
Girl, Portrait of a, Hals, 176
Girl Reading, Renoir, 233
Girls at the Piano, Renoir, 233
Girls Throwing Flowers, Hofer, 243
Girls, Two, Laurencin, 232
Gisze, George, Holbein, 169
Giuliano da Sangallo, 99
Gizeh, 2, 3
Glackens, William, 301
Gladiator, Falling, Rimmer, 280
Glass, stained, 84
Gleaners, The, Millet, 223
Glebe Farm, Constable, 192
Glessner House, Chicago, 266
Glorification of Beauty, Archipenko, 314
Glorious Victory of the Sloop Maria,
     Feininger, 304
Gloucester Cathedral, 87, 88
Glycon, 36
Gocar, Josef, 210
God Hovering over the Waters, Michel-
     angelo, 140
Goddess, Model of, Egyptian, 9, 10
Goddess, Snake, 16
Godley, Wynne, Head of, Epstein, 319
Goes, Hugo van der, 158, 326(F-2)
Goldberg, Bertrand, Associates, archi-
     tects, 278
Golden Age of Aztec Civilization, Orozco,
     248
Golden Age, Greek, 18–21, 31–35, 321
Golden door, Freiberg Cathedral, 89
Golden Hawk, Rozak, 318
Golden Stairs, Burne-Jones, 193
Golden Wedding, Ostade, 183
Gondi Palace, Florence, 99
Gonzaga, Eleanora, Titian, 148
Good Government, Allegory of, A. Loren-
     zetti, 118
Good Shepherd, 57, 60
Goodhue, Bertram, 268
Goodwin, P. L., 272
Goose, Boy with a, 38

Gorgon, 26
Gossaert, Jan, 159, 326(F-2)
Gothenburg, Sweden, 313
Gothic: architecture, 74–95; period, 322–
     323
Gothic Chippendale, 198
Gottlieb, Adolph, 247
Goujon, Jean, 202, 204
Goya, Francisco, 174–175, 327(G-1); *Self
     portrait,* 174
Gozzoli, Benozzo, 126, 127, 325(E-2);
     Self portrait, 126
Grace Church, N.Y.C., 263
Graces, Three, 52, 150
Graham, Bruce, 277
Graham, Mrs., Gainsborough, 189
Granada: Alhambra, 91; Palace of
     Charles V, 170
Granville, Ohio, 263
Graves, Morris, 308
Great Lakes, Ill., 273
Greek: architecture, 16–22; sculpture, 25–
     41; vases, 22–25
Greek Slave, Powers, 279
Greeks and Amazons, Battle of, 24, 37
Greenough, Horatio, 280
Greuze, Jean Baptiste, 217, 327(G-1)
Grimani Palace, Venice, 105
Gris, Juan, 241
Gropius, Walter, 209, 271
Gropper, William, 306
Gros, Antoine Jean, 220, 327(G-1)
Gross Clinic, Eakins, 296
Grosz, George, 244
Grotesque, Paris Cathedral, 77
Grünewald, Matthias, 167, 326(F-3)
Guard, The, Fabritius, 178
Guardi, Francesco, 153, 325(E-5)
Guardian, Graves, 308
Gudea Head, 11
Guercino, 325(E-6)
Guernica, Picasso, 239
Guggenheim Museum, N.Y.C., 276
Guglielmi, Louis, 245
Guidoriccio da Foligno, Martini, 118
Guilderland, N.Y., 264
Guillaume Jouvenal des Ursins, J. Fou-
     quet, 211
Guitar Player, Picasso, 238
Gulf Reston, Va., 277
Gupta, 322
Guston, Philip, 306, 309

Hadrian: Tomb of, 47; Villa, mosaic of,
     52
Hagar, Lipchitz, 319
Hagar in the Desert, Ghiberti, 108
Hagia Triada: sarcophagus from, 151;
     vase from, 16
Hale, Nathan, Macmonnies, 280
Halicarnassus, Mausoleum, 21, 37
Hall: of Chevaliers, Mont St. Michel, 80,
     81; of Mirrors, Versailles, 201; of the
     Two Sisters, Alhambra, 91
Hals, Frans, 176, 326(F-5)
Hamilton, Lady, Romney, 189
Hammond-Harwood House, Annapolis,
     Md., 255
Hampton Court, 184
Han period, 321, 322
Hancock House, Boston, 253
Hancock, John, Copley, 285
Hancock (John) Center, Chicago, 277
Handball, Shahn, 305
Hangar, Orly, France, 208
Harbaville triptych, 59
Hare, Young, Dürer, 168
Harem Court, of Palace of Sargon, 12
Harlequin, Picasso, 239
Harmodius, 29
Harnett, William, 293

Harp of the Winds, Martin, **299**
Harris and Abramowitz, architects, **276**
Harrisburg, Pa., 281
Harrison, Peter, 252, 254
Harrison, W. K., 274
Hartley, Marsden, 305
Harvesters, Bruegel, 160
Hassam, Childe, 301, 327(G-3)
Hatfield, Mass., 252
Hathor capital, 6
Hatshepsut, Queen, Temple of, 5
Haussonville, Comtesse d', Ingres, 219
Hawkwood, Sir John, Uccello, 125
Ha-won-je-tah, Catlin, 292
Haystacks in Snow, Monet, 229
Head: Belling, 316; Gabo, 316; Picasso,
     315
Hegeso, Grave relief of, 38
Heir, Guston, 309
Helen, David, 219
Hellenistic: art, 321; period, 21, 22, 38–
     41
Hellenistic Ruler, 48
Helsingfors, Finland, 270
Henri, Robert, 300, 327(G-3)
Henriette, Mme., Nattier, 217
Henry II of France, F. Clouet, 212
Henry II, furniture, 227, 328
Henry IV, furniture, 328
Henry VII, Chapel, 88
Henry VIII, Holbein, 169
Hepplewhite furniture, 199, 328
Hera of Samos, 25
Heraeum, The, Olympia, 17
Herculaneum: painting from, 51; Thea-
     tre, 46
Hercules, 23–25, 28
Hercules and an Amazon, 28
Hercules and Antaeus: Euphronius, 25;
     Pollaiuolo, 113, 127
Hercules Discovers His Son Telephos, 51
Hercules, Farnese, Glycon, 36
Hercules and the Hydra, Pollaiuolo, 127
Hercules with the Serpents, 52
Hermes of Andros, 36
Hermes with the Infant Dionysus, Praxit-
     eles, 35
Hermes in Repose, 41
Herod, 59
Herod, Feast of, Masolino, 124
Herring Net, Homer, 296
Herring Woman, Ostade, 182
Hesire, Panel of, 4
Hesselius, Gustavus, 284, 291; *Self por-
     trait,* 284
Hesselius, John, 285
High Yaller, Marsh, 302
Highboy, Georgian, 197
Hildesheim: Cathedral doors, 73; Knoch-
     enhaueramthaus, 89
Hilversum, Neth., 208
Hindu Pose, Matisse, 242
Hippodameia, 24
*Historical Monument of the American
     Republic,* Field, 294
Hoadley, David, 258
Hoban, James, 261
Hobbema, Meindert, 182, 183, 326(F-5),
     327(G-2)
Hofer, Karl, 243
Hoffmann, Josef, 208
Hofmann, Hans, 308
Hogarth, William, 187, 327(G-2); *Self
     portrait,* 187
Holbein, Hans, the Younger, 169, 170,
     326(F-3)
Holfernes, Donatello, 110
Hollywood, Cal., 273
Holy Family: Mantegna, 143; Sarto, 134;
     Tiepolo, 153 (see also *Madonna*)
Holy Family of the Doni, Michelangelo,
     141
Holzschuher, Heironymus, Dürer, 167

Homer, Apotheosis of, Ingres, 219
Homer, Winslow, 295, 296, 327(G-3)
Homeric Age, 321
Homewood, Baltimore, Md., 260
Honeysuckle motif, 20
Hood, Raymond, 268, 271
Hook of Holland, 208
Hope, Watts, 193
Hopper, Edward, 307
Hoppner, John, 190, 327(G-2)
Horatii, Oath of the, J. L. David, 218
Horse, 1, 8, 13, 48: Duchamp-Villon, 315
Horse Tamers, Macmonnies, 280
Horsemen, Parthenon, 32
Horses of Marly, Coustou, 205
Horses, Red, Marc, 243
Horta, Victor, 207
Horus, Temple of, 6, 10
Hospital: of the Innocents, Florence, 111; of St. Mark, Venice, 104
Hôtel: de Cluny, Paris, 82, 83; de Ville, Brussels, 82; des Invalides, Paris, 203
Houdon, Jean Antoine, 205, 206
House of Representatives, Old, Morse, 290
Houses: Medieval, 82, 83, 89; Pompeii, 45 (see also Architecture)
Housewife, The, Chardin, 216
Houston, Samuel, as Marius, 292
Howard, Catherine, Holbein, 170
Hudson River Landscape, D. Smith, 318
Hudson River School, 327(G-3)
Hundred Guilder Print, Rembrandt, 178
Hungarian sculpture, 317
Hunt, Holman, 193, 327(G-2)
Hunt, R. M., 265
Hunt, W. M., 299, 327(G-3)
Hunters in the Snow, Bruegel, 161
Huntingfield Psalter, 71
Huntington, Anna Hyatt, 283
Hyksos Invasion, 321
Hypostyle Hall: Abydos, 6, 8; Karnak, 5

I and the Village, Chagall, 244
Ictinus, 18, 19
Iffley, 70
Ikhnaton, 7
Ilaria del Carretto, Tomb of, Quercia, 108
Ile de France, 69
Illinois: Chicago, 265–269, 271, 275, 277–278, 281, 311, 315; Great Lakes, 273; Moline, 275; Oak Park, 269; Urbana, 276, 283; Waukegan, 273
Illinois Institute of Technology, Chicago, 278
Imhof, Hans, Dürer, 167
Improvisation No. 30, Kandinsky, 243
Incan period, 322
Independence Hall, Philadelphia, Pa., 259
Indian, American, 282, 291, 292
Indian art, 321–323
Indiana, Columbus, 272
Indiana, Robert, 310
Individuals, Arp, 316
Industry, Dickinson, 303
Infanta, The, Velásquez, 172
Infanta Maria Theresa, Velásquez, 173
Inferno: Maitani, 97; Pisano, 96
Ingres, J. A. Dominique, 219, 220, 327 (G-1)
Inness, George, 299, 327(G-3)
Intoxication of Wine, Clodion, 205
Ionic order, Greek, 16
Ippotamia, 51
Irish art (see Celtic art)
Ironers, Degas, 230
Isaac, Sacrifice of: Brunelleschi, 107; Ghiberti, 108
Isabel Corbo de Porcel, Doña, Goya, 174
Isabel, Infanta, Coello, 171
Isis, Temple of, 10
Islamic art, 322, 323

Isotta da Rimini, Medal to, Pisanello, 114
Issus, Battle of, 50, 51
Istanbul, Santa Sophia, 55
Italian: architecture, 62–64, 92–95, 98–106; minor arts, 154; painting, 117–153, 245, 325; sculpture, 65, 96, 97, 107–116, 205, 315–317, 324
Ivory sculpture, 57–60

Jabach, Eberhard, and Family, C. LeBrun, 214
Jackie, Warhol, 309
Jackson, Andrew, Powers, 280
Jacobean furniture, 196, 328
Jacopo da Barbari, 144, 325(E-5)
Jacopo della Quercia (see Quercia)
Jacques Coeur, House of, Bourges, 82
James II, Van Dyck, 163
Japanese art, 322, 323
Japanese Fan, The, Monet, 229
Jealous Lover of Lone Green Valley, The, Benton, 303
Jefferson, Thomas, 261–262
Jefferson, Thomas: Browere, 279; Rembrandt Peale, 288
Jenkins, Paul, 310
Jeremiah, Michelangelo, 140
Jericho, 61
Jerusalem, Spoils of, 48
Jewish Burial Ground, Ruisdael, 181
Joan of Arc: Chapu, 206; A. H. Huntington, 283; Ingres, 220
Job, Book of, Blake, 191, 192
Joel, Michelangelo, 140
Jogan period, 322
John, Augustus, 327(G-2)
John the Baptist (see *St. John*)
John Hancock Center, Chicago, 277
Johns, Jasper, 308
Johnson, Eastman, 294
Johnson House, Cambridge, Mass., 273
Johnson, Philip, 273
Johnson, Samuel, Reynolds, 188
Johnson Wax Company Building, Racine, Wisc., 270
Jones House, Hatfield, Mass., 252
Jones, Inigo, 184
Jörg, Klee, 243
Josephine, Empress of the French, Prud'hon, 217
Joshua, 61
Judgment of Paris (see *Paris*)
Judith and Holfernes: Botticelli, 130; Donatello, 110
Julia, Basilica, 42
Julius, Divus, Temple of, 42
Julius II, Raphael, 138
Julius II, Tomb of, 115
Junius Bassus, Sarcophagus, 57
Juno Moneta, Temple of, 42
Jupiter Capitolinus, Temple of, 42, 43
Jupiter Olympus, Temple of, 22
Justus of Ghent, 157

Kamakura period, 322
Kamares style vase, 16
Kandinsky, Wassily, 243
Karfiol, Bernard, 302
Karnak: capital, 6; Temple of Amon, 5; Temple of Khons, 7
Kedleston Hall, 186
Kells, Book of, 70
Kennebunk, Me., 264
Kentucky Home, Old, Johnson, 293
Kephisodotus, 37
Kermess, Rubens, 163
Kheops, pyramid of, 2
Khepren, 3: pyramid of, 2
Khnûmhotep, tomb of, 5

Khons, Temple of, 7
Khorsabad, Palace at, 12, 13
Kindred Spirits . . . , Durand, 291
King Arthur, Vischer, 166
King David, Donatello, 109
King's Chapel, Boston, Mass., 252
Kings (see Sovereigns)
Kirby Hall, Northants, Eng., 184
Kirchner, Ernst, 242
Kiss, The, Rodin, 206
Kitylos, 25
Klee, Paul, 243
Kline, Franz, 309
Klitias, 23
Knaths, Karl, 305
Kneeling Woman, Lehmbruck, 313
Kneller, Sir Godfrey, 187, 327(G-2)
Knight of Malta, Giorgione, 146
Knitting Lesson, Millet, 222
Knochenhaueramthaus, Hildesheim, 89
Knole House, Kent, Eng., 184
Knossus: amphora from, 16; Palace at, 14, 15
Ko-kak-koo-kiss . . . , Stanley, 291
Kollwitz, Käthe, 243; *Self portrait,* 243
Koppe, Richard, 306
Kouros, Noguchi, 317
Krater, 23, 24 (see also Volute-Krater; Kylix-Krater)
Kuniyoshi, Yasuo, 305; *Self portrait,* 305
Kyknos, 23
Kylix, 23, 25
Kylix-Krater, 25

La Belle Ferroniére, Leonardo, 132
La Belle Simonetta, Piero di Cosimo, 132
Laboratory, Mexico City, 274
Labranche Building, New Orleans, La., 262
Labrouste, Henri, 207
Lace Maker, The, Vermeer, 180
Lachaise, Gaston, 314
Ladder back chair, 198
LaFarge, John, 266, 327(G-3)
Lafayette, General, C. W. Peale, 287
Lafever, Minard, 262
Lake County Tuberculosis Sanatorium, Waukegan, Ill.,273
La Madeleine, Paris, 204
Lancaster, Mass., 257
Lancret, Nicolas, 214, 215, 326(F-1), 327(G-1)
Landscape, Segonzac, 234
Landscape with Castle, Ruisdael, 181
Landscape with Figures and Cattle, Gainsborough, 189
Landscape, Italian, Allston, 289
Landscape with Mill, Claude Lorrain, 213
Landscape, Moonlit, Allston, 289
Landscapists, 327(G-3)
Langhans, Karl, 166
Languedoc, 66, 68
Laocoön, 40: El Greco, 171
Lapith (see *Centaur*)
Lapowinsa, G. Hesselius, 291
Larkin Building, Buffalo, N.Y., 269
Lassaw, Ibram, 318
Last Judgment: Maitani, 97; Michelangelo, 141
Last Supper: Fra Angelico, 123; Castagno, 125; D. Ghirlandaio, 129; Giotto, 120, 121; Justus of Ghent, 157; Leonardo, 133; Sarto, 134; Tintoretto, 150
La Trinité, Caen, 69
Latrobe, Benjamin H., 260, 261, 262
Laughing Audience, Hogarth, 187
Laughing Cavalier, Hals, 176
Laurencin, Marie, 232
Laurens, Henry, 315
Lavinia, Titian, 148
Lawrence, Sir Thomas, 190, 191, 327(G-2)

Lawrie, Lee, 268, 313
Leaf and dart motif, 20
LeBrun, Charles, 201, 214, 326(F-1)
LeBrun, Nicholas, 268
LeBrun, Vigée, 218; *Self portrait*, 218
Le Corbusier, 210, 278
Leda, study for, Leonardo, 132
Le Foyer de la Danse . . . , Degas, 231
Léger, Fernand, 240
Lehmbruck, Wilhelm, 313
Lely, Sir Peter, 326(F-2)
Lemnia, Athena, 33
Le Moine (Le Moyne), François, 326
   (F-1), 327(G-1)
L'Enfant, P. C., 254, 261
Leo X, Raphael, 139
Leonardo da Vinci, 132, 133, 325(E-2)
Lescaze, William, 273
Lescot, Pierre, 202, 203
Lesson on the Lute, Terborch, 180
L'Été, Lancret, 215
Leucippus, Rape of the Daughters of,
   Rubens, 160
Lever House, N.Y.C., 274
Levi, Feast in the House of, Veronese, 151
Levine, Jack, 247
L'Hote, André, 240
Liber Vitae, 71
Liberale da Verona, 153
Liberty on the Barricade, Delacroix, 222
Libraries: New York University, N.Y.C.,
   265; St. Mark's, Venice, 104 (see also
   Bibliothèque)
Libyan Sibyl, Michelangelo, 141
Life mask, 279
Light of the World, Holman Hunt, 193
Limbourg, Pol de, 85
Limner, Mason, 284
Limoges enamel, 84, 85
Lincoln, Abraham: Barnard, 282; Brown,
   282; D.C. French, 281; Taft, 283
Lincoln Cathedral, 86
Lincoln, Mass., 273
Lincoln, Neb., 268, 281
L'Indifférent, Watteau, 215
Lindisfarne, Book of, 70
Lion, frieze of, 13
Lion Gate, Mycenae, 14
Lion Hunt, Rubens, 161
Lioness, Wounded, 13
Lipchitz, Jacques, 315, 316, 319
Lippi, Filippino, 124, 131, 325(E-2)
Lippi, Fra Filippo, 125, 126, 325(E-2);
   Self portrait, 126
Lipton, Seymour, 319
Lithograph, 175, 192, 226, 230, 243, 320
Liverpool: St. George's Hall, 186
Lochner, Stefan, 166, 326(F-3)
Logetta, Venice, 104
Loggia, 98, 272
Lombardi, The, 104
Lombardo, Pietro, 104, 105
London: Bank of England, 186; Crystal
   Palace, 207; Houses of Parliament,
   186; St. Bride's, Fleet Street, 185; St.
   Martin's in the Fields, 185; St. Mary-
   le-Bow, 185; St. Paul's Cathedral, 184,
   185; St. Stephen's Walbrook, 185;
   Whitehall, 184
Longfellow House, Cambridge, Mass.,
   252
Longhena Baldassare, 105, 106
Longhi, Pietro, 153, 325(E-5)
Longwood Plantation, Natchez, Miss., 264
Loos, Adolph, 271
Loredano, Doge, Giovanni Bellini, 144
Lorenzetti, Ambrogio, 118, 119, 325(E-1)
Lorenzetti, Pietro, 118, 325(E-1)
Lorenzo at the House of Isabella, Millais,
   193
Lorenzo di Credi, 132, 325(E-2)
Lorthet, prehistoric painting, 1
Los Angeles, Cal., 270

Lotto, Lorenzo, 148, 325(E-5)
Lotus capitals, 6
Louis XII–XVI furniture, 328
Louis XIV: Coysevox, 204; Nanteuil, 213;
   Rigaud. 213
Louis XIV furniture, 195, 227
Louis XV furniture, 195
Louis XVI furniture, 195, 196
Louisiana: Baton Rouge, 263; Edgard,
   263; New Orleans, 256, 262; New
   Roads, 256
Louvre, Paris, 202, 203
Louvre, Gallery of the, Morse, 290
Love and Life, Watts, 193
Lowboy, Georgian, 197
Lucca Cathedral, sculpture, Quercia, 108
Ludovisi, Ares, 37
Ludovisi Throne, 30
Luini, Bernardino, 325(E-4)
Luks, George, 300, 301, 327(G-3)
Luncheon of the Boating Party, Renoir,
   232
Luxor, Temple at, 6
Lyon, Pat, at His Forge, Neagle, 290
Lysicrates, Monument of, 22
Lysippus, 36, 38

Mabuse (see Gossaert)
Macmonnies, Frederick, 280
McComb, John, 259
McCormick, Sir William, Orpen, 194
McGraw-Hill Building. N.Y.C., 271
McIntire, Samuel, 257, 258
MacIver, Loren, 307
McKenzie, Voorhees and Gmelin, archi-
   tects, 268
McKim, Mead and White, architects,
   265
McNab, The, Raeburn, 190
McPhedris-Warner House, Portsmouth,
   N.H., 251, 252
Madeleine, La, Paris, 204
Maderna, Carlo, 102, 106
Madison, Wisc., 267
Madonna, 83: French Romanesque, 67;
   Verrocchio, 114
Madonna Adoring Child, Filippino Lippi,
   131
Madonna of the Annunciation, Van Eyck,
   155
Madonna with the Book, Michelangelo,
   115
Madonna of Bruges, Michelangelo, 114
Madonna of the Burgomaster Meyer, Hol-
   bein, 169
Madonna with the Canon van der Paele,
   Van Eyck, 156
Madonna del Cardellino, Raphael, 138
Madonna, Castelfranco, Giorgione, 146
Madonna of the Chair, Raphael, 138
Madonna of Chancellor Rolin, Van Eyck,
   156
Madonna and Child: Baldovinetti, 125;
   Giovanni Bellini, 144; Correggio, 149;
   Cranach, 168; Desiderio, 112; Epstein,
   314; Donatello, 112; Italian School,
   117; Fra Filippo Lippi, 126; Mantegna,
   142; Massys, 159; Murillo, 173; Pi-
   sano, 97; Pinturicchio, 137; Andrea
   della Robbia, 110; Luca della Robbia,
   111; Rossellino, 112; Van der Weyden,
   156
Madonna and Child with Angels, Filippino Lippi, 131
Madonna and Child in a Courtyard,
   Schongauer, 166
Madonna and Child with St. Anne, Leonardo, 132
Madonna and Child with Saints: Correggio, 148; P. Lorenzetti, 118; Vivarini,
   145

*Madonna and Child with SS. Jerome and
   Bernard*, Signorelli, 136
Madonna Enthroned, 88: Veneziano, 125
Madonna del Granduca, Raphael, 137
Madonna with Grapes, Gossaert, 159
Madonna of the Harpies, Sarto, 133
Madonna of the Linaiuoli, Fra Angelico,
   123
Madonna of the Magnificat, Botticelli, 130
Madonna, Medici, Michelangelo, 114
Madonna, Pesaro, Titian, 147
Madonna of the Rocks, Leonardo, 132
Madonna in a Rose Hedge, Schongauer,
   167
Madonna, Rucellai, 119
Madonna of St. Jerome, Correggio, 149
Madonna and Saints: Fra Bartolommeo,
   133; Giovanni Bellini, 144; Perugino,
   136
Madonna with SS. Catherine and Jerome,
   Moroni, 149
Madonna with SS. Paul and George, Gio-
   vanni Bellini, 144
Madonna, Sistine, Raphael, 138
Madonna with Six Angels, Botticelli, 131
Madonna of the Stairs, Michelangelo, 116
Madonna of the Trees, Giovanni Bellini,
   145
Madonna with the Violet, Lochner, 166
Madonna (see also *Christ; Holy Family;
   Virgin*)
Magi, The, 65, 73
Magi, Adoration of the: Botticelli, 130;
   Gaddi, 121; Gentile, 135; D. Ghirlan-
   daio, 129; Van der Weyden, 157
Magi Before Herod, 59
Magi, Hildesheim, 73
Magi, Journey of the, Gozzoli, 126, 127
Mahomet II, Gentile Bellini, 144
Maiano (see Benedetto)
Maids of Honor, Velásquez, 172
Maillol, Aristide, 312
Maine Islands, Marin, 304
Maine, Kennebunk, 264
Mainz Cathedral, 72
Maison Carrée, Nimes, 44
Maitani, Lorenzo, 92, 93, 97, 324
Maja Desnuda, Goya, 175
Maja Vestida, Goya, 175
Majas on a Balcony, Goya, 174
Majestà: Duccio, 117; Martini, 118
Malatesta, Sigismund, Francesca, 128
Malouel, Jean, 155, 326(F-1)
Man with a Glass of Wine, 211
Man and Horse, Egyptian, 8
Man Lighting a Pipe, Teniers, 165
Man Making Beer, Egyptian, 4
Man with a Pipe, Courbet, 225
Man in Rocker, Gallo, 311
Man with a Wine Glass, Velásquez, 172
Manchester, England, 207
Manchester Valley, Pickett, 293
Manet, Edouard, 228, 229
Mangin, Joseph, 259
Manship, Paul, 283
Mansard, Jules, 201, 203
Mantegazzi, The, 114
Mantegna, Andrea, 142, 143, 145, 325(E-4)
Mantel, Adam style, 199
Mantua, Sant' Andrea, 100
Manuscripts, 61, 70, 71, 85, 153
Marat, Death of, J. L. David, 218
Marburg, Church of St. Elizabeth, 89
Marc, Franz, 243
Marcus Aurelius, 49
Marcus Aurelius, Sacrifice of, 50
Maria Louisa of Parma, Goya, 175
Marie Antoinette, furniture of, 195
Marin, John, 304
Marina City Towers, Chicago, 278
Market Cart, Gainsborough, 189
Market Woman, Old, 41
Marriage à la Mode, Hogarth, 187

Marriage of Virgin (see *Virgin*)
Mars, Sansovino, 104
Mars, Borghese, 34
Mars Ultor, Temple of, 43
Marsh, Reginald, 302
Marshall Field Wholesale Building, Chicago, 265
Marsuppini, Carlo, Tomb of, 111
Marsyas, M ron, 30, 31
Martial Memory, Guston, 306
Martin, Homer, 299, 327(G-3)
Martin van Niewenhoven, diptych of, Memlinc, 157
Martini, Simone, 118, 325(E-1)
Mary (see *Madonna; Virgin*)
Mary Magdalene, Van der Goes, 158
Mary Magdalene, Ecstasy of, Ribera, 173
Maryland: Annapolis, 255; Baltimore, 260
Masaccio, 123, 124, 131, 325(E-2)
Mask of Tutankhamon, 8
Masolino, 124, 325(E-2)
Mason Limner, 284
Massachusetts: Andover, 296; Boston, 251–253, 257, 258, 264, 266; Cambridge, 252, 273, 282; Hatfield, 252; Lancaster, 257; Lincoln, 273; Medford, 251; New Bedford, 263; Salem, 257, 258; Topsfield, 251
Massacre of the Innocents: P. Bruegel, 160; Pisano, 96
Massacre of Scio, Delacroix, 221
Massimi Palace, Rome, 101
Massys, Quentin, 159, 326(F-2)
Mastodon, Exhuming of the First American, C. W. Peale, 287
Mater Amabilis, Gill, 312
Maternity: Millet, 223; Modigliani, 232
Matilda, Queen, 69
Matisse, Henri, 242
Matsys (see Massys)
Matthew, Van Eyck, 155
Mausoleum, Halicarnassus, 21, 37
Max Schmidt in a Single Scull, Eakins, 297
Maxentius, Basilica of, 45
Maximian, Throne of, 57, 58
Maximilian style armor, 170
Maya, Mirror of Illusions, Davies, 300
Mayan period, 322
Mede Bringing a Tribute of Horses, from Palace of Sargon II, 13
Medford, Mass., 251
Medici, Cosimo de: Gozzoli, 126; Pontormo, 134
Medici, Don Garzia de, Bronzini, 134
Medici, Giovanni di Cosimo de, Botticelli, 129
Medici, Giuliano de, A. Pollaiuolo, 113
Medici, Giuliano de, Tomb of, Michelangelo, 115
Medici, Giulio de, Raphael, 139
Medici, Lorenzo de, Vasari, 142
Medici, Lorenzo de, Tomb of, Michelangelo, 115
Medici, Marie de, Rubens, 163
Medici Palace, 126
Medici, Piero de, Gozzoli, 126
Medici, Villa of the, Rome, 106
Medici-Riccardi Palace, Florence, 98
Meeting House, Rockingham, Vt., 253
Meissonier, J. L. E., 224
Melancholia, Zerbe, 247
Meleager, 37
Mellan, Claude, 212, 213, 320
Mellini, Pietro, Benedetto, 113
Melos, Amphora from, 23
Melos, Aphrodite of, 40
Melos, Apollo from, 26
Melozzo da Forli, 135, 325(E-3)
Memlinc, Hans, 157, 158, 326(F-2)
Memmi, Lippo, 118
Memnon, Colossi of, 7

Mendelsohn, Erich, 209
Meninas, Las, Velásquez, 172
Merced Convent, Mexico City, 250
Merchants Exchange, Philadelphia, Pa., 258
Mercury, Giovanni da Bologna, 116
Mercury and the Three Graces, Tintoretto, 150
Mereruka, tomb of, 4
Merovingian, 73
Mesopotamian art, 11–13
Messel, Alfred, 270
Meštrovič, Ivan, 312
Metope: Parthenon, 31, 32; Selinus, 26; Temple of Zeus, 29
Metropolitan Life Insurance Building, N.Y.C., 269
Metsu, 326(F-5)
Mexican: architecture, 249, 250; painting, 248
Mexico City: Cathedral, 249; churches, 250; Convent of La Merced, 250; Normal School, 273; University of Mexico, 274
Meyer, Adolph, 209
Meyer-Hermann, Dr., Dix, 244
Mezzotint, 170, 191, 320
Michael, Archangel, Reni, 152
Michelangelo, 101–103, 106, 114–116, 139–141, 324, 325(E-2), 326(F-4)
Michelozzo, 98, 110, 324
Michigan: Detroit, 248; Bloomfield Hills, 272
Middelharnis Avenue, Hobbema, 182
Middle Empire (Kingdom), 5, 321
Miës van der Rohe, Ludwig, 210, 278
Mifflin, Gov. and Mrs. Thomas, Copley, 285
Migration of the Spirit, Orozco, 248
Milan, Italy: Cathedral, 95; San Satiro, 101; Sant' Ambrogio, 62; Santa Maria delle Grazie, 101, 133
Milkmaid, The, Greuze, 217
Milky Way, Origin of, Tintoretto, 150
Mill, The, Hobbema, 183
Mill Near Wijk, Ruisdael, 181
Millais, Sir J. E., 193
Milles, Carl, 313
Millet, Jean François, 222, 223, 327(G-1)
Mills, Robert, 260
Milmore, Martin, 282
Ming period, 322
Minnesota, Owatonna, 269
Minoan art, 321
Minor arts: Aegean, 15, 16; Egyptian, 9; English, 88; French, 69, 84, 85; German, 72, 73, 170; Italian, 154 (see also Chairs; Furniture; Mosaics; Vases; etc.)
Minos, Palace of, 14, 15
Minotaur, Barye, 206
Minster, York, 87
Mirko, 318
Miró, Joan, 246
Mirror of Illusions, Davies, 300
Mirror of Venus, Burne-Jones, 193
Mirrors: Empire, 196; Georgian, 197; Hepplewhite, 199
Missions, American, 249, 250
Mississippi, Natchez, 263, 264
Missouri, St. Louis, 269, 276
Mnesicles, 19, 20
Mobile: Red Petals, Calder, 317
Model, sculptor's, Egyptian, 9, 10
Models, Seurat, 234
Modena, Cathedral, 62
Modern Conveniences, Demuth, 304
Modigliani, Amadeo, 232
Moffatt-Ladd House, Portsmouth, N.H., 251, 253
Mogul, 322
Mohammedan (see Islamic)
Moholy-Nagy, Ladislaus, 317

Moissac Tympanum, 68
Mona Lisa, Leonardo, 132
Monadnock Block, Chicago, 268
Moncriff, Mrs. Scott, Raeburn, 190
Mondrian, Piet, 246
Monet, Claude, 229, 230; *Self portrait,* 230
Monks Reading, Barlach, 312
Monreale: Cathedral, 61, 64; Cloister, 64; Doors, 65
Mont St. Michel, 80, 81
Mont St. Michel, Arms, 302
Mont Ste. Victoire, Cézanne, 236
Months, The, Amiens Cathedral, 79
Monticello, Charlottesville, Va., 260, 261, 262
Montmagny, France, 208
Moore, Henry, 315, 317
Moorish architecture, 90, 91
Moorish Dance, Toulouse-Lautrec, 231
Moravian Village, Schoenbrunn, Ohio, 262
More, Sir Thomas, Rubens, 163
Morienval, Cathedral, 69
Morisot, Berthe, Manet, 228
Moro, Antonio, 160, 326(F-2,4)
Moroni, Giovanni Battista, 149, 325(E-4)
Morse, Samuel F. B., 290, 327(G-3)
Morton, Mrs. Pérez, Stuart, 286
Mosaics, 50–52, 60, 61
Moses, Michelangelo, 115
Moses, Fire Ordeal of Infant, Giorgione, 146
Moses Well, 83
Mosque, Cordova, 91
Mother, The Artist's, Whistler, 298
Mother and Child: Brush, 299; Cassatt, 301; De Hooch, 179
Mother and Child, Reclining, Umlauf, 319
Motherwell, Robert, 307
Motivo Alato, Mirko, 318
Mouldings, 20
Moulin Rouge, At the, Toulouse-Lautrec, 231
Mt. Katahdin, Hartley, 305
Mount Pleasant, Philadelphia, Pa., 255
Mount, William S., 294
Mourners, Claus Sluter, 83
Mshatta Façade, 58
Muirdach's Cross, 70
Munch, Edvard, 242
Murillo, Bartolomé Esteban, 173, 174, 326(F-4)
Muscles in Action, Boccioni, 315
Muse Leaning Against a Rock, 39
Museum: of Fine Arts, Boston, Mass., 264; of Modern Art, N.Y.C., 272
Music Lesson: Lancret, 215; Terborch, 180
My Daughters, Benson, 301
My Egypt, Demuth, 303
Mycenean art, 321
Mycenae: Lion Gate, 14; Treasury, 14
Mykerinos, pyramid of, 2
Myron, 30, 31

Nakht, scene in a tomb of, 8
Nanteuil, Robert, 213
Naos of Parthenon, 33
Napoleon Among the Plague Stricken at Jaffe, Gros, 220
Napoleon, Coronation of, J. L. David, 218 (see also *Bonaparte; Campaign*)
Narmer, palettes of, 3
Natchez, Miss., 263, 264
National Farmer's Bank, Owatonna, Minn., 269
Nativity (see *Christ*)
Nattier, Jean Marc, 216, 217
Naturalists (Italy), 325(E-6)
Nature's Wonderland, In, Doughty, 291

Nave, Durham Cathedral, 70
Naxian Sphinx, 27
Neagle, John, 290
Nebraska, Lincoln, 268
Necropolis, Relief from, 9
Nefretete, 4, 7
Neptune, Sansovino, 104
Nesiotes, 29
Never Again War, Kollwitz, 243
New Bedford, Mass., 263
New Empire (Egypt), 6–9, 321
New Hampshire: Acworth, 252; Fitzwilliam, 257; Portsmouth, 251, 252, 253, 257
New Haven, Conn., 258, 276
New Mexico, Ranchos de Taos, 250
New Orleans, La., 256, 262
New Roads, La., 256
New York: Buffalo, 267, 269; Guilderland, 264; Ticonderoga (see Hancock House); N.Y.C., 254, 259, 263, 265, 266, 268, 271, 272, 274, 276, 277, 280, 283
New York University Library, N.Y.C., 265
Newport, R.I., 252, 254
Niccolo da Uzzano, Donatello, 109
Niemeyer, Oscar, 274
Night: Epstein, 314; Michelangelo, 115
Night Watch, Rembrandt, 176
Nike, Paionius, 34
Nike Fastening Her Sandal, 34
Nike and a Fate, Phidias, 31
Nike of Samothrace, 40
Nîmes, 43, 44, 46
Ninevah, Palace at, 13
Niobe and Her Youngest Daughter, 37
Niobid, 37
Nocturne in Black and Gold, Whistler, 298
Noguchi, Isamu, 317
Noland, Kenneth, 309
Norham Castle, Turner, 191
Normal School, Mexico City, 273
Norman architecture, 70
Normandy, 68
North Carolina, Ashville, 265
Northern Italian painting, 325(E-4)
Norwegian painting, 242
Notre Dame: Paris, 74; la Grand, Poitiers, 66; du Haut, Ronchamp, 278 (see also French architecture; Cathedrals)
Nuclear Physics Laboratory, Mexico City, 274
Nude, Despiau, 312
Nude Descending the Stairs, Duchamp, 240
#5, Pollock, 308
Nuremberg: Frauenkirche, 89; Peller House, 165
Nymph of Fontainebleau, Cellini, 116
Nymph, Water, Rush, 279

Oak Park, Ill., 269
Oaks, The, Théodore Rousseau, 224
Obelisk at Luxor, 6
Odalisque, Matisse, 242
Oedipus and the Sphinx, Ingres, 219
Officer of the Guard, Géricault, 221
Officers of the Company of St. Adrian, Hals, 176
Oh, You're Jealous, Gauguin, 237
Ohio: Cincinnati, 263; Granville, 263; Schoenbrunn, 263
Oinomaos, 29
Oinochoë, 22
Old Age: Then and Now, Goya, 175
Old City Hall, Newport, R.I., 252
Old King, The, Rouault, 241
Old Kingdom (Egypt), 2–4
Old Man and Boy, D. Ghirlandaio, 128

Old Models, Harnett, 293
Old North Church, Boston, Mass., 252
Old St. Lazare Station, Paris, Monet, 230
Old State House, Boston, Mass., 253
Oldenberg, Claes, 318
Olympia: Heraeum, 17; Temple of Zeus, 18, 29
Olympia, Manet, 228
Olympieum at Acragas, 18
Opéra, Paris, 204, 206
Oppenheim, Meret, 316
Or San Michele, Florence, 97
Orange: Arch at, 47; Theatre, 46
Orcagna, Andrea, 97, 122, 324, 325(E-2)
Order of the Olympieum, 18
Orders: corn, 261; Greek, 16; tobacco, 260 (see also Doric; Ionic; Corinthian)
Orestes, 41
Orgaz, Burial of Count of, El Greco, 171
Orly, France, 208
Orozco, José Clemente, 248
Orpen, Sir William, 194, 327(G-2)
Orpheus, Milles, 313
Orpheus Asking Way to Hades, Poussin, 212
Orvieto Cathedral, 92, 93, 97, 135, 136
Osceola, Catlin, 292
Otis, Harrison Gray, house, Boston, Mass., 258
Otricoli, Zeus, 40
Oud, J. J. P., 208
Oval Still Life, Braque, 241
Owatonna, Minn., 269
Oxford, Countess of, Hoppner, 190

Padua, Arena Chapel, Giotto, 120, 121
Paele, Canon van der, Van Eyck, 156
Paestum: The Basilica, 18; Temple of Demeter, 17; Temple of Poseidon, 18
Painter and His Model, The, Picasso, 239
Painting: Aegean, 15; American, 284–311, 327; Dutch, 176–183, 235–238, 326; Egyptian, 8, 9, 52; English, 187–194, 327; Flemish, 155–165, 326; French, 211–242, 246, 326, 327; German, 166–170, 242–244, 326; Greek (see Vases, Greek); Italian, 117–153, 245, 325; Mexican, 248; Norwegian, 242; Roman, 51, 52; Russian, 243, 244; Spanish, 71, 171–175, 238–239, 244–246, 326; Swedish, 194
Paionius, 34
Palace: of Ashurnasirpal II, 11; of Charles V, Granada, 170; Crystal, 207; of Darius, 12, 13; Ducal, Venice, 95, 104, 105; of Minos, Knossus, 14, 15; Papal, Avignon, 82; of Potsdam, 165; of Sargon II, 12; Senators', Rome, 103; Versailles, 195, 201, 202
Palace at 4 A.M., Giacometti, 317
Palaestra Scene, 27
Palais de Justice, Rouen, 81
Palazzo: Cà d'Oro, Venice, 94; Contarini Fasan, Venice, 94; "Corner," Venice, 105; Farnese, Rome, 101; Foscari, Venice, 94; Gondi, Florence, 99; Grimani, Venice, 105; Loredan, Venice, 94; Massimi, Rome, 101; Medici-Riccardi, Florence, 98; Paesaro, Venice, 105; Pisani, Venice, 95; Pitti, Florence, 100; Pubblico, Siena, 94, 118; Quaratesi, Florence, 100; Rucellai, Florence, 100; Strozzi, Florence, 99; Vecchio, Florence, 94, 100; Vendramin, Venice, 105
Paleologus, John: Gozzoli, 127; Pisanello, 114
Palermo, mosaic, 61
Palettes of Narmer, 3
Palladio, Andrea, 103, 104
Pampulha, Minas Gerais, Brazil, 274

Pani, Mario, 273
Panthéon: Paris, 203; Rome, 44
Paolo Fountain, Rome, 106
Papal Palace, Avignon, 82
Parade: Blume, 245; Lassaw, 318
Paradise, Signorelli, 135
Paris: Arc de l'Etoile, 203; Bibliothèque Nationale, 207; Bibliothèque Sainte Geneviève, 207; Cathedral of Notre Dame, 76, 77; Eiffel Tower, 207; Fountain of the Innocents, Goujon, 204; Hôtel de Cluny, 82, 83; Hôtel des Invalides, 203; Louvre, 202, 203; Madeleine, 204; Opéra, 204, 206; Panthéon, 203; St. Eustache, 82; Sainte Chapelle, 80
Paris and Helen, J. L. David, 219
Paris, Judgment of: Boucher, 216; L'Hote, 240; Rubens, 161
Paris Roofs, MacIver, 307
Park Street Church, Boston, Mass., 257
Parlange Plantation House, New Roads, La., 256
Parliament, Houses of, London, 186
Parma: Cathedral of, 63, 149; Convent of San Paolo, Correggio murals, 149
Parnassus, Mantegna, 142
Parthenon, Athens, 16, 18, 19, 31–33
Parthian period, 321, 322
Pasiteles, 41
Pastoral: Boucher, 216; Lancret, 215
Pastoral Symphony, Giorgione, 146
Patinir, Joachim de, 326(F-2)
Paul III, Titian, 148
Pavement, Baptistry, Florence, 65
Pavia, Italy: Certosa of, 114; San Michelè, 63
Pavilion Sully, Louvre, Paris, 203
Paxton, Joseph, 207
Pazzi Chapel, Florence, 98
Peace: Daumier, 226; Ambrogio Lorenzetti, 118
Peace and Plenty, Inness, 299
Peale, Charles Willson, 287, 288, 327 (G-3); *Self portrait,* 287
Peale, Charles Willson, West, 288
Peale Family, C. W. Peale, 287
Peale, Raphaelle, 288
Peale, Rembrandt, 288
Peasant Dance, P. Bruegel, 159
Peasant Interior, D. Teniers, 164
Peasant at a Window, Ostade, 183
Peasants, Group of, Ostade, 182
Pectoral of Ramses II, 9
Pediment sculpture, 28
Pelike, 24
Peller House, Nuremberg, 165
Pelops, 24
Penelope (see *Ulysses*)
Penitent, The, Dürer, 167
Penn's Treaty with the Indians, West, 288
Pennsylvania: Bear Run, 270; Harrisburg, 281; Philadelphia, 254, 255, 258, 259, 264
Perdita, Romney, 189
Pére Tanguy, Van Gogh, 236
Pereira, I. R., 306
Pereira, W. L., 273
Pergamon: Acropolis, 22; Altar of Zeus, 39
Périgueux, St. Front, 66
Perrault, Claude, 203
Perret, Auguste and Gustave, 208
Persepolis: Palace at, 13; tomb at, 13
Perseus, 26
Persian: architecture, 13; period, 321, 323; sculpture, 12, 13
Persistence of Memory, Dali, 244
Person Throwing a Stone at a Bird, Miró, 246
Perugino, Pietro, 136, 137, 325(E-3)
Peruzzi, Baldassare, 101
Pesaro Palace, Venice, 105

Pessellino, Francesco, 125
Petit Trianon, Versailles, 202
Pevsner, Antoine, 316
Phenomena Point Swing and Flank, Jenkins, 310
Phidias, 31–33
Philadelphia, Pa., 254, 255, 258, 259, 264
Philae, Temple of Isis, 10
Philip the Bold, Tomb of, 83
Philip IV, Velásquez, 173
Philosophers, Three, Giorgione, 147
Phyfe, Duncan, furniture, 199, 328
Picasso, Mme., Picasso, 238
Picasso, Pablo, 238, 239, 311, 315
Piccolomini, Aeneas Silvius, Pinturicchio, 137
Pickett, Joseph, 293
Picnic in the Woods, Watteau, 214
Pierce House, Portsmouth, N.H., 257
Piero della Francesca, 128, 325(E-3)
Piero di Cosimo, 132, 325(E-3)
Pietà: Avignon, 211; Giovanni Bellini, 145; Crivelli, 142; Franco-Italian, 211; Giotto, 121; Mantegna, 142; Michelangelo, 114; Van Dyck, 163
Pietro da Cortona, 106
Pinturicchio, 137, 325(E-3)
Piranesi, 102
Pirithous, 51
Pisa: Baptistry, Pulpit, 96; Bonannus of, 65; Campanile, 63; Campo Santo frescoes, 119; Cathedral group, 63
Pisanello, 114, 324, 325(E-4)
Pisano, Andrea, 93, 97, 324, 325(E-2)
Pisano, Giovanni, 96, 97, 324, 325(E-2)
Pisano, Niccolo, 96, 324
Pissarro, Camille, 232
Pitt, Mr. . . . , C. W. Peale, 288
Pitti Palace, Florence, 100
Pius II, Pinturicchio, 137
Place du Havre, Pissarro, 232
Plans: Acropolis, 19; Chapel at Aix-la-Chapelle, 56; Amiens Cathedral, 79; Angoulême Cathedral, 67; Canterbury Cathedral, 85, 86; Chartres, 74; Cologne Cathedral, 89; Egyptian Temples, 5, 6; Florence Cathedral, 93; German Pavilion, Barcelona, 210; Palace of Minos, 14; Palace of Sargon II, 12; Paris Cathedral, 76; Parthenon, 18, 19; Cathedral of Pisa, 63; Reims Cathedral, 79; Roman house, 45; St. Front, Périgueux, 66; St. Mark's, Venice, 56; Old St. Peter's, 53; St. Sernin, Toulouse, 66; Salisbury Cathedral, 87; San Clemente, 53; San Vitale, 55; Sant' Ambrogio, 62; Santa Sophia, 55; Temple of Apollo, 18; Temple of Poseidon, 18; Theatre at Epidaurus, 21; Toledo Cathedral, 90; Tomb of Galla Placidia, 54; Villa Rotonda, 103; Washington, D.C., 261; Worms Cathedral, 72
Plankfelt, Jobst, Dürer, 167
Plantation houses, 256, 263, 264
Plateresque, 170
Plato, Raphael, 138
Ploutos, Kephisodotus, 37
Poet Laureate, Baskin, 319
Pogany, Mlle., Brancusi, 314
Possy-sur-Seine, France, 210
Poitiers, Notre Dame La Grande, 66
Polish Rider, Rembrandt, 178
Politics in an Oyster House, Woodville, 294
Pollaiuolo, Antonio, 113, 127, 324, 325 (E-2)
Pollaiuolo, Simone del, 99
Pollock, Jackson, 308
Polyclitus, 34, 35
Polyneikes, 24
Pomegranates, 11
Pompadour, Mme., Boucher, 216

Pompeii, 43, 45, 48, 50–52
Pont du Gard, Nîmes, 47
Ponte della Paglia, Prendergast, 301
Pontormo, 134, 325(E-2)
Porch, 19, 34
Porden, William, 186
Porta, Giacomo della, 102, 106
Porta Nigra, Trèves, 46
Portinari Altarpiece, Hugo Van der Goes, 158
Portinari, Candido, 274
Portland vase, 50
Portsmouth, N.H., 251, 252, 253, 257
Poseidon, 32
Poseidon, Temple of, 18
Postman, The, Van Gogh, 235
Potsdam, 165, 209
Potter, Paul, 182
Poussin, Nicholas, 212, 213, 326(F-1)
Powell House, Philadelphia, Pa., 254
Powers, Hiram, 279, 280
Prague, Czechoslovakia, 210
Prato, pulpit, Donatello, 110
Pratt, Matthew, 286
Praxiteles, 35, 36
Praying Boy, 38
Predis, Ambrogio di, 133, 325(E-4)
Predynastic jar, 2
Prehistoric art, 1, 2
Prendergast, Maurice, 301
Pre-Raphaelite Brotherhood, 193, 327 (G-2)
Presentation (see *Christ; Virgin*)
President's House, Williamsburg, Va., 255
Priebe, Karl, 247
Priest, Head of, Egyptian, 9
Priestess, fresco, 14
Primaticcio, 149, 325(E-3), 326(F-1)
Primavera, Botticelli, 130
Primavera God, Epstein, 314
Princess, Egyptian, 3
Princeton, Death of Gen. Mercer at the Battle of, Trumbull, 290
Print technique details, 320 (see also Aquatint; Engraving; Etching; Lithograph; Mezzotint; Wood Engraving; Woodcut)
Prior's Door, Ely, 70
Proculus, Paquius, fresco, 51, 52
Prometheus, Manship, 283
Pro Patria Ludus, Puvis de Chavannes, 226
Prophet Jeremiah, Michelangelo, 140
Prophet Job, Michelangelo, 140
Propylaea, The, 17, 20
Protonoe, grave relief, 38
Provence, 67
Proverbios, Los, Goya, 175
Provident Trust Company Building, Philadelphia, Pa., 264
Prudential Building, Buffalo, N.Y., 267
Prud'hon, Pierre, 217, 327(G-1)
Psalter: Arundel, 88; Huntingfield, 71
Psyche, Prud'hon, 217
Ptahhotep, Tomb of, 4
Ptolemaic period (Egypt), 10, 321
Puebla Cathedral, Mexico, 249
Pulpits: Pisa Baptistry, N. Pisano, 96; Prato, Donatello, 110; Ravello, 65; San Miniato, Florence, 65; Sant' Andrea, Pistoia, G. Pisano, 96; Siena Cathedral, N. Pisano, 96
Putto Riding a Crab, 51
Puvis de Chavannes, 225, 226, 327(G-1)
Pylon: at Edfu, 10; at Luxor, 6
Pyramid, Stepped, 2
Pyramids of Gizeh, 2, 3
Pythagoras, 76

Quaratesi Palace, Florence, 100
Queen Anne furniture, 198, 328

Quercia, Jacopo della, 108, 109, 324, 325 (E-2)
Quidor, John, 293
Quoniam Page, 70

Racine, Wisc., 270
Radio City, N.Y.C. (see Rockefeller Center)
Radio, Spirit of, Friedlander, 312
Raeburn, Sir Henry, 190, 327(G-2)
Raft of the Medusa, Géricault, 221
Raftsmen Playing Cards, Bingham, 295
Rahotep, 4
Railroad Station, Helsingfors, 270
Raimondi, Marcantonio, 141
Rain, Steam and Speed, Turner, 192
Ram's Head, Egyptian, 10
Ramses II; Colossi at Luxor, 6; Pectoral, 9; Temple at Abu Simbel, 7
Ramses II in Battle, 8
Ranchos de Taos, New Mexico, 250
Ranofer, 3
Rape of Sabine Women, Poussin, 212
Raphael, 103, 137–139, 325(E-3), 326 (F-4), 327(G-1)
Rattner, Abraham, 307
Rauschenberg, Robert, 309
Ravello, pulpit, 65
Ravenna, 54–56
Realists, The, 327(G-1)
Récamier, Mme.: J. L. David, 218; Gérard, 220
Receding Red, Pereira, 306
Reclining Figure, Moore, 315
Reconstruction, The, Rivera, 248
Red Cart, Davis, 305
Red Horses, Marc, 243
Red Sea, Crossing the, 61
Red Sun Box, Stamos, 310
Redon, Odilon, 232
Redwood Library, Newport, R. I., 254
Redwood, William, Stuart, 286
Reims Cathedral, 77, 78
Reindeer, prehistoric, 1, 2
Relief: from wall at Abydos, 8; Ludovisi Throne, 30 (see also Sculpture)
Reliquary, 84
Rembrandt, 176–178, 326(F-5); *Self portrait,* 177
Rembrandt's Mother, Dou, 178
Renaissance period, 322, 323
Rendezvous, The, Fragonard, 217
Reni, Guido, 152, 325(E-6)
Renoir, Pierre August, 232–234
Renwick, James, 263
Republic, The, D. C. French, 281
Reston, planned community, Fairfax County, Va., 277
Restoration furniture, 197
Resurrection (see *Christ*)
Reunion of the Soul and Body, Blake, 191
Revere House, Boston, Mass., 251
Revivals (architecture), 323
Reyna, J. G., 274
Reynolds, Sir Joshua, 188, 327(G-2)
Rhinoceros, prehistoric, 1
Rhode Island, Newport, 252, 254
Rhodes, sculpture, 40
Rhone, River God of, Covsevox, 205
Ribera, Jusepe de, 173, 326(F-4)
Richardson, H. H., 265, 266
Richmond, Va., 262
Riesener, 195, 196
Rigaud, Hyacinthe, 213, 214
Rimini, Italy, San Francisco, 100
Rimmer, William, 280
River God of the Rhone, Coysevox, 205
Rivera, Diego, 248
Rivers, Larry, 309
Rivière, Mme., Ingres, 219
Rizzo, 104, 105

Robbia, Andrea della, 110, 111, 324
Robbia, Luca della, 110, 111, 324
Robie House, Chicago, Ill., 269
Robinson, Mrs., Romney, 189
Roche, Kevin, 277
Rockefeller Center, N.Y.C., 272, 283, 312, 313
Rockingham, Vt., 253
Rococo furniture, 328
Rodin, Auguste, 206
Rodin, Auguste, Zorn, 194
Roebling, J. and W. A., architects, 266
Roman: architecture, 42–47; art, 321, 322, 323; painting, 51, 52; sculpture, 48–50
Romanesque: architecture and sculpture, 62–69; English (see Norman); period, 322, 323; vaulting, 68
Romano, Giulio, 103, 139, 325(E-3), 326(F-1)
Romantics, The, 327(G-1)
Romanus IV, 60
Rome, Ancient, 42–52
Rome: Arch of Constantine, 46, 49; Arch of Titus, 46, 48, 49; Basilica of Maxentius, 45; Baths of Diocletian, 44; Circus Maximus, 45; Colosseum, 45; Farnese Palace, 101; The Gesù, 106; Massimi Palace, 101; Pantheon, 44; Paolo Fountain, 106; Round Temple, 44; St. Paul's Outside the Walls, 64; St. Peter's, 53, 102, 114; San Giovanni in Laterano, 106; San Lorenzo, 53, 65; San Pietro in Montorio, 101; Santa Costanza, 54, 60; Santa Maria della Pace, 106; Senators' Palace, 103; Tomb of Hadrian, 47; Trevi Fountain, 106; Villa Madama, 103; Villa Medici, 106
Romney, George, 189, 190, 327(G-2); Self portrait, 189
Root, J. W., 265, 268
Rosa, Salvator, 152
Rospigliosi Cup, Cellini, 116
Rosselli, Cosimo, 325(E-2)
Rossellino, Antonio, 112, 324
Rossellino, Bernardo, 111, 112, 324
Rossetti, Dante Gabriel, 193, 327(G-2)
Rossi, Cardinal, Raphael, 139
Rosso, Il, 325(E-2)
Rotch House, New Bedford, Mass., 263
Rotterdam, 210
Rotund Plastic, Schlemmer, 316
Rouault, Georges, 241
Rouen: Butter Tower, 81; Cathedral, 81; House of Diane de Poitiers, 200; Palais de Justice, 81
Rouen Cathedral, Monet, 229
Round Temple, Rome, 44
Rousseau, Henri, 235
Rousseau, Théodore, 224, 327(G-1)
Roy, Pierre, 245, 246
Royal Portal, Chartres, 75
Rozak, Theodore, 318
Rubens, Nicholas, Rubens, 162
Rubens, Peter Paul, 160–163, 326(F-1,2), 327(G-1); Self portrait, 161
Rucellai Madonna, 119
Rue Transnonain, Daumier, 226
Ruisdael, Jacob van, 181, 182, 326(F-5)
Rumford, Count, Gainsborough, 189
Rupert, Prince, 170, 320
Rush, William, 279
Russian painting, 243, 244
Ryder, Albert P., 297, 327(G-3)

Saarinen, Eero, 272, 275, 276
Saarinen, Eliel, 270, 271, 272
Sabine Women, Rape of, Poussin, 212
Sailing through Marshes, Egyptian, 4
St. Agnes, Duccio, 117
St. Anna, Giotto, 120
St. Anne, altarpiece, Massys, 159

St. Anne, Madonna and Child, Leonardo, 132
St. Ansano, Martini, 118
St. Anthony, Dürer, 168
St. Augustine, Gozzoli, 127
St. Bernard, Signorelli, 136
St. Bernard, Vision of: Filippino Lippi, 131; Perugino, 137
St. Bride's, Fleet Street, London, 185
St. Castrensis, 61
St. Catherine, Moroni, 149
St. Catherine, Ecstasy of, Carracci, 152
St. Cecelia, Raphael, 137
St. Christopher Bearing the Infant Christ, 166
St. Clara, Giotto, 120
St. Damian, Church of, Giotto, 120
St. Denis, Martyrdom of, Malouel and Bellechose, 155
St. Dominic, Rosary of, Tiepolo, 153
St. Eligius, Christus, 157
St. Elizabeth, Marburg, 89
St. Etienne, Caen, 68, 69
St. Eustache, Paris, 82
St. Francis: Giotto, 120; Sassetta, 119
St. Francis of Assisi: Pampulha, Minas Gerais, Brazil, 274; Ranchos de Taos, New Mexico, 250
St. Francis: Death of, Giotto, 121
St. Francis, Vision of, Giotto, 121
St. Front, Perigueux, 66
St. George: Giovanni Bellini, 144; Donatello, 109
St. George's Hall, Liverpool, 186
St. Germer, Church at, 74
St. Gilles, Church at, 67
St. Godeberta, Cristus, 157
St. Helena, Sarcophagus of, 49
St. Jerome: Antonello, 143; Correggio, 149; Dürer, 168; Ghirlandaio, 128; Moroni, 149; Signorelli, 136
St. Joachim, Giotto, 120
St. John the Baptist: Sarto, 134; Desiderio, 112; Donatello, 109, 112; Andrea Pisano, 97; Rodin, 206; Rossellino, 112
St. John the Evangelist: Dürer, 168; Grunewald, 167
St. John, Infant, Rubens, 162
St. Juliet, Martini, 118
St. Lazare Station, Paris, Monet, 230
St. Leu d'Esserant, Church, 74
St. Louis, Mo., 269, 276
St. Margaret, Van der Goes, 158
St. Mark's, Venice, 48, 56, 57, 104
St. Martin Dividing His Cloak: El Greco, 172; Liberale da Verona, 153
St. Martin's in the Fields, London, 185
St. Mary-le-Bow, London, 185
St. Matthew, 84
St. Michael, Rouen Cathedral, 81
St. Michael's Church, Charleston, S.C., 256
St. Paul, Giovanni Bellini, 144
St. Paul, Conversion of, Caravaggio, 151
St. Paul's: Cathedral, London, 184, 185; Chapel, New York, 254; Outside the Walls, Rome, 53, 64
St. Peter: Dürer, 168; Ghiberti, 107; Filippino Lippi, 131; Masaccio, 124
St. Peter, Christ Delivering the Keys to, Perugino, 136
St. Peter, Old Basilica of, Rome, 53
St. Peter's, Rome, 102, 114
St. Sebastian: Fiorenzo di Lorenzo, 128; Mantegna, 143; Reni, 152
St. Sernin, Toulouse, 66
St. Sigismund, Piero della Francesca, 128
St. Stephen, Funeral of, Fra Filippo Lippi, 126
St. Stephen's Walbrook, London, 185
St. Therese, Bernini, 116
St. Therese, Church of, Montmagny, 208

St. Trophîme, Arles, 67
St. Ursula: Carpaccio, 145, 146; Memlinc, 157, 158
St. Vulfrand, Abbeville, 82
St. Wenceslas, Prague, 210
Sainte Chapelle, Paris, 80
Saint-Gaudens, Augustus, 281, 282
Saïte period, 9, 10, 321
Sakkâra, 2, 4
Saladin, 322
Salamanca University, 90, 170
Salem, Mass., 257, 258
Salisbury, Cathedral, 86, 87
Salle des Pas-Perdus, Daumier, 227
Saltcellar of Francis I, Cellini, 116
Salutat, Eakins, 297
Salviati, Gozzoli, 126
Samos, Hera of, 25
Samothrace, Nike of, 40
Samuel, Little, Reynolds, 188
San Antonio, Texas, 249, 250
San Antonio de Valero, San Antonio, Texas, 249
San Clement de Tahull, fresco, 71
San Clemente, Basilica of, 53
San Francesco: Assisi, 92, 118, 120; Rimini, 100
San Giorgio Maggiore, Venice, 104
San Giovanni in Laterano, Rome, 106
San José Mission, San Antonio, Tex., 250
San Lorenzo: Florence, 98, 112, 115; Rome, 53, 65
San Marco, Florence, 122, 123
San Marco, Venice, Procession in Piazza, Gentile Bellini, 144
San Maria da Mura, 71
San Martin, Tepotzotlán, Mexico, 249
San Michele, Pavia, 63
San Miniato, Florence, 63, 64, 65
San Niccolo, Bari, 64
San Paolo, Parma, Correggio mural, 149
San Pietro in Montorio, Rome, 101
San Romano, Rout of, Uccello, 124
San Satiro, Milan, 101
San Sebastian and Santa Prisca, Taxco, Mexico, 249
San Stefano Rotondo, 53
San Vitale, Ravenna, 55, 57, 60
San Xavier del Bac, Tucson, Arizona, 250
San Zeno Maggiore, Verona, 62
Sanatorium, Waukegan, Ill., 273
Sangallo, Antonio da, 101
Sanmichele, Michele, 105
Sansovino, Andrea, 104, 105, 114, 324
Sansovino, Jacopo, 324
Sant' Ambrogio, Milan, 62
Sant' Andrea: Mantua, 100; Pistoia, pulpit, 96
Sant' Apollinare Nuovo, Ravenna, 56, 61
Santa Barbara, Cal., 249
Santa Costanza, Rome, 54, 60
Santa Croce, Florence, 109, 111, 121, 122
Santa Maria de Mura, fresco, 71
Santa Maria dei Miracoli, Venice, 104
Santa Maria del Carmine, Florence, 123, 124, 131
Santa Maria della Pace, Rome, 106
Santa Maria della Salute, Guardi, 153
Santa Maria della Salute, Venice, 106
Santa Maria delle Grazie, Milan, 101, 133
Santa Maria Maddalena dei Pazzi, Florence, mural, 137
Santa Maria Novella, Florence, 93, 100, 122
Santa Sophia, Istanbul, 55
Santiago Cathedral, 71
Santísima Trinidad, Mexico City, 250
Santo Domingo, Mexico City, 250
Santo Spirito, Florence, 98
Sarah at the Tent, Ghiberti, 108
Sarcophagus: Alexander, 38; Early Christian, 57, 58; from Hagia Triada, 15;

Junius Bassus, 57; Roman, 50; of St. Helena, 49
Sardanapalus, Death of, Delacroix, 222
Sargent, Henry, 294
Sargent, John Singer, 298, 327(G-3)
Sargon II, Palace of, 12, 13
Sarto, Andrea del, 133, 134, 325(E-2)
Sassanian period, 322
Sassetta, 119
Satan, Reni, 152
Saturn, Temple of, 42, 43
Satyr, Praxiteles, 35
Satyr, Sleeping, 41
Sauroctonos, 35
Savannah, Tenn., 272
Savonarola, Fra Bartolommeo, 133
Savoye House, Possy-sur-Seine, 210
Scamozzi, 104
Scarpagnino, 104
Scattered Sunset, Hofman, 308
Scheuring, Dr., Cranach, 169
Schiavonetti, Luigi, 191
Schlemmer, Oskar, 316
Schocken Department Store, Chemnitz, Germany, 209
Schoenbrunn, Ohio, 263
Schongauer, Martin, 166, 167, 326(F-3)
School of Athens, Raphael, 138
Schoolcraft House, Guilderland, N.Y., 264
Schoolmistress, The, Fragonard, 217
Scio, Delacroix, 221
Scopas, 37
Scream, The, Munch, 242
Scribe, Seated, 4
Sculpture: Aegean, 14; American, 279–283, 292, 293, 312–319; Assyrian, 11–13; Babylonian, 11; Byzantine, 57–60; Early Christian, 57; Egyptian, 2–5, 7–10; English, 312–315, 317–319; French, 67, 68, 75–79, 83, 204–206, 312–316; German, 166, 312, 313, 316; Greek, 25–41; Hungarian, 317; Italian, 65, 96–97, 107–116, 205, 315–317, 324; Persian, 12, 13; Prehistoric, 2; Roman, 48–50; Spanish, 315; Yugoslavic, 312
Scuola di San Rocco, Venice, 105
Sea with Ships, Van de Velde, 183
Seaport at Sunset, Claude Lorrain, 213
Seashore, By the, Renoir, 234
Seated Woman: Gauguin, 237; Picasso, 239
Segonzac, André de, 234
Segovia, Aqueduct, 47
Selinus, Metope from, 26
Senators' Palace, Rome, 103
Senile Old Man Tottering Down Steps, Bingham, 295
Septimius Severus, Arch of, 42, 43, 47
Servant Girl Pouring Milk, Vermeer, 180
Seti I, 9
Seti I, Temple of, 6, 8
Settee, Adam style, 199
Seurat, Georges, 234
Seville: Cathedral, 90; Giralda, 90; Town Hall, 170
Seymour, Jane, Holbein, 169
Shahn, Ben, 305
Shaw Memorial, Saint-Gaudens, 282
Sheba, Queen of, Received by Solomon: Ghiberti, 108; Piero della Francesca, 128
Sheeler, Charles, 304
Sheikh-el-Beled, 3
Shepherds, Adoration of the, Ghirlandaio, 128
Shepherds of Arcadia, Poussin, 213
Sheraton furniture, 198, 199, 328
Sherman Monument, Saint-Gaudens, 281
Shooting of a Group of Citizens . . . , Goya, 174
Shreve, Lamb, and Harmon, architects, 271

Shrimp Girl, Hogarth, 187
Shrine of Athena, 25
Sibyl (see Sistine Chapel)
Sibyl, Temple of the, 43
Sick Lady, A, Steen, 181
Siddons, Mrs.: Gainsborough, 188; Lawrence, 191
Siddons, Mrs., as the Tragic Muse, Reynolds, 188
Siegfried and the Rhine Maidens, Ryder, 297
Siena, Italy: Cathedral, 92, 96; Library mural, Pinturicchio, 137; Palazzo Público, 94, 118
Sienese painting, 117–119, 325(E-1)
Signorelli, Luca, 135, 136, 325(E-3); Self portrait, 136
Silenus and Bacchus, 36
Simon, Robert E., Jr., 277
Singing Gallery: Donatello, 110; panel, Luca della Robbia, 110
Singing Man, Barlach, 191
Siphnians, Treasury of the 17, 27
Siqueiros, David, 248
Sisley, Alfred, 232
Sistine Chapel murals, Michelangelo, 139–141
Six Dynasties period, 322
Sixtus IV Giving Audience to Platina, Melozzo da Forli, 135
Skidmore, Owings, and Merrill, architects, 273, 274, 275, 277
Skirts of the Woods, Gainsborough, 188
Slave, Bound, Michelangelo, 115
Slave, Greek, Powers, 279
Slave Sharpening Knife, 39
Sleeping Gypsy, H. Rousseau, 235
Sleeping Satyr, 41
Sloop, Bermuda, Homer, 295
Sluter, Claus, 83
Smibert, John, 284, 285, 327(G-3); Self portrait, 284
Smith, David, 318
Smithfield, Va., 251
Smoker, The, Teniers, 164
Snake Goddess, 16
Snow at Louveciennes, Sisley, 232
Snyders, Frans, and His Wife, Van Dyck, 164
Soane, Sir John, 186
Sodom and Gomorrah, Rattner, 307
Sodoma, Il, 325(E-2)
Soldier Drinks, The, Chagall, 244
Solitude, Hopper, 307
Solomon Receiving the Queen of Sheba, Ghiberti, 108
Song of the Lark, Breton, 224
Sophocles, 38
Sorolla y Bastida, Joaquín, 194, 327(G-1)
Sortie of the Civic Guard, Rembrandt, 176
Soufflot, Jacques, 203
Soup, Daumier, 227
Source, The: Courbet, 225; Ingres, 220
South Carolina, Charleston, 256
Sovereigns, English and French, 328
Sower, The, Millet, 222
Spandrels, 49
Spanish: architecture, 70, 91, 170; painting, 71, 171–175, 194, 238, 239, 244–246, 326; sculpture, 315
Spanish Chapel, Santa Maria Novella, 122
Spano, Pippo, Andrea del Castagno, 125
Sparta, stele from, 25, 26
Spear Thrower, 27
Spearbearer, Polyclitus, 34
Spectre of the Sea, Gottlieb, 247
Speicher, Eugene, 302
Speyer Cathedral, 72
Sphinx: Egyptian, 2; Milmore, 282
Sphinx, Naxion, 27
Sphinx, Oedipus and the, Ingres, 219
Sphinxes, Avenue of, Egypt, 5
Spielers, The, Luks, 300

Spoons, Egyptian, 9
Spring: Botticelli, 130; Corot, 223
Spring in France, Avery, 308
Squarcione, 325(E-4)
Stag Hunt, prehistoric, 1
Staircase Group, C. W. Peale, 287
Stamnos, 24
Stamos, Theodoros, 310
Stanley, John Mix, 291
Starr King Mountain, Bierstadt, 292
Starry Night, Van Gogh, 238
State House, Boston, Mass., 253, 257
Steen, Jan, 181, 326(F-5)
Stein House, Garches, France, 210
Stele of Aristion, 26, 27
Stele, Cypriote, 17
Stele from Sparta, 25, 26
Sterope, 29
Steuben, Maj. Gen. William Augustin, Earl, 284
Stevenson, Robert Louis: Saint-Gaudens, 282; Sargent, 298
Stewart, A. T., Store, N.Y.C., 266
Still Life: Braque, 240, 241; Cézanne, 236; Chardin, 215; Peale, 288; Picasso, 238; Sheeler, 304
Stockholm, Sweden, 313
Stoclet Palace, Brussels, 208
Stoffels, Hendrickje, Rembrandt, 177
Stone, Edward, 272
Stonehenge, 1
Stool, Italian, 154
Storm Bird, Lipton, 319
Storrs, John, 315
Straw Hat, The, Rubens, 162
Street of Auvers, Van Gogh, 236
Street Scene, Kirchner, 242
Strickland, William, 258, 259
Stroganoff ivory, 60
Strozzi, Niccolo, Campin, 156
Strozzi Palace, Florence, 99
Stuart furniture, 196, 197
Stuart, Gilbert, 286, 327(G-3)
Sturgis, Russell, 264
Sub-Treasury Building, N.Y.C., 259
Sugar Workers, Rivera, 248
Suiko period, 322
Sullivan, Louis, 267, 269
Sully, Thomas, 290, 327(G-3); Self portrait, 290
Summer, Puvis de Chavannes, 225
Sun, Temple of, Baalbek, 43
Sun Flowers, Van Gogh, 237
Sunday on the Island of La Grand Jatte, Seurat, 234
Sung period, 322
Susa: Palace at, 13; tile from, 12
Swedish painting, 194
Swing, The, Fragonard, 217
Syndics of the Cloth Guild, Rembrandt, 177
Syracuse, Aphrodite of, 36
Syria: Mshatta Façade, 58; Basilica of Tourmanin, 54

Tabernacle: Desiderio, 112; Orcagna, 97
Tabernacle Church of Christ, Columbus, Ind., 272
Tables: Chippendale, 198; Louis XIV, 195; Noguchi, 317; Phyfe, 199; Sheraton, 199
Tabularium, 42
Taft House, Cincinnati, Ohio, 262
Taft, Lorado, 283
Tahitian Women, Gauguin, 237
Talbot Family, Lady of the, Christus, 157
Tanagra Figure, 41
T'Ang period, 322
Tangry, Mme., and Daughters, J. L. David, 219
Tapestry, 69, 84

Tapestry Weavers, Velásquez, 172
Tchelitchew, Pavel, 247
Tea Party, The, Henry Sargent, 294
Telephos, 51
Tempietto, Rome, 101
Temple: Aegina, 28; Amon, 5, 6; Apollo, 16–18; Athena, 19; Athena Nike, 20, 34; Castor and Pollux, 42; Concord, 42; at Delos, 16; Diana, 43; Divus Julius, 42; Egyptian, 5–8, 10; Fortuna Augustus, 43; Fortuna Virilis, 44; Juno Moneta, 42; Jupiter Capitolinus, Rome, 42, 43; Jupiter Olympus, 22; Mars Ultor, 43; Poseidon, 18; Queen Hatshepsut, 5; Round Temple, Rome, 44; Saturn, 42, 43; the Sibyl, Tivoli, 43; the Sun, 43; Vespasian, 42, 43; Zeus, 18, 29
Temple of the Mind, Ryder, 297
Tempyo period, 322
Teniers, David, the Younger, 164, 165, 326(F-2)
Tennessee, Savannah, 272
Tepotzotlán, Mexico, 249
Terborch, Gerard, 180, 181, 326(F-5)
Terror in Brooklyn, Guglielmi, 245
Texas, San Antonio, 249, 250
Textile, velvet, Italian, 154
Theatres: Epidaurus, 21; Herculaneum, 46; Orange, 46
Thebes, Colossi, 7
Then the Lord Answered Job . . . , Blake, 192
Theodora, Empress, 60
Theodoric, Tomb, 54
Theophilus' Son Raised by St. Peter, Filippino Lippi, 131
Thersites, 25
Theseum, The, Athens, 21
Theseus, Greek, 25
Theseus Slaying the Minotaur, Barye, 206
Thinker, The, Rodin, 206
Third Class Carriage, The, Daumier, 227
Thomas, Incredulity of, Verrocchio, 113
Thompson, Martin, 259
Thompson, Sir Benjamin, Gainsborough, 189
Thornton, William, 260
Thorpe, John, 184
Three Graces, 52, 150
Three Marys at the Tomb, Van Eyck, 155
Three Men Crying, Echaurren, 246
Three Trees, Derain, 241
Three Women, Léger, 240
Throne: of Dagobert, 73; Ludovisi, 30; of Maximian, 57, 58; Pontifical, 65
Throne Room, Knossus, 15
Ticonderoga, N.Y., 253
Tiepolo, Giovanni Battista, 153, 325 (E-5), 327(G-1)
Tiger Walking, Barye, 206
Tile from Susa, 12, 13
Time, Gropper, 306
Tintoretto, 150, 325(E-5), 326(F-4)
Tiryns, 14
Titian, 147, 148, 325(E-5), 326(F-4); *Self portrait,* 147
Titus, Arch of, 46, 48, 49
Tivoli, Temple of Sibyl, 43
Tobacco capital designed for National Capitol, 260
Tobey, Mark, 307
Tobias and the Angel, Pollaiuolo, 127
Tobit, Blindness of, Rembrandt, 178
Toilers of the Sea, Ryder, 297
Tokugawa period, 322
Toledo Cathedral, 90
Toltec period, 322
Tomb: of Leonardo Bruni, Rossellino, 111; of Darius, 13; Egyptian, 4, 5, 8; of Galla Placidia, 54; of Hadrian, 47; of Ilaria del Carreto, 108; of Julius II,

Michelangelo, 115; of Carlo Marsuppini, Settignano, 111; of Medici, Michelangelo, 115; of Philip the Bold, 83; of Theodoric, 54; Wainwright, Sullivan, 269 (see also Egyptian architecture; Mausoleum)
Topsfield, Mass., 251
Torch holder, 99
Torn Hat, Sully, 290
Tornado, The, Curry, 302
Torso, Maillol, 312
Toulouse, St. Sernin, 66
Toulouse-Lautrec, Henri de, 231
Tourmanin, Basilica at, 54
Tournai tapestry, 84
Tower of Babel, 71
Tower of the Winds, Athens, 22
Town, Ithiel, 258, 259
Toys of a Prince, Chirico, 245
Tragedy, Rush, 279
Trajan, Column of, 49
Tralles, School of, 41
Transept, Chartres Cathedral, 74
Transitional period, Greek, 18, 29, 30
Transportation Building, Chicago, 267
Travel and Transport Building, Chicago, 271
Travellers, The, Hobbema, 183
Treasury: of the Athenians, 17; of Atreus, 14; of Siphnians, 17, 27
Trees, Three, Derain, 241
Très Riches Heures, 85
Trèves, Porta Nigra, 46
Trevi Fountain, Rome, 106
Trianon, The Petit, Versailles, 202
Tribune Building, Chicago, 271
Tribute Money, Masaccio, 124
Trinité, La, Caen, 69
Trinity Church: Boston, 266; New York City, 263
Triptych, 59
Triumph of Death, 119
Trumbull, John, 290, 291, 327(G-3)
Tschacbasov, Nahum, 247
Ts'ing period, 322
Tuberculosis Clinic, Alexandria, Egypt, 272
Tucson, Arizona, 250
Tudor furniture, 328
Tura, Cosimo, 143, 325(E-4)
Turkish Bath, Ingres, 220
Turner, J. M., 190–192, 327(G-2)
Tutankhamon, mask, 8
Twachtman, John H., 327(G-3)
Twilight, Michelangelo, 115
Twilight Head, Tchelitchew, 247
Two Children are Menaced by a Nightingale, Ernst, 316
Two Citizens Engaged in a Conversation, Bingham, 295
Two Girls, Laurencin, 232
Two Little Circus Girls, Renoir, 233
Tyche of Antiocheia, 40
Tympanum: Autun, 68; Moissac, 68; Vézelay, 67
Typhon, The, 28

Uccello, Paolo, 124, 125, 325(E-2)
Uffizi, The, Florence, 94
Ulysses and Penelope, Primaticcio, 149
Umlauf, Charles, 319
Unique Forms of Continuity in Space, Boccioni, 315
United Church, New Haven, Conn., 258
United Nations Secretariat, N.Y.C., 274
United States Air Force Academy, Colorado Springs, Colo., 275
Unity Temple, Oak Park, Ill., 269
University: of Illinois, at Chicago, 275; of Illinois, at Urbana, 276; of Sala-

manca, 90, 170; of Virginia, Charlottesville, 261
Unloading Oranges, Brangwyn, 194
Upjohn, Richard, 263
Uprising, The, Daumier, 226
Urbana, Ill., 276, 283
Urbino, Duchess of, Titian, 148
Urbino, Duke of, Piero della Francesca, 128
Usher-Royall House, Medford, Mass., 251

Vaccination, Rivera, 248
Valencia, Sorolla, 194
Valor, Friedlander, 313
Vanbrugh, Sir John, 185
Vanderbilt House, N.Y.C., 265
Vanderlyn, John, 289; *Self portrait,* 289
Van de Velde, E., 326(F-5)
Van de Velde, William, 183
Van der Goes, Hugo, 158, 326(F-2)
Van der Rohe, Ludwig Miës, 210, 278
Van der Vlugt, L. C., 210
Van der Weyden, Roger, 156, 157, 326 (F-2)
Van Dyck, Anthony, 163, 164, 326(F-2); *Self portrait,* 164
Van Eyck, Hubert and Jan, 155, 156, 326(F-2)
Van Eyck, Margaret, Jan Van Eyck, 155
Van Gogh, Vincent, 235–238
Van Goyen, Jan, 326(F-5)
Van Leyden, L., 326(F-3)
Van Ostade, A., 182, 183, 326(F-5)
Vaphio Cups, 15
Varvakeion Athena, 33
Vasari, Giorgio, 94, 142, 325(E-2)
Vases: Aegean, 16; Greek, 22–25; Portland, 50
Vatican (see Melozzo da Forli; Michelangelo; Perugino; Raphael)
Vaulting: Amiens, 80; Burgos, 90; Caen, 69; Chartres, 75; Gothic, 74; Romanesque, 68; St. Eustache, Paris, 82
Vedder, Elihu, 327(G-3)
Velásquez, Diego, 172, 173, 326(F-4); *Self portrait,* 172
Velletri Athena, 33
Vendramin Palace, Venice, 105
Venetian painting, 325(E-5)
Veneziano, Domenico, 125, 325(E-3)
Venice: Cà d'Oro Palace, 94; Campanile, 104; Contarini Fasan Palace, 94; "Corner" Palace, 105; Ducal Palace, 95, 104, 105; Foscari Palace, 94; Grimani Palace, 105; Hospital of St. Mark, 104; Library of St. Mark's, 104; Loredan Palace, 94; Pesaro Palace, 105; Pisani Palace, 95; St. Mark's, 48, 56, 57; San Giorgio Maggiore, 104; Santa Maria dei Miracoli, 104; Santa Maria della Salute, 106, 153; Scuola di San Rocco, 105; Vendramin Palace, 105
Venus, Titian, 148
Venus, Birth of: Botticelli, 130; Bouguereau, 220
Venus, Capitoline, 36
Venus of Cnidos, 36
Venus Genetrix, 34
Venus, Rokeby, Velásquez, 173
Venus, Sleeping, Giorgione, 147
Venus, Toilet of, Boucher, 216
Venus Victrix, Pauline Borghese as, Canova, 205
Vermeer, Jan, 179–180, 326(F-5)
Vermont: Bennington, 257; Rockingham, 253
Verona, San Zeno Maggiore, 62
Veronese, Paolo, 150, 151, 325(E-5), 326(F-1)
Veronica, The, Mellan, 212

Verrocchio, Andrea del, 113, 114, 132, 324, 325(E-2)
Versailles, Artemis of, 40
Versailles, Palace of, 195, 201, 202
Vespasian, Temple of, 42, 43
Vespucci, Simonetta, Piero de Cosimo, 132
Vetii, House of, murals, 51, 52
Vézelay, Abbey Church, 67, 68
Vicenza, Italy: Basilica, 103, 104; Villa Rotonda, 103
Victim of the Fête, Zuloaga, 194
Vierge Dorée Portal, Amiens, 79
Vignola, Giacomo, 106
Vignon, Barthélémy, 204
Villa: Madama, Rome, 103; Medici, Rome, 106; Rotonda, Vicenza, 103
Village Festival, Teniers, 165
Violin Player, Young, Hals, 176
Virgil, Delacroix, 222
Virgin, Annunciation: Baldovinetti, 125; Benedetto da Maiano, 112; Botticelli, 131; Crivelli, 142; Donatello, 109; Fra Angelico, 122; Lorenzo di Credi, 132; Lotto, 148; Martini, 118; Rossetti, 193; Sarto, 134; Tura, 143; Van Eyck, 155
Virgin, Annunciation of the Death of the, Orcagna, 97
Virgin, Assumption: Correggio, 149; Titian, 147
Virgin, Birth of, Ghirlandaio, 129
Virgin, Coronation of: Fra Angelico, 122, 123; Fra Filippo Lippi, 125
Virgin, Death of, Caravaggio, 152
Virgin, Enthroned: Fra Bartholommeo, 133; Cimabue, 119; Giotto, 119
Virgin, Immaculate Conception, Murillo, 174
Virgin, Life of, 75
Virgin, Marriage of: Orcagna, 97; Raphael, 138
Virgin, Presentation of: T. Gaddi, 121; Giotto, 120; Tintoretto, 150
Virgin with the Siskin, Dürer, 167
Virgin, Visitation, 59, 114: Andrea Pisano, 97; Vivarini, 145
Virgin (see also *Madonna; Vierge*)
Virginia: Charles City County, 255; Charlottesville, 261, 262; Reston, 277; Richmond, 262; Smithfield, 251; Williamsburg, 255, 256
Virginia Deer, Audubon, 293
Virgins Bearing Their Crowns. . . , 61
Visage of War, Dali, 245
Vischer, Peter, the Elder, 166
Visitation (see *Virgin*)
Vivarini, Alvise, 325(E-5)
Vivarini, Antonio, 325(E-5)
Vivarini, Bartolommeo, 145, 325(E-5)
Voltaire, Houdon, 206
Volute-Krater, 24, 25
Von Werl Altarpiece, Campin, 156
Vulcan, Forge of, Velásquez, 172

Wainscot chair, Jacobean, 196

Wainwright Tomb, St. Louis, Mo., 269
Waldo, Gen. Samuel, Feke, 284
Walter, T. U., 260
Ward, James, Stuart, 286
Ward, J. Q. A., 280
Warhol, Andy, 309
Warrior, Wounded, 28
Washington, D. C.: Arena Stage, 277; Capitol, 260, 261; city plan, 261; Washington Monument, 260; White House, 261
Washington, Gen., Lafayette, and Tench Tilghman, Peale, 287
Washington, George: Brown, 280; Greenough, 280; Houdon, 205; Stuart, 286; Ward, 280
Washington Square, New York, 259: Arch, 265
Water Nymph and Bittern, Rush, 279
Waterlilies, Monet, 230
Watson and the Shark, Copley, 285
Watteau, Jean Antoine, 214, 215, 326 (F-1), 327(G-1)
Watts, George Frederick, 193, 327(G-2)
Waukegan, Ill., 273
Weathervane, Browne, 293
Weber, Max, 305, 306
Wedding Cake House, Kennebunk, Me., 263
Weese and Associates, architects, 277
Wei period, 322
Welfare Building, Great Lakes, Ill., 273
Wellington, Duke of, Lawrence, 190
Wells Cathedral, 87
Wentworth-Gardner House, Portsmouth, N.H., 253
Wertheim Department Store, Berlin, 270
West, Benjamin, 288, 327(G-3)
West, Benjamin, Stuart, 286
Westminster Abbey, 88
Westover, Va., 255
Weyden (see Van der Weyden)
Wheatfields, Ruisdael, 182
When the Morning Stars Sang Together, Blake, 191
Whistler, James, 298, 320, 327(G-3)
Whistling Boy, Duveneck, 299
White Forms, Kline, 309
White Horse, The, Gauguin, 237
White House, Washington, D.C., 261
White, Stanford, 265
Whitehall, London, 184
Whitman House, Farmington, Conn., 251
Whitman, Walt, Eakins, 296
William and Mary College, Williamsburg, Va., 255
William and Mary furniture, 197, 328
Williamsburg, Va., 255, 256
Wilson, Richard, 327(G-2)
Wimar, Charles, 292
Window on a Park, Derain, 241
Wine, Making, 60
Winged Figure from Delos, 25
Winter Solstice, Burchfield, 303
Winter Twilight, Burchfield, 303
Wisconsin: Madison, 267; Racine, 270

Wishnick Hall, Illinois Institute of Technology, Chicago, 278
Wistar, Dr. Caspar, Rush, 279
Wolfert's Will, Quidor, 293
Woman: De Kooning, 311; Lachaise, 314
Woman Combing Her Hair, Braque, 240
Woman Grinding Grain, Egyptian, 4
Woman with a Mirror, Courbet, 225
Woman with a Parasol, Renoir, 232
Woman with a Pearl, Corot, 224
Woman in a Room, Terborch, 180
Woman Seated, Toulouse-Lautrec, 231
Woman Washing Her Hands, Terborch, 181
Woman's Head, Gabo, 316
Wood, ages of, in furniture, 328
Wood engraving, 162, 194, 320
Wood, Grant, 303
Woodcut, 166, 167, 320
Woodville, Richard, 294
Woolworth Building, N.Y.C., 268
Workers' Houses, Hook of Holland, 208
World's Columbian Exposition, Chicago, 265, 267
Worms Cathedral, 72
Wren, Sir Christopher, 184, 185
Wren, Sir Christopher, Kneller, 187
Wrestlers, Greek, 27
Wright, Frank Lloyd, 269, 270, 276
Wyant, Alexander H., 327(G-3)
Wyeth, Andrew, 308
Wythe House, Williamsburg, Va., 256

Yale University, New Haven, Conn., 276
Yellow Calvary, Gauguin, 238
Yellow Seascape, Diebenkorn, 311
York Minster, 87
Young Girl, Head of a, Vermeer, 180
Young Girl Reading a Letter, Vermeer, 180
Young Man in a Fur Cap, Hals, 176
Young Men by the Sea, Beckmann, 243
Young Woman, Dürer, 167
Young Woman Reading a Letter, Vermeer, 180
Young Woman with a Water Jug, Vermeer, 179
Youths Bearing Wine Jars, Parthenon, 32
Youths Playing Ball, 27
Yugoslavic sculpture, 312

Zacharias, Van Eyck, 155
Zerbe, Karl, 247
0 through 9, Johns, 308
Zeus: Altar of Pergamon, 39; Temple of, Olympia, 18, 29
Zeus Otricoli, 40
Zoning Law, N.Y.C., 268
Zorach, William, 314, 319
Zorn, Anders, 194, 327(G-1)
Zuloaga, Ignacio, 194, 327(G-1)
Zurbarán, Francisco de, 173, 326(F-4)
Zwinger Palace, Dresden, 165